AF730573

Joshua Williams

PRINCIPLES OF THE LAW OF REAL PROPERTY

Elibron Classics
www.elibron.com

Elibron Classics series.

© 2006 Adamant Media Corporation.

ISBN 0-543-97834-6 (paperback)
ISBN 0-543-97833-8 (hardcover)

This Elibron Classics book contains the complete text of the edition published in 1877 by H. Sweet, London; Hodges, Foster & Co., Dublin; C. F. Maxwell, Melbourne.

Elibron and Elibron Classics are trademarks of Adamant Media Corporation. All rights reserved.

This book is an accurate reproduction of the original. Any marks, names, colophons, imprints, logos or other symbols or identifiers that appear on or in this book, except for those of Adamant Media Corporation and BookSurge, LLC, are used only for historical reference and accuracy and are not meant to designate origin or imply any sponsorship by or license from any third party.

INTRODUCTORY CHAPTER
OF THE CLASSES OF PROPERTY

In the early ages of Europe, property was chiefly of a substantial and visible, or what lawyers call, a corporeal kind. Trade was little practised, and consequently debts were seldom incurred. There were no public funds, and of course no funded property. The public wealth consisted principally of land, and the houses and buildings erected upon it, of the cattle in the fields, and the goods in the houses. Now land, which is immoveable and indestructible, is evidently a different species of property from a cow or a sheep, which may be stolen, killed, and eaten; or from a chair or a table, which may be broken up or burnt. No man, be he ever so feloniously disposed, can run away with an acre of land. The owner may be ejected, but the land remains where it was; and he, who has been wrongfully turned out of possession, may be reinstated into the identical portion of land from which he had been removed. Not so with moveable property; the thief may be discovered and punished; but if he has made away with the goods, no power on earth can restore them to their owner. All he can hope to obtain is a compensation in money, or in some other article of equal value.

Moveable and *immoveable* is then one of the simplest and most natural divisions of property in times of but partial civilization. In our law this division has been brought into great prominence by the circumstances of our early history.

By the Norman conquest, it is well known a vast number of Norman soldiers settled in this country. The new settlers were encouraged by their king and master; and whilst the conquered Saxons found no favour at court, they suffered a more substantial grievance in the confiscation of the lands of such of them as had opposed the Conqueror. The lands thus confiscated were granted out by the Conqueror to his followers, nor was their rapacity satisfied till the greater part of the lands in the kingdom had been thus disposed of. In these grants the Norman king and his vassals followed the custom of their own country, or what is called the feudal system. The lands granted were not given freely and for nothing; but they were given to hold of the king, subject to the performance of certain military duties as the condition of their enjoyment. The king was still considered as in some sense the proprietor, and was called the lord paramount; while the services to be rendered were regarded as incident or annexed to the ownership of the land; in fact, as the rent to be paid for it.

This feudal system of tenures, or holding of the king, was soon afterwards applied to all other lands, although they had not been thus granted out, but remained in the hands of their original Saxon owners. How this change was effected is perhaps a matter of doubt. Sir Martin Wright, who is followed by Blackstone, supposes that the introduction of tenures, as to lands of the Saxons, was accomplished at a stroke by a law of William the Conqueror, by which he required all free men to swear that they would be faithful to him as their lord. "The terms of this law," says Sir Martin Wright, "are absolutely feudal, and are apt and proper to establish that policy with all its consequences." Mr. Hallam, however, takes a different view of the subject; for while he considers it certain that the tenures of the feudal system were thoroughly established in England under the Conqueror, he yet remarks that by the transaction in question an oath of fidelity was required, as well from the great landowners themselves as from their tenants, "thus breaking in upon the feudal compact in its most essential attribute, the exclusive dependence of a vassal upon his lord". The truth appears to be that Norman customs, and their upholders and interpreters, Norman lawyers, were the real introducers of the feudal system of tenures into the law of this country. Before the conquest, landowners were subject to military duties; and to a soldier it would matter little whether he fought by reason of tenure, or for any other reason. The distinction between his services being annexed to his *land*, and their being annexed to the *tenure* of his land, would not strike him as very important. These matters would be left to those whose business it was to attend to them; and the lawyers from Normandy, without being particularly crafty, would, in their fondness for their own profession, naturally adhere to the precedents they were used to, and observe the customs and laws of their own country. Perhaps even they, in the time of the Conqueror, troubled themselves but little about the laws of landed property. The statutes of William are principally criminal, as are the laws of all half-civilized nations. Life and limb are of more importance than property; and when the former are in danger, the security of the latter is not much regarded. When the convulsions of the conquest began to subside, the Saxons felt the effects of the Norman laws, and cried out for the restoration of their own; but they were the weaker party and could not help themselves. By this time the industry of the lawyers had woven a net from which there is no escaping. But in what precise manner tenures crept in, was a question perhaps never asked in those days; and if asked, it could not probably, even then, have been minutely answered.

The system of tenure could evidently only exist as to lands and things immoveable. Cattle and other moveables were things of too perishable and insignificant a nature to be subject to any feudal liabilities, and could therefore only be bestowed as absolute gifts. No duty or service could well be annexed as the condition of their ownership. Hence a superiority became attached to all *immoveable* property, and the distinction between it and *moveables* became clearly marked; so that, whilst *lands* were the subject of the disquisitions of lawyers, the decisions of the Courts of justice, and the attention of the legislature, *moveable* property passed almost unnoticed.

Lands, houses, and immoveable property, — things capable of being held in the way above described, — were called *tenements* or *things held.* They were also denominated *hereditaments*, because, on the death of the owner, they devolved by law to his heir. So that the phrase, *lands*, *tenements* and *hereditaments*, was used by the lawyers of those times to express all sorts of property of the first or immoveable class; and the expression is in use to the present day.

The other, or moveable class of property, was known by the name of *goods* or *chattels*. The derivation of the word *chattel* has not been precisely ascertained. Both it and the word *goods* are well known to be still in use as technical terms amongst lawyers.

So great was the influence of the feudal system, and so important was the tenure or holding of lands, whether by the vassals of the crown, or by the vassals of those vassals, that for a long time immoveable property was known rather by the name of *tenements* than by any other term more indicative of its fixed and indestructible nature. In time, however, from various causes, the feudal system began to give way. The growth of a commercial spirit, the rising power of towns, and the formation of an influential middle class, combined to render the relation of lord and vassal anything but a reciprocal advantage; and at the restoration of King Charles II. a final blow was given to the whole system. Its form indeed remained, but its spirit was extinguished. The tenures of land then became less burdensome to the owner, and less troublesome to the law student; and the Courts of law, instead of being occupied with disputes between lords and tenants, had their attention more directed to controversies between different owners. It became then more obvious that the essential difference between lands and goods was to be found in the remedies for the deprivation of either; that land could always be restored, but goods could not; that, as to the one, the *real* land itself could be recovered; but, as to the other, proceedings must be had against the *person* who had taken them away. The two great classes of property accordingly began to acquire two other names more characteristic of their difference. The remedies for the recovery of lands had long been called *real* actions, and the remedies for loss of goods *personal* actions. But it was not until the feudal system had lost its hold, that lands and tenements were called *real property*, and goods and chattels *personal property*.

It appears then, that lands and tenements were designated, in later times, *real property*, more from the nature of the legal remedy for their recovery than simply because they are real things; and on the other hand, goods and chattels were called *personal property* because the remedy for their abstraction was against the person who had taken them away. Personal property has been described as that which may attend the owner's person wherever he thinks proper to go but goods and chattels were not usually called things personal till they had become too numerous and important to attend the persons of their owners.

The terms *real property* and *personal property* are now more commonly used than the old terms *tenements and hereditaments, goods and chattels*. The old terms were, indeed, suited only to the feudal times in which they originated; since those times great changes have taken place, commerce has been widely extended, loans of money at interest have become common, and the funds have engulfed an immense mass of wealth. Both classes of property have accordingly been increased by fresh additions; and within the new names of *real* and *personal* many kinds of property are now included, to which our forefathers were quite strangers; so much so that the simple division into immoveable tenements and moveable chattels is lost in the many exceptions to which time and altered circumstances have given rise. Thus, shares in canals and railways, which are sufficiently immoveable, are generally personal property; funded property is personal; whilst a dignity or title of honour, which one would think to be as locomotive as its owner, is not a chattel but a tenement. Canal and railway shares and funded property are made personal by the different acts of parliament under the authority of which they have originated. And titles of honour are real property, because in ancient times such titles were annexed to the ownership of various lands.

But the most remarkable exception to the original rule occurs in the case of a lease of lands or houses for a term of years. The interest which the lessee, or person who has taken the lease, possesses, is not his real, but his personal property; it is but a chattel, though the rent may be only nominal, and the term ninety or even a thousand years. This seeming anomaly is thus explained. In the early times, to which we have before referred, towns and cities were not of any very great and general importance; their influence was local and partial, and their laws and customs were frequently peculiar to themselves. Agriculture was then, though sufficiently neglected, yet still of far more importance than commerce; and from the necessities of agriculture arose many of our ancient rules of law. That the most ancient leases must have been principally farming leases, is evident from the specimens of which copies still remain, and also from the circumstance that the word *farm* applies as well to anything let on lease, or *let to farm*, as to a farm house and the lands belonging to it. Thus, we hear of farmers of tolls and taxes, as well as of farmers engaged in agriculture. Farming in those days required but little capital, and farmers were regarded more as bailiffs or servants, accountable for the profits of the land at an annual sum, than as having any property of their own. If the farmer was ejected from his land by any other person than his landlord, he could not, by any legal process, again obtain possession of it. His only remedy was an action for damages against his landlord, who was bound to warrant him quiet possession. The farmer could therefore be scarcely said to be the owner of the land, even for the term of the lease; for his interest wanted the essential incident of real property, the capability of being restored to its owner. Such an interest in land had, moreover, nothing military or feudal in its nature, and was, consequently, exempt from the feudal rule of descent to the eldest son as heir at law. Being thus neither real property, nor feudal tenement, it could be no more than a chattel; and when leases became longer, more valuable, and more frequent, no change was made; but to this day the owner of an estate for a term of years possesses in law merely a chattel. His leasehold estate is only his personal property, however long may be the term of years, or however great the value of the premises comprised in his lease.

There is now perhaps as much personal property in the country as real; possibly there may be more. Real property, however, still retains many of its ancient laws, which invest it with an interest and importance to which personal property has no claim. Of these ancient laws one of the most conspicuous is the feudal rule of descent, under which, as partially modified by amending acts, real property goes, when its owner dies intestate, to the *heir*, while personal property is distributed, under the same circumstances, amongst the *next of kin* of the intestate by an administrator appointed for that purpose by the Court of Probate.

Besides the division of property into real and personal, there is another classification which deserves to be mentioned, namely, that of *corporeal and incorporeal*. It is evident that all property is either of one of these classes or of the other; it is either visible and tangible, or it is not. Thus a house is corporeal, but the annual rent payable for its occupation is incorporeal. So an annuity is incorporeal; "for, though the money, which is the fruit or product of this annuity, is doubtless of a corporeal nature, yet the annuity itself, which produces that money, is a thing invisible, has only a mental existence, and cannot be delivered over from hand to hand". Corporeal property, on the other hand, is capable of manual transfer; or, as to such as is immoveable, possession may actually be given up. Frequently the possession of corporeal property necessarily involves the enjoyment of certain incorporeal rights; thus the lord of a manor, which is corporeal property, may have the advowson or perpetual right of presentation to the parish church; and this advowson, which, being a mere right to present, is an incorporeal kind of property, may be appendant or attached, as it were, to the manor, and constantly belong to every owner. But, in many cases, property of an incorporeal nature exists apart from the ownership of anything corporeal, forming a distinct subject of possession; and, as such, it may frequently be required to be transferred from one person to another. An instance of this separate kind of incorporeal property occurs in the case of an advowson or right of presentation to a church, when not appendant to any manor. In the transfer or conveyance of incorporeal property, when thus alone and self-existent, formerly lay the practical distinction between it and corporeal property. For, in ancient times, the impossibility of actually delivering up any thing of a separate incorporeal nature, rendered some other means of conveyance necessary. The most obvious was writing; which was accordingly always employed for the purpose, and was considered indispensable to the separate transfer of every thing incorporeal; whilst the transfer of corporeal property, together with such incorporeal rights as its possession involved, was long permitted to take place without any written document. *Incorporeal* property, in our present highly artificial state of society, occupies an important position; and such kinds of incorporeal property as are of a real nature will hereafter be spoken of more at large. But for the present, let us give our undivided attention to property of a *corporeal* kind; and, as to this, the scope of our work embraces one branch only, namely, that which is *real*, and which, as we have seen, being descendible to *heirs*, is known in law by the name of *hereditaments*. Estates or interests in corporeal hereditaments, or what is commonly called landed property, will accordingly form our next subject for consideration.

PART I
OF CORPOREAL HEREDITAMENTS

Before proceeding to consider the estates which may be held in corporeal hereditaments or landed property, it is desirable that the legal terms made use of to designate such property should be understood; for the nomenclature of the law differs in some respects from that which is ordinarily employed. Thus a house is by lawyers generally called a *messuage*; and the term *messuage* was formerly considered as of more extensive import than the word *house*. But such a distinction is not now to be relied on. Both the term *messuage* and *house* will comprise adjoining out-buildings, the orchard, and curtilage, or court yard, and, according to the better opinion, these terms will include the garden also. The word *tenement* is often used in law, as in ordinary language, to signify a house: it is indeed the regular synonyme which follows the term *messuage*; a house being usually described in deeds as "all that messuage or tenement." But the more comprehensive meaning of the word *tenement*, to which we have before adverted, is still attached to it in legal interpretation, whenever the sense requires. Again, the word *land* comprehends in law any ground, soil, or earth whatsoever; but its strict and primary import is arable land. It will, however, include castles, houses, and outbuildings of all binds; for the ownership of land carries with it every thing both above and below the surface, the maxim being *cujus est solum, ejus est usque ad cœlum*. A pond of water is accordingly described as *land* covered with water; and a grant of land includes all mines and minerals under the surface. This extensive signification of the word *land* may, however, be controlled by the context; as where land is spoken of in plain contradistinction to houses, it will not be held to comprise them. So mines lying under a piece of land may be excepted out of a conveyance of such land, and they will then remain the corporeal property of the grantor, with such incidental powers as are necessary to work them, and subject to the incidental duty of leaving a sufficient support to the surface to keep it securely at its ancient and natural level. In the same manner, chambers may be the subjects of conveyance as corporeal property, independently of the floors above or below them. The word *premises is* frequently used in law in its proper etymological sense of that which has been before mentioned. Thus, after a recital of various facts in a deed, it frequently proceeds "in consideration of the *premises*," meaning in consideration of the facts before mentioned; and property is seldom spoken of as *premises*, unless a description of it is contained in some prior part of the deed. Most of the words used in the description of property have however no special technical meaning, but are construed according to their usual sense; and, as to such words as have a technical import more comprehensive than their ordinary meaning, it is very seldom that such extensive import is alone relied on; but the meaning of the parties is generally explained by the additional use of ordinary words.

CHAPTER I
OF AN ESTATE FOR LIFE

It seldom happens that any subject is brought frequently to a person's notice, without his forming concerning it opinions of some kind. And such opinions carelessly picked up are often carefully retained, though in many cases wrong, and in most inadequate. The subject of property is so generally interesting, that few persons are without some notions as to the legal rights appertaining to its possession. These notions, however, as entertained by unprofessional persons, are mostly of a wrong kind. They consider that what is a man's own is what he may do what he likes with; and with this broad principle they generally set out on such legal adventures as may happen to lie before them. They begin at a point at which the lawyer stops, or at which indeed the law has not yet arrived, nor ever will; but to which it is still continually approximating. Now the student of law must forget for a time that, if he has land, he may let it, or leave it by his will, or mortgage it, or sell it, or settle it. He must humble himself to believe that he knows as yet nothing about it; and he will find that the attainment of the ample power, which is now possessed over real property, has been the work of a long period of time; and that even now a common purchase deed of a piece of freehold land cannot be explained without going back to the reign of Henry VIII., or an ordinary settlement of land without recourse to the laws of Edward I. That such should be the case is certainly a matter of regret. History and antiquities are, no doubt, interesting and delightful studies in their place; but their perpetual intrusion into modern practice, and the absolute necessity of some acquaintance with them, give rise to much of the difficulty experienced in the study of the law, and to many of the errors of its less studious practitioners.

The first thing then the student has to do is to get rid of the idea of absolute ownership. Such an idea is quite unknown to the English law. No man is in law the absolute owner of lands. He can only hold an estate in them.

The most interesting, and perhaps the most ancient of estates, is an estate for life; and with this we shall begin. Soon after the commencement of the feudal system, to which, as we have seen, our laws of real property owe so much of their character, an estate for, life seems to have been the smallest estate in conquered lands which the military tenant was disposed to accept. This estate was inalienable, unless his lord's consent could be obtained. A grant of lands to A. B. was then a grant to him as long as he could hold them, that is, during his life and no longer; for feudal donations were not extended beyond the precise terms of the gift by any presumed intent, but were taken strictly; and, on the tenant's death, the lands reverted to the lord or grantor. If it was intended that the descendants of the tenant should, at his decease, succeed him in the tenancy, this intention was expressed by additional words of grant; the gift being then to the tenant and his heirs, or with other words expressive of the intention. The heir was thus a nominee in the original grant; he took every thing from the grantor, nothing from his ancestor. So that, in such a case, "the ancestor and the heirs took equally as a succession of usufructuaries, each of whom during his life enjoyed the beneficial, but none of whom possessed, or could lawfully dispose of, the direct or absolute dominion of the property". The feudal system, however, had not long been introduced into this country before the restriction on alienation began to be relaxed. Subsequently, by a statute of Edward I. the right of every freeman to sell at his own pleasure his lands or tenements, or part thereof, was expressly recognized; at a still later period, the power of testamentary alienation was bestowed, until, at the present day, the right to dispose of property is not only established, but has become inseparable from its possession. Moreover, the old feudal rule of strict construction has long since given way to the contrary maxim, that every grant is to be construed most strongly against the grantor. Yet so deeply rooted are the feudal principles of our law of real property, that, in the case before us, the ancient interpretation remains unaltered; and a grant to A. B. simply now confers but an estate for his life, which estate, though he may part with it if he pleases, will terminate at his death, into whosoever hands it may have come.

The most remarkable effect of this antiquated rule has been its frequent defeat of the intentions of unlearned testators, who, in leaving their lands and houses to the objects of their bounty, were seldom aware that they were conferring only a life interest; though, if they extended the gift to the *heirs* of the parties, or happened to make use of the word *estate*, of some other such technical term, their gift or devise should the whole extent of the interest they had power to dispose of. "Generally speaking," says Lord Mansfield, "no common person has the smallest idea of any difference between giving a horse and a quantity of land. Common sense alone would never teach a man the difference; but the distinction, which is now clearly established, is this: — If the words of the testator denote only a *description* of the *specific estate* or *land* devised, in that case, if no words of limitation are added, the devisee has only an estate for life. But if the words denote the *quantum* of *interest* or property that the testator has in the lands devised, then the *whole* extent of such his *interest* passes by the gift to the devisee. The question, therefore, is always a question of construction, upon the words and terms used by the testator." Such questions, as may be imagined, have been sufficiently numerous. Happily by the act of parliament for the amendment of the laws with respect to wills, a construction more accordant with the plain intention of testators is now given in such cases.

If the owner of an estate for his own life should dispose thereof, the new owner will become entitled to an estate for the life of the former. This, in the Norman French, with which our law still abounds, is called an estate *pur autre vie*; and the person for whose life the land is holden is called the *cestui que vie*. In this case, as well as in that of an original grant, the new owner was formerly entitled only so long as he lived to enjoy the property, unless the grant were expressly extended to his heirs; so that, in case of the decease of the new owner, in the lifetime of the *cestui que vie*, the land was left without an occupant so long as the life of the latter continued, for the law would not allow him to re-enter after having parted with his life estate. No person having therefore a right to the property, anybody might enter on the land; and he that first entered might lawfully retain possession so long as the *cestui que vie* lived. The person who had so entered was called a *general occupant*. If, however, the estate had been granted to a man *and his heirs* during the life of the *cestui que vie*, the heir might, and still may, enter and hold possession; and in such a case he is called in law a *special occupant*, having a special right of occupation by the terms of the grant. To remedy the evil occasioned by property remaining without an owner, it was provided by a clause in a famous statute passed in the reign of King Charles II., that the owner of an estate *pur autre vie* might dispose thereof by his will; that if no such disposition should be made, the heir, as occupant, should be charged with the debts of his ancestor; or, in case there should be no special occupant, it should go to his executors or administrators, and be subject to the payment of his debts, of course only during the residue of the life of the *cestui que vie*. In the construction of this enactment a question arose, whether or not, supposing the owner of an estate *pur autre vie* died without a will, the administrator was to be entitled for his own benefit, after paying the debts of the deceased. An explanatory act was accordingly passed in the reign of King George II., by which the surplus, after payment of debts, was, in ease of intestacy, made distributable amongst the next of kin, in the same manner as personal estate. By the statute for the amendment of the laws with respect to wills, the above enactments were both replaced by more comprehensive provisions to the same effect.

When one person has an estate for the life of another, it is evidently his interest that the *cestui que vie*, or he for whose life the estate is holden, should live as long as possible; and, in the event of his decease, a temptation might occur to a fraudulent owner to conceal his death. In order to prevent any such fraud, it is provided, by an act of parliament passed in the reign of Queen Anne, that any person having any claim in remainder, reversion or expectancy, may, upon affidavit that he hath cause to believe that the *cestui que vie* is dead, or that his death is concealed, obtain an order from the Lord Chancellor for the production of the *cestui que vie* in the method prescribed by the act; and, if such order be not complied with, then the *cestui que vie* shall be taken to be dead, and any person claiming any interest in remainder, or reversion or otherwise, may enter accordingly. The act, moreover, provides, that any person having any estate *pur autre vie*, who, after the determination of such estate, shall continue in possession of any lands, without the express consent of the persons next entitled, shall be adjudged a trespasser, and may be proceeded against accordingly.

The owner of an estate for life is called a tenant for life, for he is only a *holder* of the lands according to the feudal principles of our law. A tenant, either for his own life, or for the life of another *(pur autre vie)*, hath an estate *of freehold*, and he that hath a less estate cannot have a freehold. Here, again, the reason is feudal. A life estate is such as was considered worthy the acceptance of *a free man*; a less estate was not. And it is worthy of remark, that in the earlier periods of our law an estate for a man's own life was the only life estate considered of sufficient importance to be an estate of freehold: an estate for the life of another person was not then reckoned of equal rank. But this distinction has long since disappeared; and there are now some estates which may not even last a lifetime, but are yet considered in law as life estates, and are estates of freehold. Thus, an estate granted to a woman during her widowhood is in law a life estate, though determinable on her marrying again. Every life estate also may be determined by the *civil* death of the party, as well as by his natural death; for which reason in conveyances the grant is usually made for the term of a man's *natural* life. Formerly a person, by entering a monastery, and being *professed* in religion, became dead in law. But this doctrine is now inapplicable; for there is no longer any legal establishment for professed persons in England, and our law never took notice of foreign professions. Civil death may, however, occur by outlawry. It was formerly occasioned also by attainder for treason or felony; but all attainders are now abolished.

Every tenant for life, unless restrained by covenant or agreement, has the common right of all tenants to cut wood for fuel to burn in the house, for the making and repairing of all instruments of husbandry, and for repairing the house, and the hedges and fences, and also the right to cut underwood and lop pollards in due course. But he is not allowed to cut timber, or to commit any other kind of *waste*; either by voluntary destruction of any part of the premises, which is called *voluntary* waste, or by permitting the buildings to go to ruin, which is called *permissive* waste. Of late, however, doubts have been thrown on the liability of a tenant for life for waste which is merely permissive; and the Courts of Equity have refused to interfere in the case of a tenant for life, whose estate is equitable only. But there appears to be no sufficient ground for doubting the tenant's liability where he has the legal estate vested in himself. So a tenant for life cannot plough up ancient meadow land; and he is not allowed to dig for gravel, brick, or stone, except in such pits as were open and usually dug when he came in; nor can he open new mines for coal or other minerals, nor cut turf for sale on bog lands; for all such acts would be acts of voluntary *waste*. But to continue the working of existing mines, or to cut turf for sale in bogs already used for that purpose, is not *waste*; and the tenant may accordingly carry on such mines and cut turf in such bogs for his own profit. By an old statute the committing of any act of waste was a cause of forfeiture of the thing or place wasted, in case a *writ of waste* was issued against the tenant for life. But this writ is now abolished; and a tenant for life is now liable only to damages in an action in the High Court of Justice for waste already done, or to be restrained by injunction from cutting the timber or committing any other act of waste, which he may be known to contemplate. If any of the timber is in such an advanced state that it would take injury by standing, the Court will allow it to be cut, on the money being secured for the benefit of the persons entitled on the expiration of the life estate; and the Court will allow the interest of the money to be paid to the tenant during his life. And the Settled Estates Act, 1877, now empowers the Chancery Division of the High Court, if it think proper, to authorize a sale of any timber, not being ornamental timber, growing on any settled estates. If, however, the estate is given to the tenant by a written instrument expressly declaring his estate to be *without impeachment of waste*, he is allowed to cut timber in a husbandlike manner for his own benefit, to open mines, and commit other acts of waste with impunity; but so that he does not pull down or deface the family mansion, or fell timber planted or left standing for ornament, or commit other injuries of the like nature; all of which are termed *equitable* waste; for the Court of Chancery, administering *equity*, restrained such proceedings. The Supremo Court of Judicature Act, 1873, now provides that, after the time appointed for the commencement of that act, namely, the first of November, 1875, an estate for life without impeachment of waste shall not confer, or be deemed to have conferred, upon the tenant for life any legal right to commit waste of the description known as equitable waste, unless an intention to confer such right shall expressly appear by the instrument creating such estate.

As a tenant for life has merely a limited interest, he cannot of course make any disposition of the lands to take effect after his decease; and, consequently, he can make no leases to endure beyond his own life, unless he be specially empowered so to do by the deed under which he holds. It is however provided by the Settled Estates Act, 1877, that when the settlement is made after the 1st of November, 1856, the day when the now repealed act to facilitate leases and sales of settled estates came in force, and does not contain an express declaration to the contrary, every tenant for life may demise the premises or any part thereof (except the principal mansion-house and the demesnes thereof, and other lands usually occupied therewith), for any term not exceeding twenty-one years as to estates in England, and thirty-five years as to estates in Ireland, to take effect in possession at or within one year next after the making thereof; provided that every such demise be made by deed, and the best rent that can reasonably be obtained be thereby reserved, without any fine or other benefit in the nature of a fine, which rent shall be incident to the immediate reversion; and provided that such demise be not made without impeachment of waste, and do contain a covenant for payment of the rent, and such other usual and proper covenants as the lessor shall think fit, and also a condition of re-entry on non-payment of the rent for a period of twenty-eight days after it becomes due, or for some less period to be specified in that behalf; and provided a counterpart of every deed of lease be executed by the lessee. But the execution of the lease by the lessor is to be deemed sufficient evidence that a counterpart of such lease has been duly executed by the lessee as required by the act.

Leases may also be made by the authority of the Chancery Division of the High Court, on due application, whatever may be the date of the settlement, for terms not exceeding twenty-one years as to England, and thirty-five years as to Ireland, for an agricultural or occupation lease, forty years for a mining lease, or a lease of water, water mills, way-leaves, water-leaves, or other rights or easements, sixty years for a repairing lease, and ninety-nine years for a building lease, subject to the conditions prescribed by the act; and where the Court shall be satisfied that it is the usual custom of the district, and beneficial to the inheritance, to grant leases for longer terms, any of the above leases, except agricultural leases, may be granted for such term as the Court shall direct. The best rent must be reserved; but in a mining, repairing or building lease, a peppercorn or any smaller rent may be reserved for the first five years. In the case of a mining lease, a proportion of the rent is set apart and invested, namely, one-fourth where the landlord is entitled to work the mines, otherwise three-fourths.

If a tenant for life should sow the lands, and die before harvest, his executors will have a right to the emblements or crop. And the same right will also belong to his under-tenant; with this difference, however, that if the life estate should determine by the tenant's *own act*, as by the marriage of a widow holding during her widowhood, the tenant would have no right to emblements; but the under-tenant being no party to the cesser of the estate, would still be entitled in the same manner as on the expiration of the estate by death. And with respect to tenants at rack rent, it is now provided, that where the lease or tenancy of any farm or lands held by such a tenant shall determine by the death or cesser of the estate of any landlord entitled for his life, or for any other uncertain interest, instead of claims to emblements, the tenant shall continue to hold and occupy such farm or lands until the expiration of the then current year of his tenancy, and shall then quit upon the terms of his lease or holding, in the same manner as if such lease or tenancy were then determined by effluxion of time, or other lawful means, during the continuance of his landlord's estate; and the succeeding owner will be entitled to a fair proportion of the rent from the death or cesser of the estate of his predecessor to the time of the tenant's so quitting. And the succeeding owner and the tenant respectively will, as between themselves and as against each other, be entitled to all the benefits and advantages, and be subject to the terms, conditions and restrictions to which the preceding landlord and the tenant respectively would have been entitled and subject in case the lease or tenancy had determined in the manner before mentioned at the expiration of the current year; and no notice to quit shall be necessary from either party to determine such holding.

As a consequence of the determination of the estate of a tenant for life the moment of his death, it was held in old times, that if such a tenant had let the lands reserving rent quarterly or half-yearly, and died between two rent days, no rent was due from the undertenant to anybody from the last rent day till the time of the decease of the tenant for life. But in the reign of King George II. a remedy for a proportionate part of the rent, according to the time such tenant for life lived, was given by act of parliament to his executors or administrators. Formerly, also, when a tenant for life had a power of leasing, and let the lands accordingly, reserving rent periodically, his executors had no right to a proportion of the rent, in the event of his decease between two quarter days; and, as rent is not due till midnight of the day on which it is made payable, if the tenant for life had died even on the quarter day, but before midnight, his executors lost the quarter's rent, which went to the person next entitled. But by a modern act of parliament, the executors and administrators of any tenant for life who had granted a lease since the 16th of June, 1834, the date of the act, might claim an apportionment of the rent from the person next entitled, when it should become due. This act, however, did not apply unless the demise were made by an instrument in writing. But the Apportionment Act, 1870, now provides, that after the passing of that act, which took place on the 1st of August, 1870, all rents and other periodical payments in the nature of income (whether reserved or made payable under an instrument in writing or otherwise) shall, like interest on money lent, be considered as accruing from day to day, and shall be apportionable in respect of time accordingly.

By an act of the present reign tenants for life, and some other persons having limited interests, were empowered to apply to the Court of Chancery for leave to make any permanent improvements by *draining* the lands with tiles, stones, or other durable materials, or by warping, irrigation or embankment in a permanent manner, or by erecting thereon any buildings of a permanent kind incidental or consequential to such draining, warping, irrigation or embanking, and immediately connected therewith. And if, in the opinion of the Court, such improvements would have been beneficial to all persons interested, the money expended in making such improvements, or in obtaining the authority of the Court, was to be charged on the inheritance of the lands, with interest at such rate as should have been agreed on, not exceeding five per cent. per annum, payable half-yearly; the principal money to be repaid by equal annual instalments, not less than twelve nor more than eighteen in number; or in the case of buildings, by equal annual instalments, not less than fifteen nor more than twenty-five in number. And under the provisions of more recent acts of parliament, called the Public Money Drainage Acts, tenants for life and other owners of land may obtain advances from government for works of drainage, which may be completed within five years; such advances to be repaid by a rent-charge on the land, after the rate of 6*l*. 10*s*. rent-charge for every 100*l*. advanced, and to be payable for the term of twenty-two years. By another act of parliament called the Private Money Drainage Act, 1849, the owner of any land in Great Britain or Ireland was empowered to borrow or advance money for the improvement of *each* land by works of drainage; such money, with interest not exceeding five per cent. per annum, to be charged on the inheritance of the land, in the shape of a rent-charge, for the term of twenty-two years. This act, however, is now repealed by the Improvement of Land Act, 1864, which gives a very wide definition to the phrase "improvement of land," and contains provisions facilitating the raising of money by way of encourage that purpose. The rate of interest to be charge not to exceed five per cent. per annum, and the term for repayment is not to exceed twenty-five years. These loans are under the superintendence of the Inclosure Commissioners for England and Wales, Ireland under that of the Commissioners for Works in Ireland. But the authority to issue certificates of the redemption of the loans of public money belongs to the Board of Inland Revenue. An act, styled the "Limited Owners Residences Act, 1870, Amendment Act, 1871", now provides that the following shall be improvements within the meaning of the Improvement of Land Act, 1864, namely, the erection of a mansion-house and such other usual and necessary buildings, outhouses and offices as commonly appurtenant thereto and held and enjoyed therewith, and the completion of any mansion-house and such appurtenances as aforesaid, and the improvement of and addition to any mansion-house and such appurtenances as aforesaid already erected, and the improvement of and addition to any house which is capable of being converted into a mansion-house suitable to the estate on which the same stands, so as such improvement and addition be of a permanent nature; provided that every such mansion-house so erected or enlarged or converted is suitable to the estate on which it stands as a residence for the owner of such estate. But the sum charged on any estate under settlement in respect of mansion and other buildings before mentioned is not to exceed two years' net rental of the whole estate. In all other respects, improvements which a tenant for life may wish to make must be paid for out of his own pocket.

Tenants for life under wills are empowered, by recent acts of parliament, to convey in certain cases, under the direction of the Chancery Division of the High Court, the whole estate in the lands of which they are tenants for life. Such conveyances are made only when the concurrence of the other parties cannot be obtained, and a sale or mortgage of the lands is required for the payment of the debts of the testator. These powers, however, are given to the tenant for life for the sake of making a title to the property; and are more for the benefit of the creditors of the late testator, than for the advantage of the tenant for life, who is, in these cases, merely the instrument for carrying into effect the decree of the Court; and the powers given by these acts are now a great measure superseded by the provisions of the act to consolidate and amend the laws relating to the conveyance and transfer of real and personal property rented in mortgagees and trustees. More recently, however, an act was passed, to which we have already referred, to facilitate leases and sales of settled estates. This act, and the acts by which, it was led, have now been repealed, amended and consolidated by the Settled Estates Act, 1877. Under this act, if the Chancery Division of the High Court should deem it proper and consistent with a due regard for the interest of all parties entitled, a sale of any settled estate may be ordered to be made. And the money to be raised on any such sale is to be paid either to trustees of whom the Court shall approve, or into Court, and is to be applied to the following purposes, namely, the redemption of the land tax, or of any incumbrance affecting the hereditaments sold or any other hereditaments settled in. the same way, or the purchase of other hereditaments to be settled in the same manner, or in the payment to any person becoming absolutely entitled. And the money is in the meantime to be invested in some or one of the investments in which cash under the control of the Court is for the time being authorized to be invested, and the interest or dividends paid to the tenant for life. But the powers of the are not to be exercised if an express declaration that they shall not be exercised in the settlement.

The following new provision is contained in the settled Estates Act, 1877, and is very important to tenants for life and other owners of limited estates. The Court is empowered, if it shall deem it proper and consistent with a due regard for the interests of all parties who are or may hereafter be entitled under the settlement, and subject to the provisions and restrictions contained in the act, to sanction any action, defence, petition to Parliament, parliamentary opposition, or other proceedings appearing to the Court necessary for the protection of any settled estate, and to order that all or any part of the costs and expenses in relation thereto be raised and paid by means of a sale or mortgage of or charge upon all or any part of the settled estate, or out of the rents and profits thereof, or out of any monies or investments representing monies liable to be laid out in the purchase of hereditaments to be settled in the same manner as the settled estate, or out of the income of such monies or investments, or out of any accumulations of rents, profits or income.

In addition to estates for life expressly created by the acts of the parties, there are certain life interests, created by construction and operation of law, possessed by husbands and wives in each other's land. These interests will be spoken of in a future chapter. There are also certain other life estates held by persons subject to peculiar laws; such as the life estates held by beneficed clergymen. These estates are exceptions from the general law; and a discussion of them, in an elementary work like the present, would tend rather to confuse the student than to aid him in his grasp of those general principles, which it should be his first object to comprehend.

CHAPTER II
OF AN ESTATE TAIL

The next estate we shall notice is an estate tail, or an estate given to a man *and the heirs of his body*. This is such an estate as will, if left to itself, descend, on the decease of the first owner, to all his lawful issue, — children, grand-children, and more remote descendants, so long as his posterity endures, — in a regular order and course of descent from one to another: and, on the other hand, if the first owner should die without issue, his estate, if left alone, will then determine. An estate tail may be either *general*, that is, to the heirs of his body generally and without restriction, in which case the estate will be descendible to every one of his lawful posterity in due course; or *special*, when it is restrained to certain heirs of his body, and does not go to all of them in general; thus, if an estate be given to a man and the heirs of his body by a particular wife; here none can inherit but such as are his issue by the wife specified. Estates tail may be also in *tail male*, or in *tail female*: an estate in *tail male* cannot descend to any but males, and male descendants of males; and cannot, consequently, belong to any one who does not bear the surname of his ancestor from whom he inherited: so an estate in *tail, female* can only descend to females, and female descendants of females. Special estates tail, confined to the issue by a particular wife, are not now common; the most usual kinds of estates tail now given are estates in tail general, and in tail male. Tail female scarcely ever occurs.

The owner of an estate tail is called a *donee* in tail, and the person who has given him the estate tail is called the *donor*. And here it may he remarked, that such correlative words as *donor* and *donee*, *lessor* and *lessee*, and many others of a like termination, are used in law to distinguish the person from whom an act proceeds, from the person for or towards whom it is done. The owner of an estate tail is also called a *tenant in tail*, for he is as much a *holder* as a tenant for life. But an estate tail is a larger estate than an estate for life, as it may endure so long as the first owner of the estate has any issue of the kind mentioned in the gift. It is consequently an estate of *freehold*. We shall now proceed to give a short history of this estate; in doing which it will be necessary to advert to the origin and progress of the general right of alienation of lands.

It will readily be supposed that a mere system of life estates, continually granted by feudal lords to their tenants, would not long continue; the son of the tenant would naturally be the first person who would hope to succeed to his father's tenancy: accordingly we find that the holding of lands by feudal tenants soon became hereditary, permission being granted to the heirs of the tenant to succeed on the decease of their ancestor. By the term "heirs" it is said that the issue of the tenant were at first only meant; collateral relations, such as brothers and cousins, being excluded; the true feudal reason of this construction is stated by Blackstone to be, that what was given to a man for his personal service and personal merit ought not to descend to any but the heirs of his person. But in our own country it appears that, at any rate in the time of Henry II., collateral relations were admitted to succeed as heirs; so that an estate which had been granted to a man and his heirs descended, on his decease, not only to his offspring, but also, in default of offspring, to his other relations in a defined order of succession. Hence if it were wished to confine the inheritance to the offspring of the donee, it became necessary to limit the estate expressly to him *and the heirs of his body*, making what was then called a *conditional gift*, by reason of the condition implied in the donation, that if the donee died without such particular heirs, or in case of the failure of such heirs at any time, the land should revert to the donor. The most usual species of grant appears, however, to have been that to a man *and his heirs* generally; but, on the right of alienation seems to have arisen in the like manner with regard to estates granted in both the methods, it will be desirable, in considering the origin of this right, to include in our remarks as well an estate granted to a man *and his heirs*, as an estate confined to *the heirs of the body* of the grantee.

In whichever method the estate might have been other granted, it is evident that, besides the tenant, there were two other parties interested in the lands; one, the person who was the expectant heir of the tenant, and who had, under the gift, a hope of succeeding his ancestor in the holding of the lands; the other, the lord, who had made the grant, and who had a right to the services reserved during the continuance of the tenancy, and also a possibility of again obtaining the lands on the failure of the heirs mentioned in the gift. An alienation of the lands by the tenant might therefore, it is evident, defeat the rights of one or both of the above parties. Let us, therefore, consider, in the first place, the origin and progress of the right of alienation as it affected the interest of the expectant heir; and, secondly, the origin and progress of this right as it affected the interest of the lord.

The right of an ancestor to defeat the expectation of his heir was not fully established at the time of Henry II. For it appears from the treatise of Glanville, written in that reign, that a larger right of alienation was possessed over lands which a man had acquired by purchase, than over those which had descended to him as the heir of some deceased person: and even over purchased lands the right of alienation was not complete, if the tenant had any heir of his own body; so that if lands had been given to a man *and his heirs* generally, he was able to disappoint the expectation of his collateral heirs, but he could not entirely disinherit the heirs sprung of his own body. For certain purposes, however, alienation of part of the lands was allowed to defeat the heirs of his body; thus part of the lands might be given by the tenant with his daughter on her marriage, and part might also be given for religious uses. Such gifts as these were, however, as we shall presently see, almost the only kinds of alienation, in ancient times, which occasioned any serious detriment to the heir; and the allowing of such gifts may accordingly be considered as an important step in the progress of the right of alienation. For, when lands were given to a daughter on her marriage, the daughter and her husband, or the donees in *frank-marriage*, as they were called, held the lands granted, to them and the heirs of their two bodies *free from all manner of service* to the donor or his heirs (a mere oath of fealty or fidelity excepted), until the fourth degree of consanguinity from the donor was passed; and when lands were given to religious uses, the grantees in *frankalmoign*, as they were called, were for ever free from every kind of earthly or temporal service. Little or nothing, therefore, in these cases, remained for the heir of the grantor. But the other modes of alienation which then prevailed were very different in their results, as well from such gifts as above described, as from the ordinary sales of landed property which occur in modern times. Ready money was then extremely scarce; large fortunes, acquired by commercial enterprise, were not then expended in the purchase of country seats. The auction mart was not then established; such a thing as an absolute sale for a sum of money paid down was scarcely to be met with. The alienation of lands rather assumed the form of perpetual leases, granted in consideration of certain services or rents to be from time to time performed or paid. This Method was, in feudal language, termed *subinfeudation*. In all the old conveyances, almost without exception, the lands are given to the grantee and his heirs, to hold as tenants of the grantor and his heirs, at certain rents or services; and when no particular service was reserved, it was understood that the grantee held of the grantor, subject to the same services as the grantor held of his superior lord. As, therefore, it cannot be supposed that gifts should be made without some fair equivalent, and as such equivalent, in the shape of rent or service, would descend to the heir in lieu of the land, we may fairly presume that alienation, as ordinarily practised in early times, was not so great a disadvantage to the heir as might at first be supposed: and this circumstance may perhaps help to account for that which at any rate is an undoubted fact, that the power of an absolute, ancestor to destroy the expectation of his heirs, whether merely collateral or heirs of his body, soon became absolute. In whichever way the grant were made, whether to the ancestor *and his heirs*, or to him and the *heirs of his body*, we find that by the time of Henry III. the heir was completely in his ancestor's power, so far as related to any lands of which the ancestor had possession. Bracton, who wrote in this reign, expressly lays it down, that the heir acquires nothing from the gift made to his ancestor. The very circumstance that land was given to a person and his heirs, or to him and the heirs of his body, enabled him to convey an interest in the land, to last as long as his heirs in the one case, or the heirs of his body in the other, continued to exist. And from the time of Bracton, a gift to a man *and his heirs* generally has enabled the grantee, either entirely to defeat the expectation of his heir by an absolute conveyance, or to prejudice his enjoyment of the descended lands by obliging him to satisfy any debts or demands, to the value of the lands, according to his ancestor's discretion. With respect to lands granted to a man and the *heirs of his body*, the power of the ancestor is not *now* so complete. The means by which this right of alienation was in this case curtailed will appear in the account we shall now give of the origin and progress of the right of alienation as it affected the interest of the lord.

The interest of the lord was evidently of two kinds; his interest in the rent and services during the continuance of the tenancy, and his chance or possibility of again obtaining the land on failure of the heirs of his tenant. On the former of these interests, the inroad of alienation appears to have been first made. The tenants, by taking upon themselves to make grants of part of their lands to strangers to hold of themselves, prejudiced the security possessed by the lord for the due performance of the services of the original tenure. And accordingly we find it enacted in Magna Charta, that no freeman should give or sell any more of his land than to as what remained might be sufficient to answer the services he owed to his lord. The original services reserved on any conveyance were, however, always a charge on the land while in the hands of the under-tenants, and could be distrained for by the lord; although the enforcement of such services was doubtless rendered less easy by the division of the lands into various ownerships. The infringement on the lord's interest, expectant on the failure of the heirs of his tenant, appears to have been the last step in the progress of alienation. As the advantages of a free power of disposition became apparent, a new form of grant came into general use. The lands were given not only to the tenant and his heirs, but to him and his heirs, *or to whomsoever he might wish to give or assign the land*, or with other words expressly conferring on the tenant the power of alienation. In this case, if the tenant granted, or underlet as it were, part of his land, then, on his decease and failure of his heirs, the tenant's grantee had still a right to continue to hold as tenant of the superior lord; and such superior lord then took the place of landlord, which the original tenant or his heirs would have occupied had he or they been living. And if the tenant, instead of thus underletting part of his land, chose to dispose of the whole, he was at liberty so to do, by substituting, if he thought fit, a new tenant in his own place. Grants of lands with liberty of alienation, as they became more frequent, appear in process of time to have furnished the rule by which all grants were construed. During the long and feeble reign of Henry III. this change to the disadvantage of the lord appears to have taken place; for at the beginning of the next reign it seems to have been established that, in whatever form the grant were made, the fact of the existence of an expectant heir enabled the tenant to alienate, not only as against his heirs, but also as against the lord. If therefore lands were given to a man and his heirs, he could at once dispose of them; and if lands were granted to a man and the heirs of his body, he could at once dispose of them as against the heirs of his body. And he was able, the moment he had issue born — that is, the moment he had an expectant heir of the kind mentioned in the gift — to alienate the lands as against the lord also; and the alienee and his heirs had a right to hold, not only during the existence of the issue, but also after their failure. The original intention of such gifts was therefore in a great measure defeated; originally, on failure of the issue the lands reverted to the donor; but now nothing was requisite but the mere birth of issue to give the donee a complete power of disposition.

The mere existence of an expectant heir having thus grown up into a reason for alienation, the barons of the time of Edw. I. began to feel how small was the possibility, that the lands, which they had granted by conditional gifts to their tenants and the heirs of their bodies, should ever revert to themselves again; whilst at the same time they perceived the power of their own families weakened by successive alienations. To remedy these evils, and to keep up that feudal system, which landlords ever held in high esteem, but on which the necessities of society ever made silent yet sure encroaches, it was enacted in the reign of Edw. I. by the famous statute De Donis Conditionalibus, — and no doubt as was then thought finally enacted, — that the will of the donor, according to the form in the deed of gift manifestly expressed, should be from thenceforth observed; so that they, to whom the tenement was given, should have no power to alien it, whereby it should fail to remain unto their own issue after their death, or to revert unto the donor or his heirs, if issue should fail.

Since the passing of this statute, an estate given to a man and the heirs of his body has been always called an estate tail, or, more properly, an estate in fee tail (feudum talliatum). The word fee (feudum) anciently meant any estate feudally held of another person; but its meaning is now confined to estates of inheritance, — that is, to estates which may descend to heirs; so that a fee may now be said to mean an inheritance. The word tail is derived from the French word tattler, to cut, the inheritance being, by the statute De Donis, cut down and confined to the heirs of the body strictly; but, though an estate tail still bears a name indicative of a restriction of the inheritance from any interruption in its course of perpetual descent from father to son, we shall find that in fact the right to establish such exclusive perpetual descent has long since been abolished. Inconvenience When the statute began to operate, the inconvenience of strict en tails, of the strict entails, created under its authority, became sensibly felt: children, it is said, grew disobedient when they knew they could not be set aside; farmers were deprived of their leases; creditors were defrauded of their debts; and innumerable latent entails were produced to deprive purchasers of the land they had fairly bought; treasons also were encouraged, as estates tail were not liable to forfeiture longer than for the tenant's life. The nobility, however, would not consent to a repeal, which was many times attempted by the commons, and for about two hundred years the statute remained in force. At length the power of alienation was once more introduced, by means of a quiet decision of the judges, in a case which occurred in the twelfth year of the reign of King Edward IV. In this case, called *Taltarum's case*, the destruction of an entail was accomplished by judicial proceedings collusively taken against a tenant in tail for the recovery of the lands entailed. Such proceedings were not at that period quite unknown to the English law, for the monks had previously hit upon a similar device, for the purpose of evading the statutes of Mortmain, by which open conveyances of lands to their religious houses had been prohibited; and this device they had practised with considerable success till restrained by act of parliament. In the case of which we are now speaking, the law would not allow the entail to be destroyed simply by the recovery of the lands entailed, by a friendly plaintiff on a fictitious title; this would have been too barefaced; and in such a case the issue of the tenant, claiming under the gift to him in tail, might have recovered the lands by means of a writ of *formedon*, so called because they claimed *per formam doni*, according to the form of the gift, which the statute had declared should be observed. The alienation of the lands entailed was effected in a more circuitous mode, by judicial sanction being given to the following proceedings, which afterwards came into frequent and open use, and had some little show of justice to the issue, though without any of its reality. The tenant in tail, on the collusive action being brought, was allowed to bring into Court some third person, presumed to have been the original grantor of the estate tail. The tenant then alleged that this third person had *warranted* the title; and accordingly begged that he might defend the title which he had so warranted. This third person was accordingly called on; who, in fact, had had nothing I to do with the matter; but, being a party in the scheme, he admitted the alleged warranty, and then allowed judgment to go against him by default. Whereupon, judgment was given for the demandant or plaintiff, to recover the lands from the tenant in tall; and the tenant in tail had judgment empowering him to recover a recompence in lands of *equal value* from the defaulter, who had thus cruelly failed in defending his title. If any such lands *had* been recovered under the judgment, they would have been held by the tenant for an estate tail, and would have descended to the issue, in lieu of those which were lost by the warrantor's default. But the defaulter, on whom the burden was thus cast, was a man who had no lands to give, some man of straw, who could easily be prevailed on to undertake the responsibility; and, in later times, the crier of the Court was usually employed. So that, whilst the issue had still the judgment of the Court in their favour, unfortunately for them it was against the wrong person; and virtually their right was defeated, and the estate tail was said to be *barred*. Not only were the issue barred of their right, but the donor, who had made the grant, and to whom the lands were to revert on failure of issue, had his reversion barred at the same time. So also all estates which the donor might have given to other persons, expectant on the decease of the tenant in tail without issue, (and which estates are called *remainders* expectant on the estate tail,) were equally barred. The demandant, in whose favour judgment was given, became possessed of an estate in fee simple in the lands; an estate the largest allowed by law, and bringing with it the fullest powers of alienation, as will be hereafter explained; and the demandant, being a friend of the tenant in tail, of course disposed of the estate in fee simple according to his wishes.

Such a piece of solemn juggling could not long have held its ground, had it not been supported by its substantial benefit to the community; but, as it was, the progress of events tended only to make that certain which at first was questionable; and proceedings on the principle of those above related, under the name of suffering *common recoveries*, maintained their ground, and long continued in common use as the undoubted privilege of every tenant in tail. The right to suffer a common recovery was considered as the inseparable incident of an estate tail, and every attempt to restrain this right was held void. Complex, however, as the proceedings above related may appear, the ordinary forms of a *common recovery* in later times were more complicated still. The lands were in the first place conveyed, by a deed called the recovery deed, to person against whom the action was to be brought, and who was called the tenant to the *præcipe* or writ. The proceedings then took place in the Court of Common Pleas, which had an exclusive jurisdiction in all real actions. A regular writ was issued against the tenant to the *præcipe* by another person, called the *demandant*; the tenant in tail was then required by the tenant to the *præcipe* to warrant his title according to a supposed engagement for that purpose; this was called vouching the tenant in tail to warranty. The tenant in tail, on being vouched, then vouched to warranty in the same way the crier of the court, who was called the common vouchee. The demandant then craved leave to imparl or confer with the last vouchee in private, which was granted by the court; and the vouchee, having thus got out of court, did not return; consequence of which, judgment was given in the manner before mentioned, on which a regular writ was directed to the sheriff to put the demandant into possession. The proceedings, as may be supposed, necessarily passed through numerous hands, so that mistakes were not unfrequently made, and great expense was always incurred. To remedy this evil, an act of parliament was accordingly passed in the year 1833, on the recommendation of the commissioners on the law of real property. This act, which in the wisdom of its design, and the skill of its execution, is quite a model of legislative reform, abolished the whole of the cumbrous and suspicious-looking machinery of common recoveries. It has substituted in their place a simple deed, executed by the tenant in tail and in-rolled in the Chancery Division of the High Court of Justice: by such a deed, a tenant in tail in possession is now enabled to dispose of the lands entailed for an estate in fee simple; thus at once defeating the claims of his issue, and of all persons having any estates in remainder or reversion.

A common recovery was not, in later times, the only way in which an estate tail might be barred. There was another assurance as effectual in defeating the claim of the issue, though it was inoperative as to the remainders and reversion. This assurance was a fine. Fines were in *themselves*, though not in their operation on estates tail, of far higher antiquity than common recoveries. They were not, like recoveries, actions at law carried out through every stage of the process; but were fictitious actions, commenced and then compromised by leave of the Court, whereby the lands in question were acknowledged to be the right of one of the parties. They were called *fines* from their having anciently put an *end*, as well to the pretended suit, as to all claims not made within a year and a day afterwards, a summary method of ending all disputes, grounded on the solemnity and publicity of the proceedings as taking place in open Court. This power of barring future claims was taken from fines in the reign of Edward III.; but it was again restored, with an extension however of the time of claim to five years, by statutes of Richard III. and Henry VII.; by which statutes also provision was made for the open proclamation of all fines several times in Court, during which proclamation all pleas were to cease; and in order that a fine might operate as a bar after non-claim for five years, it was necessary that it should be *levied*, as it was said, with proclamations. But now, by a statute of the present reign, all fines heretofore levied in the Court of Common Pleas shall be conclusively deemed to have been levied with proclamations, and shall have the force and effect of fines with proclamations. A judicial construction of the statute of Henry VII., quite apart, as it should seem, from its real intention, gave to a fine by a tenant in tail the force of a bar to his issue after non-claim by them for five years after the fine; and this construction was confirmed by a statute of the reign of Henry VIII., which made the bar immediate. Since this time the effect of fines in barring an entail, so far as the issue were concerned, remained unquestioned till their abolition; which took place at the same time, and by the same act of parliament, as the abolition of common recoveries. A deed inrolled in the Chancery Division of the High Court has now been substituted, as well for a fine, as for a common recovery.

Although strict and continuous entails have long been virtually abolished, their remembrance seems still to linger in many country places, where the notion of *heir land*, that must perpetually descend from father to son, is still to be met with. It is needless to say that such a notion is quite incorrect. In families where the estates are kept up from one generation to another, settlements are made every few years for this purpose; thus in the event of a marriage, a life estate merely is given to the husband; the wife has an allowance for pin money during the marriage, and a rent-charge or annuity by way of jointure for her life, in case she should survive her husband. Subject to this jointure, and to the payment of such sums as may be agreed on for the portions of the daughters and younger sons of the marriage, *the eldest son who may be born of the marriage is made by the settlement tenant in tail*. In case of his decease without issue, it is provided that the second son, and then the third, should in like manner be tenant in tail; and so on to the others; and in default of sons, the estate is usually given to the daughters. By this means the estate is tied up till some tenant in tail attains the age of twenty-one years; when he is able, with the consent of the father, who is tenant for life, to bar the entail with all the remainders. Dominion is thus again acquired over the property, which dominion is usually exercised in a re-settlement on the next generation; and thus the property is preserved in the family. Primogeniture, therefore, as it obtains among the landed gentry of England, is a *custom* only, and not a *right*; though there can be no doubt that the custom has originated in the right, which was enjoyed by the eldest son, as heir to his father, in those days when estates tail could not be barred. Primogeniture, as a custom, has been the subject of much remark. Where family honours or family estates are to be preserved, some such device appears necessary. But, in other cases, strict settlements of the kind referred to seem fitted rather to maintain the posthumous pride of present owners, than the welfare of future generations. The policy of the law is now in favour of the free disposition of all kinds of property; and as it allows estates tail to be barred, so it will not permit the object of an entail to be accomplished by other means, any farther than can be done by giving estates to the unborn children of *living persons*. Thus an estate given to the children of an *unborn child* would be absolutely void. The desire of individuals to keep up their name and memory has often been opposed to this rule of law, and many shifts and devices have from time to time been tried to keep up a perpetual entail, or something that might answer the same end. But such contrivances have invariably been defeated; and no plan can be now adopted by which lauds can with certainty be tied up, or fixed as to their future destination, for a longer period than the lives of existing persons and a term of twenty-one years after their decease.

Whenever an estate tail is not an estate in possession, but is preceded by a life interest to be enjoyed by some other person prior to the possession of the lands by the tenant in tail, the power of such tenant in tail to acquire an estate in fee simple in remainder expectant on the decease of the tenant for life is subject to some limitation. In the time when an estate tail, together with the reversion, could only be barred by a recovery, it was absolutely necessary that the first tenant for life, who had the possession of the lands, should concur in the proceedings; for no recovery could be suffered, unless on a feigned action brought against the feudal holder of the possession. This technical rule of law was also a valuable check on the tenant in tail under every ordinary settlement of landed property; for, when the eldest son (who, as we have seen, is usually made tenant in tail) came of age, he found that, before he could acquire the dominion expectant on the decease of his father, the tenant for life, he must obtain from his father consent for the purpose. Opportunity was thus given for providing that no ill use should be made of the property. When recoveries were abolished, the consent formerly required was accordingly still preserved, with some little modification. The act abolishing recoveries has established the office of *protector*, which almost always exists during the continuance of such estates under the settlement as may precede an estate tail. And the consent of the protector is required to be given, either by the same deed by which the entail is barred, or by a separate deed, to be executed on or before the day of the execution of the former, and to be also inrolled in the Chancery Division of the High Court at or previously to the time of the inrolment of the deed which bars the entail. Without such consent, the remainders and reversion cannot be barred. In ordinary cases the protector is the first tenant for life under the settlement, in analogy to the old law; but a power is given by the act, to any person entailing lands, to appoint, in the place of the tenant for life, any number of persons, not exceeding three, to be together protector of the settlement during the continuance of the preceding estates; and, in such a case, the consent of such persons only need be obtained in order to effect a complete bar to the estate tail, and the remainders and reversion. The protector is under no restraint in giving or withholding his consent, but is left entirely to his own discretion. If he should refuse to consent, the tenant in tail may still bar his own issue; as he might have done before the act by levying a fine; but he cannot bar estates in remainder or reversion. The consequence of such a limited bar is, that the tenant acquires a disposable estate in the land for so long as he has any issue or descendants living, and no longer; that is, so long as the estate tail would have lasted had no bar been placed on it. This is called a base fee. But, when his issue fail, the persons having estates in remainder or reversion become entitled. When the estate tail is in possession, that is, when there is no previous estate for life or otherwise, there can very seldom be any protector, and the tenant in tail may, at any time by deed duly inrolled, bar the entail, remainders, and reversion at his own pleasure. And where a previous estate for life exists, it does not confer the office of protector, unless it be created by the same settlement which created the estate tail; so that a tenant in tail in remainder expectant on an estate for life, created by some prior deed or will, may bar the entail, remainders, and reversion, without the consent of the tenant for life under such prior deed or will.

The above-mentioned right of a tenant in tail to bar the entail is subject to a few exceptions; which, though of not very frequent occurrence, it may be as well to mention. And, first, estates tail granted by the crown as the reward for public services cannot be barred so long as the reversion continues in the crown. This restriction was imposed by an act of parliament of the reign of Henry VIII., and it has been continued by the act by which fines and recoveries were abolished, and by the act to facilitate leases and sales of settled estates, so far as regards any sale or lease beyond the term of twenty-one years. There are also some cases in which entails have been created by particular acts of parliament, and cannot be barred.

Again, an estate tail cannot be barred by any person who is *tenant in tail after possibility of issue extinct*. This can only happen where a person is tenant in *special* tail. For instance, if an estate be given to a man and the heirs of his body by his present wife; in this case, if the wife should die without issue, he would become tenant in tail after possibility of issue extinct; the possibility of his having issue who could inherit the estate tail would have become extinct on the death of his wife. A tenancy of this kind can never arise in an ordinary estate in tail general or tail male; for, so long as a person lives, the law considers that the possibility of issue continues, however improbable it may be from the great age of the party. Tenants in tail after possibility of issue extinct were prohibited from suffering common recoveries by a statute of the reign of Elizabeth, and a similar prohibition is contained in the Act for the Abolition of Fines and Recoveries. But, as we have before remarked, tenancies in special tail are not now common. In modern times, when it is intended to make a provision for the children of a particular marriage, estates are given directly to the unborn children, which take effect as they come into existence; whereas in ancient times, as we shall hereafter see, it was not lawful to give any estate directly to an unborn child.

The last exception is one that can only arise in the case of grants and settlements made before the passing of the Act for the Abolition of Fines and Recoveries; for the future it has been abolished. It relates to women who are tenants in tail of lands of their husbands, or lands given by any of his ancestors. After the decease of the husband, a woman so tenant in tail *ex provisione viri* was prohibited by an old statute from suffering a recovery without the assent, recorded or inrolled, of the heirs next inheritable to her, or of him or them that next after her death should have an estate of inheritance, (that is, in tail or in fee simple,) in the lands: she was also prohibited from levying a fine under the same circumstances by the statute which confirmed to fines their force in other cases. This kind of tenancy in tail very rarely occurs in modern practice, having been superseded by the settlements now usually made on the unborn children of the marriage.

It is important to observe that an estate tail can only be barred by an actual conveyance by deed, duly inrolled according to the act of parliament by which a deed was substituted for a common recovery or fine. Thus every attempt by a tenant in tail to leave the lands entailed by his will, and every contract to sell them, not completed in his lifetime by the proper bar, will be null and void as against his issue claiming under the entail, or as against the remaindermen or reversioners, (that is, the owners of estates in remainder or reversion,) should there be no such issue left.

A tenant in tail may cut down timber for his own benefit, and commit what waste he pleases, without the necessity of barring the entail for that purpose. A tenant in tail was moreover empowered by a statute of Henry VIII. to make leases, under certain restrictions, of such of the lands entailed as had been most commonly let to farm for twenty years before; but such leases were not to exceed twenty-one years, or three lives, from the day of the making thereof, and the accustomed yearly rent was to be reserved. This power was however of little use; for leases under this statute, though binding on the issue, were not binding on the remainderman or reversioner, and consequently had not that certainty of enjoyment which is the great inducement to the outlay of capital, and the consequent improvement of landed property; and this statute has been recently repealed. The Act for the Abolition of Fines and Recoveries now empowers every tenant in tail in possession to make leases by deed, without the necessity of inrolment, for any term not exceeding twenty-one years, to commence from the date of the lease, or from any time not exceeding twelve calendar months from the date of the lease, where a rent shall be thereby reserved, which, at the time of granting such lease, shall be a rack-rent, or not less than five-sixth parts of a rack-rent.

It has been observed that, in ancient times, estates tail were not subject to forfeiture for high treason beyond the life of the tenant in tail. This privilege they were deprived of by an act of parliament passed in the reign of Henry VIII., by which all estates of inheritance (under which general words estates tail were covertly included) were declared to be forfeited to the king upon any conviction of high treason. But the act "to abolish forfeitures for treason and felony and to otherwise amend the law relating thereto" now provides, that after the passing of that act, which took place on the 4th July, 1870, no confession, verdict, inquest, conviction or judgment of or for any treason or felony or felo de se shall cause any attainder or corruption of blood or any forfeiture or escheat. The attainder of the ancestor did not of itself prevent the descent of an estate tail to his issue, as they claimed from the original donor, *per formam doni*; and, therefore, on attainder for murder, an estate tail still descended to the issue. By virtue of another statute of the reign of Henry VIII., estates tail are charged, in the hands of the heir, with debts due from his ancestor to the crown, by judgment, recognizance, obligation, or other specialty, although the *heir* shall not be comprised therein. And all arrears and debts due to the crown, by accountants to the crown, whose yearly or total receipts exceed three hundred pounds, were, by a later statute of the reign of Elizabeth, placed on the same footing. But estates tail, if suffered to descend, were not subject to the debts of the deceased tenant owing to private individuals. By an act passed at the commencement of Her present Majesty's reign debts, for the payment of which any judgment, decree, order or rule had been given or made by any court of law or equity, were made binding on the lands of the debtor, as against the issue of his body, and also as against all other persons whom he might, without the assent of any other person, cut off and debar from any remainder or reversion. But a more recent statute has enacted that no such judgment, decree, order or rule to be entered up after the 29th of July, 1864, the date of the act, shall affect any land until such land shall have been actually delivered in execution. An estate tail may also be barred and disposed of on the bankruptcy of a tenant in tail, for the benefit of his creditors, to the same extent as he might have barred or disposed of it for his own benefit.

In addition to the liabilities above mentioned are the rights which the marriage of a tenant in tail confers on the wife, if the tenant be a man, or on the husband, if the tenant be a woman; an account of which will be contained in a future chapter on the relation of husband and wife. But, subject to these rights and liabilities, an estate tail, if not duly barred, will descend to the issue of the donee in due course of law; all of whom will be necessarily tenants in tail, and will enjoy the same powers of disposition as their ancestor, the original donee in tail. The course of descent of an estate tail is similar, so far as it goes, to that of an estate in fee simple, an explanation of which the reader will find in the fourth chapter.

If an estate *pur autre vie* should be given to a person and the heirs of his body, a *quasi entail*, as it is called, will be created, and the estate will descend, during its continuance, in the same manner as an ordinary estate tail. But the owner of such an estate in possession may bar his issue, and all remainders, by an ordinary deed of conveyance, without any inrolment under the statute for the abolition of fines and recoveries. If the estate tail be in remainder expectant on an estate for life, the concurrence of the tenant for life is necessary to enable the tenant in tail to defeat the subsequent remainders.

CHAPTER III
OF AN ESTATE IN FEE SIMPLE

An estate in fee simple *(feudum simplex)* is the greatest estate or interest which the law of England allows any person to possess in landed property. A tenant in fee simple is he that holds lands or tenements to him *and his heirs*; so that the estate is descendible, not merely to the heirs *of his body*, but to *collateral* relations, according to the rules and canons of descent. An estate in fee simple is of course an estate of *freehold*, being a larger estate than either an estate for life, or in tail.

It is not, however, the mere descent of an estate in fee simple to collateral heirs, that has given to this estate its present value and importance: the unfettered right of alienation, which is now inseparably incident to this estate, is by far its most valuable quality. This right has been of gradual growth: for, as we have seen, estates were at first inalienable by tenants, without their lord's consent; and the heir did not derive his title so much from his ancestor as from the lord, who, when he gave to the ancestor, gave also to his heirs. In process of time, however, the ancestor acquired, as we have already seen, the right, first, of disappointing the expectations of his heir, and then of defeating the interests of his lord. The alienations, by which these results were effected were, as will be remembered, either the subinfeudation of parts of the land, to be holden of the grantor, or the conveyance of the whole, to be holden of the superior lord. It was impossible to make a grant of part of the lands to be holden of the superior lord without his consent; for, the services reserved on any grant were considered as entire and indivisible in their nature. The tenant, consequently, if he wished to dispose of part of his lands, was obliged to create a tenure between his grantee and himself, by reserving to himself and his heirs such services as would remunerate him for the services, which he himself was liable to render to his superior lord. In this manner the tenant became a lord in his turn; and the method, which the tenants were thus obliged to adopt, when alienating part of their lands, was usually resorted to by choice, whenever they had occasion to part with the whole; for the *immediate* lord of the holder of any lands had advantages of a feudal nature which did not belong to the superior lord when any mesne lordship intervened; it was therefore desirable for every feudal lord, that the *possession* of the lands should always be holden by his own immediate tenants. The barons at the time of Edward I. accordingly, perceiving that, by the continual subinfeudations of their tenants, their privileges as superior lords were gradually encroached on, proceeded to procure an enactment in their own favour with respect to estates in fee simple, as they had then already done with regard to estates tail. They did not, however, in this case, attempt to restrain the practice of alienation altogether, but simply procured a prohibition of the practice of subinfeudation; and at the same time obtained, for their tenants, facility of alienation of parts of their lands, to be holden of the chief lords.

The statute by which these objects were effected is known by the name of the statute of *Quia emptores*; so called from the words with which it commences. It enacts, that from thenceforth it shall be lawful to every freeman to sell at his own pleasure his lands and tenements or part thereof, so nevertheless that the feoffee (or purchaser) shall hold the same lands or tenements of the same chief lord of the fee, and by the same services and customs, as his feoffor held them before. And it further enacts, that, if he sell any part of such his lands or tenements to any person, the feoffee shall hold that part immediately of the chief lord, and shall be forthwith charged with so much service as pertaineth, or ought to pertain, to the said chief lord, for such part, according to the quantity of the land or tenement so sold. This statute did not extend to those who held of the king as tenants *in capite*, who were kept in restraint for some time longer. Free liberty of alienation was however subsequently acquired by them; and the right of disposing of an estate in fee simple, by act *inter vivos*, is now the undisputed privilege of every tenant of such an estate.

The alienation of lands by will was not allowed in this country, from the time the feudal system became completely rooted, until many years after alienation *inter vivos* had been sanctioned by the statute of *Quia emptores*. The city of London, and a few other favoured places, formed exceptions to the general restraint on the power of testamentary alienation of estates in fee simple; for in these places tenements might be devised by will, in virtue of a special custom. In process of time, however, a method of devising lands by will was covertly adopted by means of conveyances to other parties, *to such uses* as the person conveying should appoint by his will. This indirect mode of devising lands was intentionally restrained by the operation of a statute, passed in the reign of King Henry VIII., known by the name of the Statute of Uses, to which we shall hereafter have occasion to make frequent reference. But only five years after the passing of this statute, lands were by a further statute expressly rendered devisable by will. This great change in the law was effected by statutes of the 32nd and 34th of Henry VIII. But even by these statutes the right to devise was partial only, as to lands of the then prevailing tenure; and it was not till the restoration of King Charles II., when the feudal tenures were abolished, that the right of devising freehold lands by will became complete and universal. At the present day, every tenant in fee simple so fully enjoys the right of alienating the lands he holds, either in his lifetime or by his will, that most tenants in fee think themselves to be the lords of their own domains; whereas, in fact, all landowners are merely tenants in the eye of the law, as will hereafter more clearly appear.

Blackstone's explanation of an estate in fee simple is, that a tenant in fee simple holds to him and his heirs for ever, generally, absolutely and simply, without mentioning *what* heirs, but referring that to his own pleasure, or the disposition of the law. But the idea of nominating an heir to succeed to the inheritance has no place in the English law, however it might have obtained in the Roman jurisprudence. The heir is always appointed by the law, the maxim being *Solus Deus hœredem facere potest, non homo*; and all other persons, whom a tenant in fee simple may please to appoint as his successors, are not his *heirs* but his *as-*

signs. Thus, a purchaser from him in his lifetime, and a devisee under his will, are alike *assigns* in law, claiming in opposition to, and in exclusion of the *heir*, who would otherwise have become entitled.

With respect to certain persons, exceptions occur to the right of alienation. Before the Naturalization Act, 1870, if an *alien* or foreigner, under no allegiance to the crown, purchased an estate in lands, the crown might at any time have asserted a right to such estate; unless it were merely a lease taken by a subject of a friendly state for the residence or occupation of himself or his servants, or the purpose of any business, trade, or manufacture, for a term not exceeding twenty-one years. For the conveyance to an alien of any greater estate in lands in this country, was a cause of forfeiture to the Queen, who, after an inquest of office had been held for the purpose of finding the truth of the facts, might have seized the lands accordingly. Before office found, that is, before the verdict of any such inquest of office had been given, an alien might have made a conveyance to a natural-born subject; and such conveyance would have been valid for all purposes, except to defeat the prior right of the crown, which would have still continued. No person is considered an alien who is born within the dominions of the crown, even though such person may be the child of an alien, unless such alien should be the subject of a hostile prince. And in *Calvin's case*, a person born in Scotland after the accession of James I. to the crown of England, was held to be a natural-born subject, and consequently entitled to hold lands in England, although the two kingdoms had not then been united. Again, the children of the Queen's ambassadors are natural-born subjects by the Common Law; and, by several acts of parliament, the privileges of natural-born subjects have been accorded to the lawful children, though born abroad, of a natural-born father, and also to the grandchildren on the father's side of a natural-born subject; and more recently, the children of a natural-born mother, though born abroad, were rendered capable of taking any real or personal estate. It was also provided that any woman, who should be married to a natural-born subject or person naturalized, should be taken to be herself naturalized, and have all the rights and privileges of a natural-born subject. And by a statute of the reign of William the Third all the king's natural-born subjects were enabled to trace their title by descent through their alien ancestors. Any foreigner may be made a denizen by the Queen's letters patent, and capable as such of acquiring lands by purchase, though not by descent, or may be naturalized by act of parliament. But the Naturalization Act, 1870, now provides that real and personal property of every description may be taken, acquired, held and disposed of by an alien in the same manner in all respects as by a natural-born British subject; and a title to real and personal property of every description may be derived through, from or in succession to an alien in the same manner in all respects as through, from or in succession to a natural-born British subject. This act repeals many of the former statutes with respect to aliens, and contains several important amendments of the general law on this subject.

Infants, or all persons under the age of twenty-one years, and also *idiots* and *lunatics*, though they may hold lands, are incapacitated from making a binding disposition of any estate in them. The conveyances of infants are generally voidable only, and those of lunatics and idiots appear to be absolutely void, unless they were made by feoffment with livery of seisin before the year 1845. But by a recent act of parliament, every infant, not under twenty if a male, and not under seventeen if a female, is empowered to make a valid and binding settlement on his or her marriage, with the sanction of the Chancery Division of the High Court. If, however, any disentailing assurance shall have been executed by an infant tenant in tail under the provisions of the act, and such infant shall afterwards die under age, such disentailing assurance shall thereupon become absolutely void. Under certain circumstances, also, for the sake of making a title to lands, infants have been empowered, by modern acts of parliament, to make conveyances of fee simple and other estates, under the direction of the Chancery Division of the High Court. And more extensive powers, with respect to the estates of idiots and lunatics, have been given to their *committees*, or the persons who have had committed to them the charge of such idiots and lunatics. Power is also given to the Chancery Division of the High Court in the case of infants, and to the Lord Chancellor or either of the Lords Justices, intrusted by virtue of the Queen's sign manual with the care of the persons and estates of idiots and lunatics, by a simple order, to vest in any other person the lands of which any infant, idiot or lunatic may be seised or possessed upon any trust or by way of mortgage. The Supreme Court of Judicature Act, 1875, provides that any jurisdiction usually vested in the Lords Justices of Appeal in Chancery, or either of them, in relation to the persons and estates of idiots, lunatics and persons of unsound mind, shall be exercised by such judge or judges of the High Court of Justice or Court of Appeal as may be intrusted by the Queen's sign manual with the care and commitment of the custody of such persons and estates.

Married women are under a limited incapacity to alienate, as will hereafter appear. And before the abolition of forfeiture for treason and felony persons attainted for these crimes could not, by any conveyance which they might make, defeat the right to their estates, which their attainder gave to the crown, or to the lord, of whom their estates were holden.

There are certain objects, also, in respect of which the alienation of lands is restricted. In the reign of George II. an act was passed, commonly called the Mortmain Act, the object of which, as expressed in the preamble, was to prevent improvident alienations or dispositions of landed estates, by languishing or dying persons, to the disherison of their lawful heirs. This statute provides that no lands or hereditaments, nor any money, stock, or other personal estate, to be laid out in the purchase of any lands or hereditaments, shall be conveyed or settled for any charitable uses, unless by deed indented, sealed and delivered in the presence of two or more credible witnesses, twelve calendar months at least before the death of the donor or grantor, including the days of the execution and death, and inrolled in the High Court of Chancery within six calendar months next after the execution thereof; and unless such stock be transferred six calendar months at least before the death of the donor or grantor, including the days of the transfer and death; and unless the same be made to take effect in possession for the charitable use intended immediately from the making thereof, and be without any power of revocation, reservation, trust, condition, limitation, clause, or agreement whatsoever, for the benefit of the donor or grantor, or of any person or persons claiming under him. Provided always, that nothing therein before mentioned relating to the sealing and delivering of any deed twelve calendar months at least before the death of the grantor, or to the transfer of any stock six calendar months before the death of the grantor, shall extend to any purchase of any estate or interest in lands or hereditaments, or any transfer of stock to be made really and bona fide for a full and valuable consideration actually paid at or before the making of such conveyance or transfer, without fraud or collusion. And all gifts, conveyances and settlements for any charitable uses whatsoever made in any other manner or form than by that act is directed, are declared to be absolutely and to all intents and purposes null and void. Gifts to either of the two Universities, or any of their colleges, or to the college of Eton, Winchester or Westminster, for the support and maintenance of the scholars only upon those foundations, are excepted. It will be seen that in consequence of this act no gift of any estate in land for charitable purposes can be made by will. By an act of parliament passed on the 25th July, 1828, the title to lands then already purchased for valuable consideration for charitable purposes is rendered valid, notwithstanding the want of an indenture duly attested and inrolled; but the act is retrospective merely.

The stringency of the provisions in the Mortmain Act has often been felt to be unnecessarily great, especially with regard to that part of the act which provides that there shall be no reservation or clause whatever for the benefit of the donor or grantor. And several acts have recently been passed to amend the law relating to the conveyance of land for charitable uses. One act, which was passed on the 17th of May, 1861, provides that no assurance for charitable uses shall be void by reason of the deed or assurance not being indented, or not purporting to be indented, nor by reason of such deed or assurance, or any deed forming part of the same transaction, containing any grant or reservation of any peppercorn or other nominal rent, or of any mines or minerals or easement, or any covenants or provisions as to the erection, repair, position, or description of buildings, the formation or repair of streets or roads, drainage or nuisance, or any covenants or provisions of the like nature, for the use and enjoyment as well of the hereditaments comprised in such deed or assurance as of any other adjacent or neighbouring hereditaments, or any right of entry on non-payment of any such rent, or on breach of any such covenant or provision, or any stipulations of the like nature, for the benefit of the donor or grantor, or of any person or persons claiming under him; nor in the case of copyholds by reason of the assurance not being made by deed; nor in the case of such assurances, made bona fide on a sale for a full and valuable consideration, by reason of such consideration consisting wholly or partly of a rent, rent-charge, or other annual payment, reserved or made payable to the vendor or to any other person, with or without a right of re-entry for non-payment thereof: provided that in all reservations authorized by the act, the donor, grantor or vendor shall reserve the same benefits for his representatives as for himself. The act further provides, that in all cases where the charitable uses of any deed or assurance thereafter to be made for conveyance of any hereditaments for any charitable uses shall be disclosed by any separate deed, the deed of conveyance need not be inrolled: but it will be void, unless such separate deed be inrolled in the Chancery Division of the High Court within six calendar months next after the making or perfecting of the deed for conveyance.

This act, it will be observed, provided only for the reservation of a *nominal* rent, except in the case of an assurance made bonâ fide on a sale for a full and valuable consideration; so that a gift of land to a charity, reserving a pecuniary rent or rent-charge to the grantor, would still have been void. Moreover no alteration was made in that part of the Mortmain Act which relates to the execution of the deed twelve calendar months at least before the death of the grantor. The only exception which that act allowed was in the case of a purchase of land bonâ fide, for a full and valuable consideration actually paid *at or before* the making of the conveyance. If on a purchase a rent were reserved to the vendor, it is clear that the full consideration was not actually paid at the making of the conveyance. There was nothing in the new act, as there was certainly nothing in the former one, to preserve such a conveyance from becoming void by the decease of the vendor within twelve calendar months from the date of the deed. This oversight in the act has been provided for by a more recent statute, which enacts that every full and bonâ fide valuable consideration which shall consist either wholly or partly of a rent or other annual payment reserved or made payable to the vendor or grantor, or to any other person, shall, for the purposes of the Mortmain Act, be as valid and have the same force and effect as if such consideration had been a sum of money actually paid at or before the making of such conveyance without fraud or collusion.

With regard to deeds and assurances already made it has been provided by another act, that all money really and bona fide expended before the 16th of May, 1862, the date of the act, in the substantial and permanent improvement, by building or otherwise for any charitable use, of land held for such charitable use, shall be deemed equivalent to money actually paid by way of consideration for the purchase of the said land. It has also been provided, that every deed or assurance by which any land shall have been demised for any term of years for any charitable use shall, for the purposes of the Mortmain Act, be deemed to have been made to take effect for the charitable use thereby intended immediately from the making thereof, if the term for which such land shall have been thereby demised was made to commence and take effect in possession at any time within one year from the date of such deed or assurance. And it has been further provided, with respect to all deeds and assurances under which possession is held for any charitable uses, that if made bona, fide for a full and valuable consideration, actually paid at or before the making of such deed or assurance, or reserved by way of rent, rent-charge, or other annual payment, or partly paid and partly so reserved, no such deed or assurance shall be void within the Mortmain Act, if it was made to take effect in possession for the charitable uses intended immediately from the making thereof, and without any power of revocation, and has been inrolled in the Court of Chancery before the 17th of May, 1866. And all conveyances to charitable uses made upon such full and valuable consideration as aforesaid, and under which possession is held for such uses, are rendered valid where any separate deed declaring the uses has alone been inrolled, or where such separate deed shall have been executed within six calendar months from the 13th of May, 1864, and inrolled before the 17th of May, 1866. Where the original deed creating any charitable trust has been lost, the Chancery Division of the High Court is empowered to authorize the inrolment in its stead of any subsequent deed by which the trusts may sufficiently appear. And power is now given to the clerk of inrolments in Chancery for the time being to inrol any conveyance for charitable uses, if he be satisfied that the same was made really and bonâ fide for full and valuable consideration actually paid at or before the making and perfecting thereof, or reserved by way of rent-charge or other annual payment, or partly paid and partly reserved as aforesaid, without fraud or collusion, and that at the time of the application to the said clerk possession or enjoyment is held under such instrument, and that the omission to inrol the same in proper time has arisen from ignorance or inadvertence, or from the destruction thereof by time or accident. When land has been already devoted to charitable purposes, the conveyance thereof to other trustees, or to another charity, does not fall within the purview of the Mortmain Act, and accordingly requires no special attestation or inrolment. The acknowledgment of deeds prior to inrolment in the Chancery Division of the High Court is now abolished.

All endowed charities are now placed under the control of the Charity Commissioners for England and Wales. Endowed schools were for a time placed under the care of certain commissioners, called the Endowed School Commissioners. But all their powers and duties are now transferred to and imposed on the Charity Commissioners. An official trustee of charity lands has been appointed, in whom may be vested, by order of the Chancery Division of the High Court or of any judge having jurisdiction, any charity lands whenever the trustees do not or will not act, or there are no trustees, or none certainly known, or where any of the trustees are under age, lunatic or of unsound mind, or otherwise incapable of acting, or out of the jurisdiction of the Court, or where a valid appointment of new trustees cannot be made, or shall be considered too expensive. But it is now provided that where the trustees of a charity have power to determine on any disposition of any property of the charity, a majority, who are present at a meeting of their body duly constituted and vote on the question, shall have, and be deemed to have always had, full power to execute and do all such assurances, acts and things as may be requisite for carrying any such disposition into effect; and all such assurances, acts and things shall have the same effect as if they were respectively executed and done by all such trustees and by the official trustee of charity lands.

An important exception to the Mortmain Act has been introduced by acts of parliament passed to afford further facilities for the conveyance and endowment of sites for schools, by which one witness only is rendered sufficient for such a conveyance, and the death of the donor or grantor within twelve calendar months from the execution of the deed will not render it void. But by these acts the necessity of inrolment does not appear to have been dispensed with. These acts contain many other provisions for facilitating the erection of schools for the education of the poor. And, by more recent acts of parliament, provision has been made for the conveyance of sites for literary and scientific and other similar institutions; for facilitating grants of land for the recreation of adults, and as play-grounds for children; and also to afford further facilities for the conveyance of land for sites for places of religious worship and for burial places. A further important inroad upon the Mortmain Act has also been made by an act, which provides, that all alienations, except by will, bonâ fide made after the passing of that act to a trustee or trustees on behalf of any society or body of persons associated together for religious purposes, or for the promotion of education, arts, literature, science, or other like purposes, of land for the erection thereon of a building for such purposes or any of them, or whereon a building used or intended to be used for such purposes or any of them shall have been erected, shall be exempt from the provisions of the Mortmain Act, and from the provisions of the 2nd section of the act 24 Vict. c. 9: provided such disposition shall have been really and bona fide made for a full and valuable consideration actually paid upon or before the making thereof, or reserved by way of rent, rent-charge, or other annual payment, or partly paid and partly reserved as aforesaid, without fraud or collusion, and provided that each such piece of land shall not exceed two acres in extent or area in each case. The deed or instrument of disposition may at any time be inrolled in the Chancery Division of the High Court if thought fit. And by a more recent statute all gifts and assurances of land of any tenure, by deed, or by will or codicil, for the purposes only of a public park, a school-house for an elementary school, or a public museum, are rendered valid notwithstanding the Statutes of Mortmain. But every such will or codicil, and every such deed made otherwise than for full and valuable consideration, must be made twelve calendar months at least before the death of the testator or grantor, and must be inrolled in the books of the charity commissioners within six calendar months next after the time when the same shall come into operation. But the act does not authorize any gift by will or codicil of more than twenty acres of land for any one public park, or of more than two acres of land for any one public museum, or of more than one acre of land for any one school-house.

Again, no conveyance can be made to any *corporation*, unless a licence to take lands has been granted to it by the crown. Formerly, licence from the lord, of whom a tenant in fee simple held his estate, was also necessary to enable him to alienate his lands to any corporation. For, this alienation to a body having perpetual existence was an injury to the lord, who was then entitled to many advantages, to be hereafter detailed, so long as the estate was in private hands; but in the hands of a corporation these advantages ceased. In modern times, the rights of the lords having become comparatively trifling, the licence of the crown alone has been rendered by parliament sufficient for the purpose. And it is now provided that any incorporated charity may, with the consent of the charity commissioners, invest money arising from any sale of land belonging to the charity, or received by way of equality of exchange or partition, in the purchase of land; and may hold such land or any land acquired by way of exchange or partition, for the benefit of such charity, without any licence in mortmain. It is further provided, that all corporations and trustees in the United Kingdom holding monies in trust for any public or charitable purpose may invest such monies on any real security authorized by or consistent with the trusts on which such monies are held, without being deemed thereby to have acquired or become possessed of any land within the meaning of the laws relating to mortmain or of any prohibition or restraint against the holding of land by such corporations or trustees contained in any charter or act of parliament. And no contract for or conveyance of any interest in land made bonâ fide for the purpose only of such security shall be deemed void by reason of any noncompliance with the conditions and solemnities required by the Mortmain Act. Provision has been lately made for the incorporation of trustees of charities for religious, educational, literary, scientific and public charitable purposes by means of a certificate of registration of the trustees as a corporate body, to be granted by the Charity Commissioners of England and Wales, with power to hold and convey lands in the same manner as the trustees might do without such incorporation. Every joint-stock company registered under the Joint-Stock Companies Acts has also power to hold lands; but no company formed for the purpose of promoting art, science, religion, charity or any other like object, not involving the acquisition of gain by the company or by the individual members thereof, shall, without the sanction of the Board of Trade, hold more than two acres of land; but the Board of Trade may, by licence under the hand of one of their principal or assistant secretaries, empower any such company to hold lands in such quantity and subject to such conditions as they think fit.

By a statute of the reign of Elizabeth, conveyances of landed estates, and also of goods, made for the purpose of delaying, hindering or defrauding creditors, are void as against them; unless made upon *good*, which here means *valuable*, consideration, and *bonâ fide*, to any person not having, at the time of the conveyance, any notice of such fraud. And, by a subsequent statute of the same reign, voluntary conveyances of any estate in lands, tenements, or other hereditaments whatsoever, and conveyances of such estates made with any clause of revocation at the will of the grantor, are also void as against subsequent purchasers for money or other valuable consideration. The effect of this enactment is, that any person who has made a voluntary settlement of landed property, even on his own children, may afterwards sell the same property to any purchaser; and the purchaser, even though he have full notice of the settlement, will hold the lands without danger of interruption from the persons on whom they had been previously settled. But if the settlement be founded on any valuable consideration, such as that of an intended marriage, it cannot be defeated.

The methods by which a tenant in fee simple can alienate his estate in his lifetime will be reserved for future consideration, as will also the subject of alienation by testament. As a tenant in fee simple may alienate his estate at his pleasure, so he is under no control in his management of the lands, but may open mines, cut timber, and commit waste of all kinds, grant leases of any length, and charge the lands with the payment of money to any amount. Fee simple estates are moreover subject, in the hands of the heir or devisee, to *debts* of all kinds contracted by the deceased tenant. This liability to what may be called an involuntary alienation, has, like the right of voluntary alienation, been established by very slow degrees. It appears that, in the early periods of our history, the heir of a deceased person was bound, to the extent of the inheritance which descended to him, to pay such of the debts of his ancestor as the goods and chattels of the ancestor were not sufficient to satisfy. But the spirit of feudalism, which attained to such a height in the reign of Edward I., appears to have infringed on this ancient doctrine; for we find it laid down by Britton, who wrote in that reign, that no one should be held to pay the debt of his ancestor, whose heir he was, to any other person than the king, unless he were by the deed of his ancestor especially bound to do so. On this footing the law of England long continued. It allowed any person, by any deed or writing under seal (called a special contract or specialty) to bind or charge his heirs, as well as himself, with the payment of any debt, or the fulfilment of any contract: in such a case the heir was liable, on the decease of his ancestor, to pay the debt or fulfil the contract, to the value of the lands which had descended to him from the ancestor, but not further. The lands so descended were called *assets* by descent, from the French word *assez*, enough, because the heir was bound only so far as he had lands descended to him enough or sufficient to answer the debt or contract of his ancestor. If, however, the heir was not expressly named in such bond or contract, he was under no liability. When the power of testamentary alienation was granted, a debtor, who had thus bound his heirs, became enabled to defeat his creditor, by devising his estate by his will to some other person than his heir; and, in this case, neither heir nor devisee was under any liability to the creditor. Some debtors, however, impelled by a sense of justice to their creditors, left their lands to trustees in trust to sell them for the payment of their debts, or, which amounts to the same thing, charged their lands, by their wills, with the payment of their debts. The creditors then obtained payment by the bounty of their debtor; and the Court of Chancery, in distributing this bounty, thought that "equality was equity," and consequently allowed creditors by simple contract to participate equally with those who had obtained bonds binding the heirs of the deceased. In such a case the lands were called *equitable assets*. At length an act of William and Mary made void all devises by will, as against creditors by specialty in which the heirs were bound, but not further or otherwise; but devises or dispositions of any lands or hereditaments for the payment of any real and just debt or debts were exempted from the operation of the statute. Creditors, however, who had no specialty binding the heirs of their debtor, still remained without remedy against either heir or devisee; unless the debtor chose of his own accord to charge his lands by his will with the payment of his debts; in which case, as we have seen, all creditors were equally entitled to the benefit. So that, till within the last few years, a landowner might incur as many debts as he pleased, and yet leave behind him an unencumbered estate in fee simple, unless his creditors had taken proceedings in his lifetime, or he had entered into any bond or specialty binding his heirs. At length, in 1807, the fee simple estates of deceased *traders* were rendered liable to the payment, not only of debts in which their heirs were bound, but also of their simple contract debts, or debts arising in ordinary business. By a subsequent statute, the above enactments were consolidated and amended, and facilities were afforded for the sale of such estates of deceased persons as were liable by law, or by their own wills, to the payment of their debts. But, notwithstanding the efforts of a Romilly were exerted to extend so just a liability, the lands of all deceased persons, not traders at the time of their death, continued exempt from their debts by simple contract, till the year 1833; when a provision, which, but a few years before, had been strenuously opposed, was passed without the least difficulty. All estates in fee simple, which the owner should not by his will have charged with, or devised subject to, the payment of his debts, were then rendered liable to be administered in the Court of Chancery, for the payment of all the just debts of the deceased owner, as well debts due on simple contract as on specialty. But, out of respect to the ancient law, the act provided that all creditors by special contract, in which the heirs were bound, should be paid the full amount of the debts due to them before any of the creditors by simple contract, or by specialty in which the heirs were not bound, should be paid any part of their demands. If, however, the debtor should by his last will have charged his lands with, or devised them subject to, the payment of his debts, such charge was still valid, and every creditor, of whatever kind, had an equal right to participate in the produce. Hence arose this curious result, that a person who had incurred debts, both by simple contract, and by specialty in which he had bound his heirs, might, by merely charging his lands with the payment of his debts, place all his creditors on a level, so far as they might have occasion to resort to such lands; thus depriving the creditors by specialty of that priority to which they would otherwise have been entitled. This anomaly has now been remedied by an act which provides that, in the administration of the estate of any person who shall die on or after the 1st of January, 1870, no debt or liability of such person shall be entitled to any priority or preference by reason merely that the same is secured by or arises under a bond, deed or other instrument under seal, or is otherwise made or constituted a specialty debt; but all the creditors of such person, as well specialty as simple contract, shall be treated as standing in equal degree and be paid accordingly out of the assets of such deceased person, whether such assets are legal or equitable: provided that the act shall not prejudice or affect any lien, charge or other security which any creditor may hold or be entitled to for the payment of his debt. And a more recent act further provides, that in the administration by the High Court of Justice thereby established of the assets of any person who may die after the commencement of that act, and whose estate may prove to be insufficient for the payment in full of his debts and liabilities, the same rules shall prevail and be observed as to the respective rights of secured and unsecured creditors, and as to debts and liabilities proveable, and as to the valuation of annuities and future and contingent liabilities respectively, as may be in force for the time being under the law of bankruptcy with respect to the estates of persons adjudged bankrupt; and all persons who, in any such case, would be entitled to prove for and receive dividends out of the estate of any such deceased person, may come in under the decree or order for the administration of such estate, and make such claims against the same, as they may respectively be entitled to by virtue of that act.

A creditor who has taken legal proceedings against his debtor, for the recovery of his debt, in the debtor's lifetime, and has obtained the *judgment* of a Court of law in his favour, has long had a great advantage over creditors who have waited till the debtor's decease. The first enactment which gave to such a creditor a remedy against the lands of his debtor was made in the reign of Edward I., shortly before the passing of the statute of *Quia Emptores*, which sanctioned the full and free alienation of fee simple estates. By this enactment it is provided, that, when a debt is recovered or acknowledged in the King's Court, or damages awarded, it shall be thenceforth *in the election* of him that sueth for such debt or damages to have a writ of *fieri facias* unto the sheriff of the lands and goods, or that the sheriff deliver to him all the chattels of the debtor (saving only his oxen and beasts of his plough), and *the one half of his land*, until the debt be levied according to a reasonable price or extent. The writ issued by the Court to the sheriff, under the authority of this statute, was called a writ of *elegit*; so named, because it was stated in the writ that the creditor had elected *(elegit)* to pursue the remedy which the statute had thus provided for him. One moiety only of the land was allowed to be taken, because it was necessary, according to the feudal constitution of our law, that, whatever were the difficulties of the tenant, enough land should be left him to enable him to perform the services due to his lord. The statute, it will be observed, was passed prior to the time when the alienation of estates in fee simple was sanctioned by parliament; and there can be no doubt, that long after the passing of this statute the vendors and purchasers of landed property held a far less important place in legal consideration than they do at present. This circumstance may account for the somewhat harsh construction, which was soon placed on this statute, and which continued to be applied to it, until its replacement by an enlarged and amended act of modern date. It was held, that, if at the time when the judgment of the Court was given for the recovery of the debt, or awarding the damages, the debtor had lands, but afterwards sold them, the creditor might still, under the writ with which the statute had furnished him, take a moiety of the lands out of the hands of the purchaser. It thus became important for all purchasers of lands to ascertain, that those from whom they purchased had no *judgments* against them. For, if any such existed, one moiety of the lands would still remain liable to be taken out of the hands of the purchaser to satisfy the judgment debt or damages. It was also held that if the debtor purchased lands after the date of the judgment, and then sold them again, even these lands would be liable, in the hands of the purchaser, to satisfy the claims of the creditors under the writ of *elegit*. In consequence of the construction thus put upon the statute, judgment debts became incumbrances upon the title to every estate in fee simple, which it was necessary to discover and remove previously to every purchase. To facilitate purchasers and others in their search for judgments, an alphabetical docket or index of judgments was provided by an act of William and Mary, to be kept in each of the courts, open to public inspection and search. But, by an enactment of the present reign these dockets have now been closed, and the ancient statute is, with respect to purchasers, virtually repealed.

The rights of judgment creditors to follow the lands of their debtors in the hands of purchasers, were remodelled by an act of parliament of the present reign, passed for the purpose of extending the remedies of creditors against the property of their debtors. The old statute extended only to one half of the lands of the debtor; but, by this act, the whole of the lands, and all other hereditaments of the debtor, could be taken under the writ of *elegit*. The power of the judgment creditor to take lands out of the hands of purchasers was no longer left to depend on a forced construction, such as that applied to the old statute; for this act expressly extended the remedy of the judgment creditor to lands of which the debtor should *have been* seised or possessed at the time of entering up the judgment, *or at any time afterwards*. But, as we shall presently see, this extensive power has since been much curtailed. The judgment creditor was also expressly provided with a remedy in equity, that is, in the Court of Chancery, as well as at law. And the remedies provided by the act were extended, in their application, to all decrees, orders, and rules made by the courts of equity and of common law, and by the Lord Chancellor or the Lords Justices in matters of bankruptcy, and by the Lord Chancellor in matters of lunacy, for the payment to any person of any money or costs. But before purchasers, mortgagees, or creditors could be affected under the provisions of this act, the name, abode and description of the debtor, with the amount of the debt, damages, costs or money recovered against him, or ordered by him to be paid, together with the date of registration, and other particulars, were required to be registered in an index which the act directed to be kept for the warning of purchasers, at the office of the Court of Common Pleas. This registration was required to be repeated every five years; but the purchaser was bound if the judgment, decree, order, or rule were registered within five years before the execution of the conveyance to him, although more than five years should have elapsed since the last previous registration. If, however, the judgment, &c., were not so registered, or re-registered, the purchaser was not affected thereby, even though he should have had express notice of its existence; but the judgment creditor did not, by omitting to re-register, necessarily lose his priority, if once obtained, over subsequent judgments, though duly registered. And, by a further enactment, it was provided, in favour of purchasers without notice of any such judgments, decrees, orders or rules, that none of such judgments, &c., should bind or affect any lands, tenements, or hereditaments, or any interest therein, as against such purchasers without notice, further or otherwise, or more extensively in any respect, although duly registered, than a judgment of one of the superior courts would have bound such purchasers before the last-mentioned act, when it had been duly docketed according to the law then in force. More recently it was provided, that no judgment to be entered up after the 23rd of July, 1860, should affect any land as to a bona fide purchaser for valuable consideration, or a mortgagee (whether such purchaser or mortgagee had notice or not of such judgment), unless a writ or other due process of execution of such judgment should have been issued and registered, as provided by the act, before the execution of the conveyance or mortgage to him, and the payment of the purchase or mortgage money by him. And no such judgment, nor any writ of execution or other process thereon, was to affect any land as to a bona fide purchaser or mortgagee, although execution or other process should have issued thereon and have been duly registered, unless such execution or other process should be executed and put in force within three calendar months from the time when it was registered. A registry of writs of execution was also provided; but as the entry was required to be made in alphabetical order by the names of the persons in whose behalf the judgments were registered, and not by the names of the debtors, it was still necessary to search for judgments in the registry above referred to.

An act has at length been passed which entirely deprives all future judgments of their lien on real estates. This act, which was passed on the 29th of July, 1864, provides that no future judgment shall affect any land, of whatever tenure, until such land shall have been actually delivered in execution by virtue of a writ of *elegit*, or other lawful authority, in pursuance of such judgment. In the construction of the act, the term "judgment" is to be taken to include registered decrees, orders of courts of equity and bankruptcy, and other orders having the operation of a judgment. Every writ, by virtue whereof any land shall have been actually delivered in execution, must be registered in the manner provided by the last-mentioned act, but in the name of the debtor against whom such writ or process is issued, instead of, as under that act, in the name of the creditor. And no other registration of the judgment is to be deemed necessary for any purpose. Every creditor to whom any land of his debtor shall have been actually delivered in execution by virtue of any judgment, and whose writ shall have been duly registered, may obtain from the Chancery Division of the High Court, upon petition in a summary way, an order for the sale of his debtor's interest in such land. The other judgment creditors, if any, are to be served with notice of the order for sale; and the proceeds of the sale are to be distributed amongst the persons who may be found entitled thereto, according to their priorities. And every person claiming any interest in such land through or under the debtor, by any means subsequent to the delivery of such land in execution as aforesaid, is bound by every such order for sale, and by all the proceedings consequent thereon. This act extends not only to judgments, but also to statutes and recognizances. Statutes merchant and statutes staple, which are here referred to, are modes of securing money that have long been obsolete. Recognizances are entered into before a court of record or a magistrate; and, like judgments, they were a charge on lands until the passing of this act. An act has been recently passed to render judgments obtained in England, Scotland and Ireland, effectual in any other part of the United Kingdom.

Lands in either of the counties palatine of Lancaster or Durham were affected both by judgments of the courts at Westminster, and also by judgments of the Palatine Court. These latter judgments had, within the county palatine, the same effect as judgments of the courts at Westminster; and an index for their registration was established in each of the counties palatine, similar to the index of judgments at the Common Pleas. And by a statute of the present reign it was provided, that no judgment, decree, order or rule *of any court* should bind lands in the counties palatine, as against purchasers, mortgagees, or creditors, until registration in the court of the county palatine in which the lands were situate. And the same provisions as to re-registration within five years as applied to the registry of the Court of Common Pleas applied also to these registries. Lands in the county palatine of Chester, and in the principality of Wales, have been placed by a modern statute exclusively within the jurisdiction of the courts at Westminster: and by another statute the palatinate jurisdiction within the county of Durham, which formerly belonged to the Bishop of Durham, has been transferred to the crown. The Supreme Court of Judicature Act, 1873, transfers to the High Court of Justice thereby established the jurisdiction of the Court of Common Pleas at Lancaster and of the Court of Pleas at Durham, and any jurisdiction of the Court of Appeal in Chancery of the county palatine of Lancaster. But the jurisdiction of the Court of Chancery of the county palatine of Lancaster is not thereby abolished.

Debts due, or which might have become due, to the crown, from persons who were accountants to the crown, and debts of record, or by bond or specialty, due from other persons to the crown, were, until recently, binding on their estates in fee simple when sold, as well as when devised by will, or suffered to descend to the heir at law. But any two of the Commissioners of the Treasury were empowered, upon such terms as they might think proper, to certify by writing under their hands, that any lands of any crown debtor, or accountant to the crown, should be held by the purchaser or mortgagee thereof discharged from all further claims of her Majesty, her heirs or successors, in respect of any debt or liability of the debtor or accountant to whom such lands belonged. And a similar power was more recently given to any two of the commissioners, or other principal officers, of any public department with respect to any crown bond or other security concerning or incident to any such department; or if there were only one such commissioner or officer then the power was vested in him. To obviate the dangerous liability of purchasers to crown debts, an index was opened at the Common Pleas of the names of crown debtors; and lands could not be charged, in the hands of purchasers, with these liabilities, unless the name, abode and description of the debtor, with other particulars, were inserted in the proper index. And from the 31st of December,

1859, the provisions already mentioned for the re-registry of judgments every five years were applied to crown debts; and notice of any crown debt not duly re-registered was rendered of no avail against a purchaser. But now no debts or liabilities to the crown incurred after the 1st of November, 1865, shall affect any land as to a bona fide purchaser for valuable consideration or a mortgagee, whether such purchaser or mortgagee have or have not notice thereof, unless a writ or process of execution has been issued and registered before the execution of the conveyance or mortgage to such purchaser or mortgagee and the payment by him of the purchase or mortgage money. The registration is effected as follows: — A minute of the name of the person against whom the writ or process is issued and of the date of the issuing thereof, and of the amount for which it is issued, is left with the senior Master of the Common Pleas Division of the High Court, who forthwith enters the same in a boob by the name, in alphabetical order, of the person against whom the writ or process is issued; and no other registration of the writ or process or of the debt or liability is now necessary for any purpose.

Actions at law and suits in equity respecting the lands will also bind a purchaser as well as the heir or devisee; that is, he must abide by the result, although he may be ignorant that any such proceedings are depending. A provision has accordingly been made for the registration of every *lis pendens*; and no *lis pendens* binds a purchaser or mortgagee without express notice thereof, unless and until it is duly registered; and the registration to be binding must be repeated every five years. And the Court before whom the property sought to be bound is in litigation is now empowered, on the determination of the *lis pendens*, or during its pendency if satisfied that the litigation is not prosecuted bonâ fide, to order the registration to be vacated without the consent of the party by whom the *lis pendens* was registered. The index of pending suits, together with the indexes of writs of execution, are accordingly searched previously to every purchase of lands; and, if the name of the vendor should be found in either, the debt or liability must be got rid of, before the purchase can be safely completed.

Another instance of involuntary alienation for the payment of debts, occurs on the bankruptcy of any person, in which event the whole of his freehold, as well as his personal estate, is now vested in the creditors' trustee, by virtue of his appointment, in trust for the whole body of the creditors. On the insolvency of any person his whole estate formerly vested in the provisional assignee of the Court for the Relief of Insolvent Debtors, from whom it was transferred to assignees appointed by the Court, vesting in them by virtue of their appointment, and without any conveyance, in trust for the benefit of the creditors of the insolvent, according to the provisions of the act for amending the laws for the relief of insolvent debtors. The whole of these laws are however now repealed, and all debtors, whether traders or not, are subject to the provisions of the last act to consolidate and amend the law of bankruptcy.

So inherent is the right of alienation of all estates (except estates tail, in which, as we have seen, the right is only of a modified nature), that it is impossible for any owner, by any means, to divest himself of this right. And in the same manner the liability of estates to involuntary alienation for payment of debts cannot by any means be got rid of. So long as any estate is in the hands of any person, so long does his power of disposition continue, and so long also continues his liability to have the estate taken from him to satisfy the demands of his creditors. When, however, lands or property are given by one person for the benefit of another, it is possible to confine the duration of the gift within the period in which it can be personally enjoyed by the grantee. Thus land, or any other property, may be given to trustees in trust for A. until he shall dispose of the same, or shall become bankrupt, or until any act or event shall occur, whereby the property might belong to any other person or persons; and this is frequently done. On the bankruptcy of A., or on his attempting to make any disposition of the property, it will in such a case not vest in the trustee for his creditors, or follow the intended disposition; but the interest which had been given to A. will thenceforth entirely cease; in the same manner as where lands are given to a person for life, his interest terminates on his decease. But, although another person may make such a gift for A.'s benefit, A. would not be allowed to make such a disposition of his own property in trust for himself. An exception to this rule of law occurs in the case of a woman, who is permitted to have property settled upon her in such a way, that she cannot when married make any disposition of it during the coverture or marriage; but this mode of settlement is of comparatively modern date. There are also certain cases in which the personal enjoyment of property is essential to the performance of certain public duties, and in which no alienation of such property can be made; thus a benefice with cure of souls cannot be directly charged or encumbered; so offices concerning the administration of justice, and pensions and salaries given by the state for the support of the grantee in the performance of present or future duties, cannot be aliened; though pensions for past services are, generally speaking, not within the rule.

In addition to the interests which may be created by alienation, either voluntary or involuntary, there are certain rights conferred by law on husbands and wives in each other's lands, by means of which the descent of an estate, from an ancestor to his heir, may partially be defeated. These rights will be the subject of a future chapter. If, however, the tenant in fee simple should not have disposed of his estate in his lifetime, or by his will, and if it should not be swallowed up by his debts, his lands will descend (subject to any rights of his wife) to the heir at law. The heir, as we have before observed, is a person appointed by the law. He is called into existence by his ancestor's decease, for no man during his lifetime can have an heir. *Nemo est hæres viventis*. A man may have an *heir apparent*, or an *heir presumptive*, but until his decease he has no *heir*. The heir *apparent* is the person, who, if he survive the ancestor, must certainly be his heir, as the eldest son in the lifetime of his father. The heir *presumptive* is the person, who, though not certain to be heir at all events, should he survive, would yet be the heir in case of the ancestor's immediate decease. Thus an only daughter is the heiress presumptive of her father: if he were now to die, she would at once be his heir; but she is not certain of being heir; for her father may have a son, who would supplant her, and become heir apparent during the father's lifetime, and his heir after his decease. An heir at law is the only person in whom the law of England vests property, whether he will or not. If I make a conveyance of land to a person in my lifetime, or leave him any property by my will, he may, if he pleases, disclaim taking it, and in such case it will not vest in him against his will. But an heir at law, immediately on the decease of his ancestor, becomes presumptively possessed, or seised in law, of all his lands. No disclaimer that he may make will have any effect, though, of course, he may, as soon as he pleases, dispose of the property by an ordinary conveyance. A title as heir at law is not nearly so frequent now as it was in the times when the right of alienation was more restricted. And when it does occur, it is often established with difficulty. This difficulty arises more from the nature of the facts to be proved, than from any uncertainty in the law. For the rules of descent have now attained an almost mathematical accuracy, so that, if the facts are rightly given, the heir at law can at once be pointed out. The accuracy of the law has arisen by degrees, by the successive determination of disputed points. Thus, we have seen that, in the early feudal times, an estate to a man and his heirs simply, which is now an estate in fee simple, was descendible only to his offspring, in the same manner as an estate tail at the present day; but in process of time collateral relations were admitted to succeed. When this succession of collaterals first took place is a question involved in much obscurity; we only know that in the time of Henry II. the law was settled as follows: — In default of lineal descendants, the brothers and sisters came in; and if they were dead, their children; then the uncles and their children; and then the aunts and their children; males being always preferred to females. Subsequently, about the time of Henry III., the old Saxon rule, which divided the inheritance equally amongst all males of the same degree, and which had hitherto prevailed as to all lands not actually the subjects of feudal tenure, gave place to the feudal law, introduced by the Normans, of descent to the eldest son or eldest brother; though among females the estate was still equally divided, as it is at present. And, about the same time, all descendants *in infinitum* of any person, who would have been heir if living, were allowed to inherit by right of representation. Thus, if the eldest son died in the lifetime of his father, and left issue, *that* issue, though a grandson or granddaughter only, was to be preferred in inheritance before any younger son. The father, moreover, or any other lineal ancestor, was never allowed to succeed as heir to his son or other descendant; neither were kindred of the half-blood admitted to inherit. The rules of descent, thus gradually fixed, long remained unaltered. Lord Hale, in whose time they had continued the same for above 400 years, was the first to reduce them to a series of canons; which were afterwards admirably explained and illustrated by Blackstone, in his well-known Commentaries; nor was any alteration made till the enactment of the act for the amendment of the law of inheritance, A.D. 1833. By this act, amongst other important alterations, the father is heir to his son, supposing the latter to leave no issue; and all lineal ancestors are rendered capable of being heirs; relations of the half-blood are also admitted to succeed, though only on failure of relations in the same degree of the whole blood. The act has, moreover, settled a doubtful point in the law of descent to distant heirs. The rules of descent, as modified by this act, will be found at large in the next chapter.

CHAPTER IV
OF THE DESCENT OF AN ESTATE IN FEE SIMPLE

We shall now proceed to consider the rules of the descent of an estate in fee simple, as altered by the act for the amendment of the law of inheritance. This act does not extend to any descent on the decease of any person, who may have died before the first of January, 1834. For the rules of descent prior to that date, the reader is referred to the Commentaries of Blackstone, and to Watkins's Essay on the Law of Descents.

1. The first rule of descent now is, that inheritances shall lineally descend, in the first place, to the issue of the last purchaser *in infinitum*. The word *purchase* has in law a meaning more extended than its ordinary sense: it is possession to which a man cometh not by title of descent: a devisee under a will is accordingly a purchaser in law. And, by the act, the purchaser from whom descent is to be traced is defined to be, the last person who had a right to the land, and who cannot be proved to have acquired the land by descent, or by certain means which render the land part of, or descendible in the same manner as, other land acquired by descent. This rule is an alteration of the old law, which was, that descent should be traced from the person who last had the feudal possession or *seisin*, as it was called; the maxim being *seisina facit stipitem*. This maxim, a relict of the troublesome times when right without possession was worth but little, sometimes gave occasion to difficulties, owing to the uncertainty of the question, whether possession had or had not been

taken by any person entitled as heir; thus, where a man was entering into a house by the window, and when half out and half in, was pulled out again by the heels, it was made a question, whether or not this entry was sufficient, and it was adjudged that it was. These difficulties cannot arise under the new act; for now the heir to be sought for is not the heir of the person *last possessed*, but the heir of the *last person entitled who did not inherit*, whether he did or did not obtain the possession, or the receipt of the rents and profits of the land. The rule, as altered, is not indeed altogether free from objection; for it will be observed that, not content with making a title to the land equivalent to possession, the act has added a new term to the definition, by directing descent to be traced from the last person entitled *who did not inherit*. So that if a person who has become entitled as heir to another should die intestate, the heir to be sought for is not the heir of such last owner, but the heir of the person from whom such last owner inherited. This provision, though made by an act consequent on the report of the Real Property Commissioners, was not proposed by them. The Commissioners merely proposed that lands should pass to the heir of the *person last entitled*, instead, as before, of the *person last possessed*; thus facilitating the discovery of the heir, by rendering a mere title to the lands sufficient to make the person entitled the stock of descent, without his obtaining the feudal possession, as before required. Under the old law, descent was confined within the limits of the family of the *purchaser*; but now no person who can be shown to have inherited can be the stock of descent, except in the case of the total failure of the heirs of the purchaser; in every other case, descent must be traced from the last *purchaser*. The author is bound to state that the decision of the Courts of Exchequer and the Exchequer Chamber, in the recent case of *Muggleton* v. *Barnett*, is opposed to this view of the construction of the statute. The reasons which have induced the author to think that decision erroneous will be found in Appendix A.

2. The second rule is, that the male issue shall be admitted before the female.

3. The third rule is, that where two or more of the male issue are in equal degree of consanguinity to the purchaser, the eldest only shall inherit; but the females shall inherit all together. The last two rules are the same now as before the recent act; accord-

ingly, if a man has two sons, William and John, and two daughters, Susannah and Catherine, William, the eldest son, is the heir at law, in exclusion of his younger brother John, according to the third rule, and of his sisters, Susannah and Catherine, according to rule 2, although such sisters should be his seniors in years. If, however, William should die without issue, then John will succeed, by the second rule, in exclusion of his sisters; but if John also should die without issue, the two sisters will succeed in equal shares by the third rule as being together heir to their father.

Primogeniture, or the right of the eldest among the males to inherit, was a matter of far greater consequence in ancient times, before alienation by will was permitted, than it is at present. Its feudal origin is undisputed; but in this country it appears to have taken deeper root than elsewhere; for a total exclusion of the younger sons appears to be peculiar to England: in other countries, some portion of the inheritance, or some charge upon it, is, in many cases at least, secured by law to the younger sons. From this ancient right has arisen the modern English custom of settling the family estates on the eldest son; but the right and the custom are quite distinct: the right may be prevented by the owner making his will; and a conformity to the custom is entirely at his option.

When two or more persons together form an heir, they are called in law *coparceners*, or, more shortly, *parceners*. The term is derived, according to Littleton, from the circumstance that the law will constrain them to make partition; that is, any one may oblige all the others so to do. Whatever may be thought of this derivation, it will serve to remind the reader that coparceners are the only kind of joint owners, to whom the ancient common law granted the power of severing their estates without mutual consent; as the estate in coparcenary was cast on them by the act of the law, and not by their own agreement, it was thought right that the perverseness of one should not prevent the others from obtaining a more beneficial method of enjoying the property. This compulsory partition was formerly effected by a writ of partition, a proceeding now abolished. The modern method is by a judge of the Chancery Division of the High Court in chambers, or more rarely by a commission issued for the purpose by that Court. Partition, however, is most frequently made by voluntary agreement between the parties, and for this purpose a deed has, by a modern act of parliament, been rendered essential in every case. The inclosure commissioners for England and Wales have also power to effect partitions, by virtue of modern enactments which will be found mentioned at the end of the chapter on Joint Tenants and Tenants in Common. When partition has been effected, the lands allotted are said to be held in *severally*; and each owner is said to have the *entirety* of her own parcel. After partition, the several parcels of land descend in the same manner as the undivided shares, for which they have been substituted; the coparceners, therefore, do not by partition become *purchasers*, but still continue to be entitled by descent. The term *coparceners* is not applied to any other joint owners, but only to those who have become entitled as coheirs.

4. The fourth rule is, that all the lineal descendants *in infinitum* of any person deceased shall represent their ancestor; that is, shall stand in the same place as the person himself would have done had he been living. Thus, in the case above mentioned, on the death of William the eldest son, leaving a son, that son would succeed to the whole by right of representation, in exclusion of his uncle John, and of his two aunts Susannah and Catherine; or had William left a son and daughter, such daughter would, after the decease of her brother without issue, be, in like manner, the heir of her grandfather, in exclusion of her uncle and aunts.

The preceding rules of descent apply as well to the descent of an estate tail, if not duly barred, as to that of an estate in fee simple. The descent of an estate tail is always traced from the purchaser, or donee in tail, that is, from the person to whom the estate tail was at first given. This was the case before the act, as well as now; for, the person who claims an entailed estate as heir claims only according to the express terms of the gift, or, as it is said, *per formam doni*. The gift is made to the donee, or purchaser, and the heirs of his body; all persons, therefore, who can become entitled to the estate by descent, must answer the description of heirs of the purchaser's body; in other words, must be *his* lineal heirs. The second and third rules also equally apply to estates tail, unless the restriction of the descent to heirs male or female should render unnecessary the second, and either clause of the third rule. The fourth rule completes the canon, so far as estates tail are concerned; for, when the issue of the donee are exhausted, such an estate must necessarily determine. But the descent of an estate in fee simple may extend to many other persons, and accordingly requires for its guidance additional rules, with which we now proceed.

5. The fifth rule is, that on failure of lineal descendants, or issue of the purchaser, the inheritance shall descend to his nearest lineal ancestor. This rule is materially different from the rule which prevailed before the passing of the act. The former rule was, that, on failure of lineal descendants or issue of the person last seised (or feudally possessed), the inheritance should descend to his *collateral* relations, being of the blood of the first purchaser, subject to the three preceding rules. The old law never allowed lineal relations in the ascending line (that is, parents or ancestors) to succeed as heirs. But, by the new act, descent is to be traced through the ancestor, who is to be heir in preference to any person who would have been entitled to inherit, either by tracing his descent through such lineal ancestor, or in consequence of there being no descendant of such lineal ancestor. The exclusion of parents and other lineal ancestors from inheriting under the old law was a hardship of which it is not easy to see the propriety; nor is the explanation usually given of the origin perhaps quite satisfactory. Bracton, who is followed by Lord Coke, compares the descent of an inheritance to that of a falling body, which never goes upwards in its course. The modern explanation derives the origin of collateral heirships, in exclusion of lineal ancestors, from gifts of estates (at the time when inheritances were descendible only to issue or lineal heirs) made, by the terms of the gift, to be descendible to the heirs of the donee, in the same manner as an ancient inheritance would have descended. This was called a gift of a *feudum novum*, or new inheritance, to hold *ut feudum antiquum*, as an ancient one. Now, an ancient inheritance, — one derived in a course of descent from some remote lineal ancestor — would of course be descendible to all the issue or *lineal* heirs of such ancestor, including, after the lapse of many years, numerous families, all *collaterally* related to one another; an estate newly granted, to be descendible *lit feudum antiquum*, would therefore be capable of descending to the collateral relations of the grantee, in the same manner as a really ancient inheritance, descended to him, would

have done. But an ancient inheritance could never go to the father of any owner, because it must have come from his father to him, and the father must have died before the son could inherit: in grants of inheritances to be descendible as ancient ones, it followed, therefore, that the father or any lineal ancestor could never inherit. So far, therefore, the explanation holds; but it is not consistent with every circumstance; for an elder brother has always been allowed to succeed as heir to his younger brother, contrary to this theory of an ancient lineal inheritance, which would have previously passed by every elder brother, as well as the father. The explanation of the origin of a rule, though ever so clear, is however a different thing from a valid reason for its continuance; and, at length, the propriety of placing the property of a family under the care of its head, is now perceived and acted on; and the father is heir to each of his children, who may die intestate, and without issue, as is more clearly pointed out by the next rule.

6. The sixth rule is, that the father and all the male paternal ancestors of the purchaser, and their descendants, shall be admitted, before any of the female paternal ancestors or their heirs; all the female paternal ancestors and their heirs, before the mother or any of the maternal ancestors, or her or their descendants; and the mother and all the male maternal ancestors, and her and their descendants, before any of the female maternal ancestors, or their heirs. This rule is a development of the ancient canon, which requires that, in collateral inheritances, the male stocks should always be preferred to the female; and it is analogous to the second rule above given, which directs that in lineal inheritances the male issue shall be admitted before the female. This strict and careful preference of the male to the female line was in full accordance with the spirit of the feudal system, which, being essentially military in its nature, imposed obligations by no means easy for a female to fulfil; and those who were unable to perform the services could not expect to enjoy the benefits. The feudal origin of our laws of descent will not, however, afford a complete explanation of this preference; for such lands as continued descendible after the Saxon custom of equal division, and not according to the Norman and feudal law of primogeniture, were equally subject to the preference of males to females, and descended in the first place exclusively to the sons,

who divided the inheritance between them, leaving nothing at all to their sisters. The true reason of the preference appears to lie in the degraded position in society, which, in ancient times, was held by females; a position arising from their deficiency in that kind of might, which then too frequently made the right. The rights given by the common law to a husband over his wife's property (rights now generally controlled by proper settlements previous to marriage), show the state of dependence to which, in ancient times, women must have been reduced. The preference of males to females has been left untouched by the recent act for the amendment of the law of descents; and the father and all his most distant relatives have priority over the mother of the purchaser: she cannot succeed as his heir until all the paternal ancestors of the purchaser, both male and female, and their respective families, have been exhausted. The father, as the nearest male lineal ancestor, of course stands first, supposing the issue of the purchaser to have failed. If the father should be dead, his eldest son, being the brother of the purchaser, will succeed as heir in the place of his father, according to the fourth rule; unless he be of the half blood to the purchaser, which case is provided for by the next rule, which is: —

7. That a kinsman of the half blood shall be capable of being heir; and that such kinsman shall inherit next after a kinsman in the same degree of the whole blood, and after the issue of such kinsman when the common ancestor is a male, and next after the common ancestor, when such ancestor is a female. This introduction of the half blood is also a new regulation; and, like the introduction of the father and other lineal ancestors, it is certainly an improvement on the old law, which had no other reason in its favour than the feudal maxims, or rather fictions, on which it was founded. By the old law, a relative of the purchaser of the half blood, that is, a relative connected by one only, and not by both of the parents, or other ancestors, could not possibly be heir; a half brother, for instance, could never-enjoy that right which a cousin of the whole blood, though ever so distant, might claim in his proper turn. The exclusion of the half blood was accounted for in a manner similar to that by which the exclusion of all lineal ancestors was explained; but a return to practical justice may well compensate a breach in a beautiful theory. Relatives of the half blood now take their proper and natural place in the or-

der of descent. The position of the half blood next after the common ancestor, when such ancestor is a female, is rather a result of the sixth rule, than an additional independent regulation, as will appear hereafter.

8. The eighth rule is, that in the admission of female paternal ancestors, the mother of the more remote male paternal ancestor, and her heirs, shall be preferred to the mother of a less remote male paternal ancestor, and her heirs; and, in the admission of female maternal ancestors, the mother of the more remote male maternal ancestor, and her heirs, shall be preferred to the mother of a less remote male maternal ancestor, and her heirs. The eighth rule is a settlement of a point in distant heirships, which very seldom occurs, but which has been the subject of a vast deal of learned controversy. The opinion of Blackstone and Watkins is now declared to be the law.

9. A further rule of descent has now been introduced by a recent statute, which enacts that, where there shall be a total failure of heirs of the purchaser, or where any land shall be descendible as if an ancestor had been the purchaser thereof, and there shall be a total failure of the heirs of such ancestor, then and in every such case the land shall descend, and the descent shall thenceforth be traced, from the person last entitled to the land, as if he had been the purchaser thereof. This enactment provides for such a case as the following. A purchaser of lands may die intestate, leaving an only son and no other relations. On the death of the son intestate there will be a total failure of the heirs of the purchaser; and previously to this enactment the land would have escheated to the lord of the fee, as explained in the next chapter. But now, although there be no relations of the son on his father's side, yet he may have relations on the part of his mother, or his mother may herself be living: and these persons, who were before totally excluded, are now admitted in the order mentioned in the sixth rule.

The rules of descent above given will be better apprehended by a reference to the accompanying table, taken, with a little modification, from Mr. Watkins's Essay on the Law of Descents. In this table, Benjamin Brown is the purchaser, from whom the descent is to be traced. On his death intestate, the lands will accordingly descend first to his eldest son, by Ann Lee, William Brown; and from him (2ndly) to *his* eldest son, by Sarah Watts,

Isaac Brown. Isaac dying without issue we must now seek the heir of the *purchaser*, and not the heir of Isaac. William, the eldest son of the purchaser, is dead; but William may have had other descendants, besides Isaac his eldest son; and, by the fourth rule, all the lineal descendants *in infinitum* of every person deceased shall represent their ancestor. We find accordingly that William had a daughter Lucy by his first wife, and also a second son, George, by Mary Wood, his second wife. But the son George, though younger than his half sister Lucy, yet being a male, shall be preferred according to the second rule; and he is therefore (3rdly) the next heir. Had Isaac been the purchaser, the case would have been different; for, his half brother George would then have been postponed, in favour of his sister Lucy of the whole blood, according to the seventh rule. But now Benjamin is the purchaser, and both Isaac and George are equally his grandchildren. George dying without issue, we must again seek the heir of his grandfather Benjamin, who now is undeniably (4thly) Lucy, she being the remaining descendant of his eldest son. Lucy dying like wise without issue, her father's issue become extinct; and we must still inquire for the heir of Benjamin Brown the purchaser, whom we now find to be (5thly) John Brown, his only son by his second wife. The land then descends from John to (6thly) *his* eldest son Edmund, and from Edmund (7thly) to his only son James. James dying without issue, we must once more seek the heir of the purchaser, whom we find among the yet living issue of John. John leaving a daughter by his first wife, and a son and a daughter by his second wife, the lands descend (8thly) to Henry his son by Frances Wilson, as being of the male sex; but he dying without issue, we again seek the heir of Benjamin, and find that John left two daughters, but by different wives; these daughters, being in the same degree and both equally the children of their common father whom they represent, shall succeed (9thly) in equal shares. One of these daughters dying without issue in the lifetime of the other, the other shall then succeed to the whole as the only issue of her father. But the surviving sister dying also without issue, we still pursue our old inquiry, and seek again for the heir of Benjamin Brown the purchaser.

The issue of the sons of the purchaser is now extinct; and, as he left two daughters, Susannah and Catherine, by different wives, we shall find, by the second and third rules, that they next inherit (10thly) in equal shares as heirs to him. Catherine Brown, one of the daughters, now marries Charles Smith, and dies, in the lifetime of her sister Susannah, leaving one son, John. The half share of Catherine must then descend to the next heir of her father Benjamin, the purchaser. The next heirs of Benjamin Brown, after the decease of Catherine, are evidently Susannah Brown and John Smith, the son of Catherine. And in the first edition of the present work it was stated that the half share of Catherine would, on her decease, descend to them. This opinion has been very generally entertained. On further research, however, the author inclined to the opinion that the share of Catherine would, on her decease, descend entirely to her son (11thly) by right of representation; and that, as respects his mother's share, he and he only, is the right heir of the purchaser. The reasoning which led the author to this conclusion will be found in the Appendix. This point is now established by judicial decision.

If Susannah Brown and John Smith should die without issue, the descendants of the purchaser will then have become extinct; and Joseph Brown, the father of the purchaser, will then (12thly), if living, be his heir by the fifth and sixth rules. Bridget, the sister of the purchaser, then succeeds (13thly), as representing her father, in preference to her half brother Timothy, who is only of the half blood to the purchaser, and is accordingly postponed to his sister by the seventh rule. But next to Bridget is Timothy (14thly) by the same rule, Bridget being supposed to leave no issue.

On the decease of Timothy without issue, all the descendants of the father will have failed, and the inheritance will next pass to Philip Brown (15thly), the paternal grandfather of the purchaser. But the grandfather being dead, we must next exhaust his issue, who stand in his place, and we find that he had another son, Thomas (16thly), who accordingly is the next heir; and, on his decease without issue, Stephen Brown (17thly), though of the half blood to the purchaser, will inherit, by the seventh rule, next after Thomas, a kinsman in the same degree of the whole blood. Stephen Brown dying without issue, the descendants of the grandfather are exhausted; and we must accordingly still keep, according to the sixth rule, in the male paternal line, and seek the paternal great grandfather of the purchaser, who is (18thly) Robert Brown; and who is represented, on his decease, by (19thly) Daniel Brown, his son. After Daniel and his issue follow, by the same rule, Edward (20thly) and his issue (21stly) Abraham.

All the male paternal ancestors of the purchaser, and their descendants, are now supposed to have failed; and by the sixth rule, the female paternal ancestors and their heirs are next admitted. By the eighth rule, in the admission of the female paternal ancestors, the mother of the more remote male paternal ancestor, and her heirs, shall be preferred to the mother of a less remote male paternal ancestor and her heirs. Barbara Finch (22ndly), and her heirs, have therefore priority both over Margaret Pain and her heirs, and Esther Pitt and her heirs; Barbara Finch being the mother of a more remote male paternal ancestor than either Margaret Pain or Esther Pitt. Barbara Finch being dead, her heirs succeed her; *she* therefore must now be regarded as the stock of descent, and her heirs will be the right heirs of Benjamin Brown the purchaser. In seeking for her heirs inquiry must first be made for her issue; now her issue by Edward Brown has already been exhausted in seeking for his descendants; but she might have had issue by another husband; and such issue (23rdly) will accordingly next succeed. These issue are evidently of the half blood to the purchaser. But they are the right heirs of Barbara Finch; and they are accordingly entitled to succeed next after her, without the aid they might derive from the position expressly assigned to them by the seventh rule. The common ancestor of the purchaser and of the issue is Barbara Finch, a female; and, by the united operation of the other rules, these issue of the half blood succeed next after the common ancestor. The latter part of the seventh rule is, therefore, explanatory only, and not absolutely necessary. In default of issue of Barbara Finch, the lands will descend to her father Isaac Finch (24thly), and then to his issue (25thly), as representing him. If neither Barbara Finch, nor any of her heirs, can be found, Margaret Pain (26thly), or her heirs, will be next entitled, Margaret Pain being the mother of a more remote male paternal ancestor than Esther Pitt; but next to Margaret Pain and her heirs will be Esther Pitt (27thly), or her heirs, thus closing the list of female paternal ancestors.

Next to the female paternal ancestors and their heirs comes the mother of the purchaser, Elizabeth Webb, (28thly) (supposing her to be alive), with respect to whom the same process is to be pursued as has before been gone over with respect to Joseph Brown, the purchaser's father. On her death, her issue by John Jones (29thly) will accordingly next succeed, as representing her, by the fourth rule, agreeably to the declaration as to the place of the half blood contained in the seventh rule. Such issue becoming extinct, the nearest male maternal ancestor is the purchaser's maternal grandfather, William Webb (30thly), whose issue (31stly) will be entitled to succeed him. Such issue failing, the whole line of male maternal ancestors and their descendants must be exhausted, by the sixth rule, before any of the female maternal ancestors, or their heirs, can find admission; and when the female maternal ancestors are resorted to, the mother of the more remote male maternal ancestor, and her heirs, is to be preferred, by the eighth rule, to the mother of the less remote male maternal ancestor, and her heirs. The course to be taken is, accordingly, precisely the same as in pursuing the descent through the paternal ancestors of the purchaser. In the present table, therefore, Harriet Tibbs (32ndly), the maternal grandmother of the purchaser, is the person next entitled, no claimants appearing whose title is preferable; and, should she be dead, her heirs will be entitled next after her. On the failure of the heirs of the purchaser, the person last entitled is, as we have seen, to be substituted in his place, and the same course of investigation is again to be pursued with respect to the person last entitled as has already been pointed out with respect to the last purchaser.

It should be carefully borne in mind, that the above-mentioned rules of descent apply exclusively to estates in land, and to that kind of property which is denominated *real*, and have no application to money or other personal estate, which is distributed on intestacy in a manner which the reader will find explained in the author's treatise on the law of personal property.

A new exception to the law of descent has been made by the Land Transfer Act, 1875, which enacts that upon the death of a bare trustee intestate as to any corporeal or incorporeal hereditament of which such trustee was seised in fee simple, such hereditament shall vest, like a chattel real, in the legal personal representative from time to time of such trustee; but this enactment does not apply to lands registered under the Land Transfer Act. A bare trustee may, perhaps, be defined as a person who has no beneficial interest in the property of which he is seised nor any active duty to perform in respect of it.

CHAPTER V
OF THE TENURE OF AN ESTATE IN FEE SIMPLE

The most familiar instance of a tenure is given by a common lease of a house or land for a term of years; in this case the person letting is still called the *landlord*, and the person to whom the premises are let is the *tenant*; the terms of the tenure are according to the agreement of the parties, the rent being usually the chief item, and the rest of the terms of tenure being contained in the covenants of the lease; but, if no rent should be paid, the relation of landlord and tenant would still subsist, though of course not with the same advantage to the landlord. This, however, is not a freehold tenure; the lessee has only a chattel interest, as has been before observed; but it may serve to explain tenures of a freehold kind, which are not so familiar, though equally important. So, when a lease of lands is made to a man *for his life*, the lessee becomes tenant to the lessor, although no rent may be reserved; here again a tenure is created by the transaction, during the life of the lessee, and the terms of the tenure depend on the agreement of the parties. So, if a gift of land should be made to a man *and the heirs of his body*, the donee in tail, as he is called, and his issue, would be the tenants of the donor as long as the entail lasted, and a freehold tenure would thus be created.

But if a gift should be made to a man *and his heirs*, or for an estate in fee simple, it would not now be lawful for the parties to create a tenure between themselves, as in the case of a gift for life, or in tail. For by the statute of *Quia emptores*, we have seen that it was enacted, that from thenceforth it should be lawful for every free man to sell, at his own pleasure, his lands or tenements, or part thereof, so nevertheless that the feoffee, or purchaser, should hold the same lands or tenements of the same chief lord of the fee, and by the same services and customs as his feoffor, the seller, held them before. The giver or seller of an estate in fee simple is then himself but a tenant, with liberty of putting another in his own place. He may have under him a tenant for years, or a tenant for life, or even a tenant in tail, but he cannot now, by any kind of conveyance, place under himself a tenant of an estate in fee simple. The statute of *Quia emptores* now forbids any one from making himself the lord of such an estate; all he can do is to transfer his own tenancy; and the purchaser of an estate in fee simple must hold his estate of the same chief lord of the fee, as the seller held before him. The introduction of this doctrine of tenures has been already noticed, and it still prevails throughout the kingdom; for it is a fundamental rule, that all the lands within this realm were originally derived from the crown (either by express grant or tacit intendment of law), and therefore the Queen is sovereign lady, or lady paramount, either mediate or immediate, of all and every parcel of land within the realm.

The rent, services and other incidents of the tenure of estates in fee simple were, in ancient times, matters of much variety, depending as they did on the mutual agreements which, previously to the statute of *Quia emptores*, the various lords and tenants made with each other; though still they had their general laws, governing such cases as were not expressly provided for. The lord was usually a baron, or other person of power and consequence, to whom had been granted an estate in fee simple in a tract of land. Of this land he retained as much as was necessary for his own use, as his own demesne, and usually built upon it a mansion or manor house. Part of this demesne was in the occupation of the villeins of the lord, who held various small parcels at his will, for their own subsistence, and cultivated the residue for their lord's benefit. The rest of the cultivable land was granted out by the lord to various freeholders, subject to certain stipulated rents or services, as "to plough ten acres of arable land, parcel of that which remained in the lord's possession, or to carry his dung unto the land, or to go with him to war against the Scots". The barren lands which remained formed the lord's wastes, over which the cattle of the tenants were allowed to roam in search of pasture. In this way manors were created, every one of which is of a date prior to the statute of *Quia emptores*, except, perhaps, some which may have been created by the king's tenants in capite with licence from the crown. The lands held by the villeins were the origin of copyholds, of which more hereafter. Those granted to the free men were subject to various burdens, according to the nature of the tenure. In the tenure by knights' service, then the most universal and honourable species of tenure, the tenant of an estate of inheritance, that is, of an estate of fee simple or fee tail, was bound to do *homage* to his lord, kneeling to him, professing to become his man, and receiving from him a kiss. The tenant was moreover at first expected, and afterwards obliged, to render to his lord pecuniary *aids*, to ransom his person, if taken prisoner, to help him in the expense of making his eldest son a knight, and in providing a portion for the eldest daughter on her marriage. Again, on the death of a tenant, his heir was bound to pay a fine, called a *relief*, on taking to his ancestor's estate. If the heir were under age, the lord had, under the name of *wardship*, the custody of the body and lands of the heir, without account of the profits, till the age of twenty-one years in males, and sixteen in females: when the wards had a right to require possession, or sue out their *livery*, on payment to the lord of half a year's profits of their lands. In addition to this, the lord possessed the right of marriage *(maritagium)*, or of disposing of his infant wards in matrimony, at their peril of forfeiting to him, in case of their refusing a suitable match, a sum of money equal to the value of the marriage: that is, what the suitor was willing to pay down to the lord as the price of marrying his ward; and double the market value was to be forfeited, if the ward presumed to marry without the lord's consent. The king's tenants *in capite* were moreover subject to many burdens and restraints, from which the tenants of other lords were exempt. Again, every lord who had two tenants or more, had a right to compel their attendance at the court baron of the manor, to which his grants to them had given existence; this attendance was called *suit of court*, and the tenants were called free-suitors. And to every species of lay tenure, as distinguished from clerical, and whether of an estate in fee simple, in tail, or for life, or otherwise, there was inseparably incident a liability for the tenant, whenever called upon, to take an oath *of fealty* or fidelity to his lord.

At the present day, however, a much greater simplicity and uniformity will be found in the incidents of the tenure of an estate in fee simple, for there is now only one kind of tenure by which such an estate can be held; and that is the tenure *of free and common socage*. The tenure of free and common socage is of great antiquity; so much so, that the meaning of the word *socage* is the subject only of conjecture. Comparatively few of the lands in this country were in ancient times the subject of this tenure: the lands in which estates in fee simple were thus held, appear to have been among those which escaped the grasp of the Conqueror, and remained in the possession of their ancient Saxon proprietors. The owners of fee simple estates, held by this tenure, were not villeins or slaves, but freemen; hence the term *free socage*. No military service was due, as the condition of the enjoyment of the estates. Homage to the lord, the invariable incident to the military tenures, was not often required; but the services, if any, were usually of an agricultural nature: a fixed rent was sometimes reserved; and in process of time the agricultural services appear to have been very generally commuted into such a rent. In all cases of annual rent, the *relief* paid by the heir, on the death of his ancestor, was fixed at one year's rent. Frequently no rent was due; but the owners were simply bound to take, when required, the oath of fealty to the lord of whom they held, to do suit at his court, if he had one, and to give him the customary aids for knighting his eldest son and marrying his eldest daughter. This tenure was accordingly more beneficial than the military tenures, by which fee simple estates, in most other lands in the kingdom, were held. True, the actual military service, in respect of lands, became gradually commuted for an *escuage* or money payment, assessed on the tenants by knights' service from time to time, first at the discretion of the crown, and afterwards by authority of parliament; and this commutation appears to have generally prevailed from so early a period as the time of Henry II. But the great superiority of the socage tenure was still felt in its freedom from the burdens of wardship and marriage, and other exactions, imposed on the tenants of estates in fee held by the other tenures. The wardship and marriage of an infant tenant of an estate held in socage devolved on his nearest relation, (to whom the inheritance could not descend,) who was strictly accountable for the rents and profits. As the commerce and wealth of the country increased, and the middle classes began to feel their own power, the burdens of the other tenures became insupportable; and an opportunity was at last seized of throwing them off. Accordingly, at the restoration of King Charles II., an act of parliament was insisted on and obtained, by which all tenures by knights' service, and the fruits and consequences of tenures in capite, were taken away, and all tenures of estates of inheritance in the hands of private persons (except copyhold tenures) were turned into free and common socage; and the same were for ever discharged from homage, wardships, values and forfeitures of marriage, and other charges incident to tenure by knights' service, and from aids for marrying the lord's daughter and for making his son a knight.

The right of wardship or guardianship of infant tenants having thus been taken away from the lords, the opportunity was embraced of giving to the father a right of appointing guardians to his children. It was accordingly provided by the same act of parliament, that the father of any child under age and not married at the time of his death, may, by deed executed in his lifetime, or by his will in the presence of two or more credible witnesses, in such manner and from time to time as he shall think fit, dispose of the custody and tuition of such child during such time as he shall remain under the age of one-and-twenty years, or any lesser time, to any person or persons in possession or remainder. And this power was given, whether the child was born at his father's decease or only *in ventre sa mère* at that time, and whether the father were within the age of one-and-twenty years, or of full age. But it seems that the father, if under age, cannot now appoint a guardian by *will*; for the Wills Act now enacts, that no will made by any person under the age of twenty-one years shall be valid. In other respects, however, the father's right to appoint a guardian still continues as originally provided by the above-mentioned statute of Charles II. The guardian so appointed has a right to receive the rents of the child's lands, for the use of the child, to whom, like a guardian in socage, he is accountable when the child comes of age. A guardian cannot be appointed by the mother of a child, or by any other relative than the father.

A *rent* is not now often paid in respect of the tenure of an estate in fee simple. When it is paid, it is usually called a *quit rent*, and is almost always of a very trifling amount: the change in the value of money in modern times will account for this. The *relief* of one year's quit rent, payable by the heir on the death of his ancestor, in the case of a fixed quit rent, was not abolished by the statute of Charles, and such relief is accordingly still due. Suit of court also is still obligatory on tenants of estates in fee simple, held of any manor now existing. And the oath of fealty still continues an incident of tenure, as well of an estate in fee simple, as of every other estate, down to a tenancy for a mere term of years; but in practice it is seldom or never exacted.

There is yet another incident of the tenure of estates in fee simple; an incident, which has existed from the earliest times, and is still occasionally productive of substantial advantage to the lord. As the donor of an estate for life has a certain reversion on his tenant's death, and as the donor of an estate in tail has also a reversion expectant on the decease of his tenant, and failure of his issue, but subject to be defeated by the proper bar, so the lord, of whom an estate in fee simple is held, possesses, in respect of his lordship or seignory, a similar, though more uncertain advantage, in his right of *escheat*; by which, if the estate happens to end, the lands revert to the lord, by whose ancestors or predecessors they were anciently granted to the tenant. When the tenant of an estate in fee simple dies, without having alienated his estate in his lifetime, or by his will, and without leaving any heirs, lineal or collateral, either of the purchaser, or of the person last entitled to the lands, such lands *escheat* (as it is called) to the lord of whom they were held. Bastardy is the most usual cause of the failure of heirs; for a bastard is in law *nullius filius*; and, being nobody's son, he can consequently have no brother or sister, or any other heir than an heir of his body. If such a person, therefore, were to purchase lands, that is, to acquire an estate in fee simple in them, and were to die possessed of them without having made a will, and without leaving any issue, the lands would escheat to the lord of the fee, for want of heirs. Again, before forfeitures for treason and felony were abolished, sentence of death pronounced on a person convicted of high treason or murder, or of abetting, procuring, or counselling the same, caused his blood to be attainted or corrupted, and to lose its inheritable quality. In cases of high treason, the crown became entitled by forfeiture to the lands of the traitor; but in the other cases the lord, of whom the estate was held, became entitled by *escheat* to the lands, after the death of the attainted person; subject, however, to the Queen's right of possession for a year and a day, and of committing waste, called the Queen's year, day and waste, — a right usually compounded for. When an escheat occurs, the crown most frequently obtains the lands escheated, in consequence of the before-mentioned rule, that the crown was the original proprietor of all the lands in the kingdom. But if there should be any lord of a manor, or other person, who could prove that the estate so terminated was held of him, he, and not the crown, would be entitled. In former times, there were many such mesne or intermediate lords; every baron, according to the feudal system, had his tenants, and they, again, had theirs. The alienation of lands appears, indeed, as we have seen, to have most generally, if not universally, proceeded on this system of subinfeudation. But now the fruits and incidents of tenure of estates in fee simple are so few and rare, that many such estates are considered as held directly of the crown, for want of proof as to who is the intermediate lord; and the difficulty of proof is increased by the fact before mentioned, that, since the statute of *Quia emptores*, passed in the reign of Edward I., it has not been lawful to create a tenure of an estate in fee simple; so that every lordship or seignory of an estate in fee simple bears date at least as far back as that reign: to this rule the few seignories, which may have been subsequently created by the king's tenants in capite, form the only exception.

A small occasional *quit rent*, with its accompanying *relief*, — *suit* of the *Court* Baron, if any such exists, — an oath *of fealty* never exacted, — and a right *of escheat* seldom accruing, — are now, it appears, therefore, the ordinary incidents of the tenure of an estate in fee simple. There are, however, a few varieties in this tenure which are worth mentioning; they respect either the *persons* to whom the estate was originally granted, or the *places* in which the lands holden are situate. And, first, respecting the persons: The ancient tenure of *grand serjeanty* was where a man held his lands of the king by services to be done in his own proper person to the king, as, to carry the banner of the king, or his lance, or to be his marshal, or to carry his sword before him at his coronation, or to do other like services: when, by the statute of Charles II., this tenure, with the others, was turned into free and common socage, the honorary services above described were expressly retained. The ancient tenure of *petit serjeanty* was where a man held his land of the king, "to yield him yearly a bow, or a sword, or a dagger, or a knife, or a lance, or a paire of gloves of maile, or a paire of gilt spurs, or an arrow, or divers arrowes, or to yield such other small things belonging to warre": this was but socage in effect, because such a tenant was not to do any personal service, but to render and pay yearly certain things to the king. This tenure therefore still remains unaffected by the statute of Charles II.

Next, as to such varieties of tenure as relate to places: — These are principally the tenures of gavel-kind, borough-English, and ancient demesne. The tenure of gavelkind, or as it has been more correctly styled, socage tenure, subject to the custom of gavelkind, prevails chiefly in the county of Kent, in which county all estates of inheritance in land are presumed to be holden by this tenure until the contrary is shown. The most remarkable feature of this kind of tenure is the descent of the estate, in case of intestacy, not to the eldest son, but to all the sons in equal shares, and so to brothers and other collateral relations, on failure of nearer heirs. It is also a remarkable peculiarity of this custom, that every tenant of an estate of freehold (except of course an estate tail) is able, at the early age of fifteen years, to dispose of his estate by feoffment, the ancient method of conveyance to be hereafter explained. There is also no escheat of gavelkind lands upon a conviction of murder; and some other peculiarities of less importance belong to this tenure. The custom of gavelkind is generally supposed to have been a part of the ancient Saxon law, preserved by the struggles of the men of Kent at the time of the Norman conquest; and it is still held in high esteem by the inhabitants, so that whilst some lands in the county, having been originally held by knights' service, are not within the custom, and others have been disgavelled, or freed from the custom, by various acts of parliament, any attempt entirely to extinguish the peculiarities of this tenure has uniformly been resisted. There are a few places, in other parts of the kingdom, where the course of descent follows the custom of gavelkind; but it may be doubted whether the tenure of gavelkind, with all its accompanying peculiarities, is to be found elsewhere than in the county of Kent.

Tenure subject to the custom of Borough-English prevails in several cities and ancient boroughs, and districts adjoining to them; the tenure is socage, but, according to the custom, the estate descends to the *youngest son* in exclusion of all the other children. The custom does not in general extend to collateral relations; but by special custom it may, so as to admit the youngest *brother*, instead of the eldest. Estates, as well in tail as in fee simple, descend according to this custom.

The tenure of ancient demesne exists in those manors, and in those only, which belonged to the crown in the reigns of Edward the Confessor and William the Conqueror, and in Domesday Book are denominated *Terræ Regis Edwardi*, or *Terræ Regis*. The tenants are freeholders, and possess certain ancient immunities, the chief of which is a right to sue and be sued only in their lord's court. Before the abolition of fines and recoveries, these proceedings, being judicial in their nature, could only take place, as to lands in ancient demesne, in the lord's court; but, as the nature of the tenure was not always known, much inconvenience frequently arose from the proceedings being taken by mistake in the usual Court of Common Pleas at Westminster; and these mistakes have given to the tenure a prominence in practice which it would not otherwise have possessed. Such mistakes, however, have been corrected, as far as possible, by the act for the abolition of fines and recoveries; and for the future, the substitution of a simple deed, in the place of those assurances, renders such mistakes impossible. So that this peculiar kind of socage tenure now possesses but little practical importance.

So much then for the tenure of free and common socage, with its incidents and varieties. There is yet another kind of ancient tenure still subsisting, namely, the tenure of *frankalmoign*, or free alms, already mentioned, by which the lands of the church are for the most part held. This tenure is expressly excepted from the statute 12 Car. II. c. 24, by which the other ancient tenures were destroyed. It has no peculiar incidents, the tenants not being bound even to do fealty to the lords, because, as Littleton says, the prayers and other divine services of the tenants are better for the lords than any doing of fealty. As the church is a body having perpetual existence, there is moreover no chance of any escheat. This tenure is therefore a very near practical approach to that absolute dominion on the part of the tenant, which yet in theory the law never allows.

CHAPTER VI
OF JOINT TENANTS AND TENANTS IN COMMON

A gift of lands to two or more persons in joint tenancy is such a gift as imparts to them, with respect to all other persons than themselves, the properties of one single owner. As between themselves, they must, of course, have separate rights; but such rights are equal in every respect, it not being possible for one of them to have a greater interest than another in the subject of the tenancy. A joint tenancy is accordingly said to be distinguished by unity of *possession*, unity of *interest*, unity of *title*, and unity of the *time* of the commencement of such title. Any estate may be held in joint tenancy; thus, if lands be given simply to A. and B. without further words, they will become at once joint tenants for life. Being regarded, with respect to other persons, as but one individual, their estates will necessarily continue so long as the longer liver of them exists. While they both live, as they must have several rights between themselves, A. will be entitled to one moiety of the rents and profits of the land, and B. to the other; but after the decease of either of them, the survivor will be entitled to the whole during the residue of his life. So, if lands be given to A. and B. and the heirs of their two bodies; here, if A. and B. be persons who may possibly intermarry, they will have an estate in special tail, descendible only to the heirs of their two bodies: so long as they both live, they will be entitled to the rents and profits in equal shares; after the decease of either, the survivor will be entitled for life to the whole; and, on the decease of such survivor, the heir of their bodies, in case they should have intermarried, will succeed by descent, in the same manner as if both A. and B. had been but. one ancestor. If, however, A. and B. be persons who cannot at any time lawfully intermarry, as, if they be brother and sister, or both males, or both females, a gift to them and the heirs of their two bodies will receive a somewhat different construction. So long as it is possible for a unity of interest to continue, the law will carry it into effect: A. and B. will accordingly be regarded as one person, and will be entitled jointly during their lives. While they both live their rights will be equal; and, on the death of either, the survivor will take the whole, so long as he may live. But, as they cannot intermarry, it is not possible that any one person should be heir of both their bodies: on the decease of the survivor, the law, therefore, in order to conform as nearly as possible to the manifest intent, that the heir of the body of each of them should inherit, is obliged to sever the tenancy, and divide the inheritance between the heir of the body of A., and the heir of the body of B. Each heir will accordingly be entitled to a moiety of the rents and profits, as tenant in tail of such moiety. The heirs will now hold in a manner denominated tenancy in common; instead of both having the whole, each will have an undivided half, and no further right of survivorship will remain.

An estate in fee simple may also be given to two or more persons as joint tenants. The unity of this kind of tenure is remarkably shown by the words which are made use of to create a joint tenancy in fee simple. The lands intended to be given to joint tenants in fee simple are limited to them *and their heirs*, or to them, *their heirs and assigns*, although the heirs of one of them only will succeed to the inheritance, provided the joint tenancy be allowed to continue: thus, if lands be given to A., B. and C. *and their heirs*, A., B. and C. will together be regarded as one person; and, when they are all dead, but not before, the lands will descend to the heirs of the artificial person (so to speak) named in the gift. The survivor of the three, who together compose the tenant, will, after the decease of his companions, become entitled to the whole lands. While they all lived each had the whole; when any die, the survivors or survivor can have no more. The heir of the survivor is, therefore, the person who alone will be entitled to inherit, to the entire exclusion of the heirs of those who may have previously died. A joint tenancy in fee simple is far more usual than a joint tenancy for life or in tail. Its principal use in practice is for the purpose of vesting estates in trustees, who are invariably made joint tenants. On the decease of one of them, the whole estate then vests at once in the survivors or survivor of them, without devolving on the heir at law of the deceased trustee, and without being affected by any disposition which he may have made by his will; for joint tenants are incapable of devising their respective shares by will; they are not regarded as having any separate interests, except as between or amongst themselves, whilst two or more of them are living. Trustees, therefore, whose only interest is that of the persons for whom they hold in trust, are properly made joint tenants; and so long as any one of them is living, so long will every other person be excluded from the legal possession of the lands to which the trust extends. But on the decease of the surviving trustee, the lands will devolve on the devisee under his will, or on his heir at law, who will remain trustee till the lands are conveyed to some other trustee duly appointed.

As joint tenants together compose but one owner, it follows, as we have already observed, that the estate of each must arise at the same time; so that if A. and B. are to be joint tenants of lands, A. cannot take his share first, and then B. come in after him. To this rule, however, an exception has been made in favour of conveyances taking effect by virtue of the Statute of Uses, to be hereafter explained; for it has been held that joint tenants under this statute may take their shares at different times; and the exception appears also to extend to states created by will. A further consequence of the unity of joint tenants is seen in the fact, that if one of them should wish to dispose of his interest in favour of any of his companions, he may not make use of any mode of disposition operating merely as a conveyance of lands from one stranger to another. The legal possession or seisin of the whole of the lands belongs to each one of the joint tenants of an estate of freehold; no delivery can, therefore, be made to him of that which he already has. The proper form of assurance between joint tenants is, accordingly, a release by deed, and this release operates rather as an extinguishment of right than as a conveyance; for the whole estate is already supposed to be vested in each joint tenant, as well as his own proportion. And in the Norman French, with which our law abounds, two persons holding land in joint tenancy are said to be seised *per mie et per tout*.

The incidents of a joint tenancy, above referred to, last only so long as the joint tenancy exists. It is in the power of any one of the joint tenants to *sever* the tenancy; for each joint tenant possesses an absolute power to dispose, in his lifetime, of his own share of the lands, by which means he destroys the joint tenancy. Thus, if there be three joint tenants of lands in fee simple, any one of them may, by any of the usual modes of alienation, dispose during his lifetime, though not by will, of an equal undivided third part of the whole inheritance. But should he die without having made such disposition, each one of the remaining two will have a similar right in his lifetime to dispose of an undivided moiety of the whole. From the moment of severance, the unity of interest and title is destroyed, and nothing is left but the unity of possession; the share which has been disposed of is at once discharged from the rights and incidents of joint tenancy, and becomes the subject of a tenancy in common. Thus, if there be three joint tenants, and any one of them should exercise his power of disposition in favour of a stranger, such stranger will then hold one undivided third part of the lands, as tenant in common with the remaining two.

Tenants in common are such as have a unity of possession, but a distinct and several title to their shares. The shares in which tenants in common hold are by no means necessarily equal. Thus, one tenant in common may be entitled to one-third, or one-fifth, or any other proportion of the profits of the land, and the other tenant or tenants in common to the residue. So, one tenant in common may have but a life or other limited interest in his share, another may be seised in fee of his, and the owners of another undivided share may be joint tenants as between themselves, whilst as to the others they are tenants in common. Between a joint tenancy and tenancy in common, the only similarity that exists is therefore the unity of possession. A tenant in common is, as to his own undivided share, precisely in the position of the owner of an entire and separate estate.

When the rights of parties are distinct, that is, for instance, when they are not all trustees for one and the same purpose, both a joint tenancy and a tenancy in common are inconvenient methods for the enjoyment of property. Of the two a tenancy in common is no doubt preferable; inasmuch as a certain possession of a given share is preferable to a similar chance of getting or losing the whole, according as the tenant may or may not survive his companions. But the enjoyment of lands in *severally* is far more beneficial than either of the above modes. Accordingly it is in the power of any joint tenant or tenant in common to compel his companions to effect a *partition* between themselves, according to the value of their shares. This partition was formerly enforced by a writ of partition, granted by virtue of statutes passed in the reign of Henry VIII. Before this reign, as joint tenants and tenants in common always become such by their own act and agreement, they were without any remedy, unless they all agreed to the partition; whereas we have seen that co-parceners, who become entitled by act of law, could always compel partition. In modern times, the Court of Chancery was found to be the most convenient instrument for compelling the partition of estates; and by a modern statute, the old writ of partition, which had already become obsolete, was abolished. The Supreme Court of Judicature Act, 1873, has transferred this jurisdiction to the High Court of Justice thereby established. Whether the partition be effected through the agency of the Court, or by the mere private agreement of the parties, mutual conveyances of their respective undivided shares must be made, in order to carry the partition into complete effect. With respect to joint tenants, these conveyances ought, as we have seen, to be in the form of releases; but tenants in common, having separate titles, must make mutual conveyances, as between strangers; and by a modern statute it is provided, that a partition shall be void at law, unless made by deed. If any of the parties entitled should be infants under age, lunatic, or of unsound mind, and consequently unable to execute a conveyance, the Court has power to carry out its own decree for a partition by making an order, which will vest their shares in such persons as the Court shall direct. Another very convenient mode of effecting a partition is, by application to the inclosure commissioners for England and Wales, who are empowered by recent acts of parliament to make orders under their hands and seal for the partition and exchange of lands and other hereditaments, which orders are effectual without any further conveyance or release.

An act has now passed to amend the law relating to partition. By this act the Court of Chancery was empowered to direct a sale of the property instead of a partition, whenever a sale and distribution of the proceeds appeared to the Court to be more beneficial to the parties interested. The jurisdiction of the Court of Chancery in all these matters is now transferred to the High Court of Justice as from the first of November, 1875. If the parties interested to the extent of a moiety or upwards request a sale, the Court shall, unless it sees good reason to the contrary, direct a sale of the property accordingly. And if any party interested requests a sale the Court may, if it thinks fit, unless the other parties interested or some of them undertake to purchase the share of the party requesting a sale, direct a sale of the property. This alteration of the law, which was some time since suggested by the author, has, in his humble judgment, effected a substantial improvement.

CHAPTER VII
A FEOFFMENT

Having now considered the most usual freehold estates which are holden in lands, and the varieties of holding arising from joint tenancies and tenancies in common, we proceed to the means to be employed for the transfer of these estates from one person to another. And here we must premise that, by enactments of the present reign, the conveyance of estates has been rendered, for the future, a matter independent of that historical learning which was formerly necessary. But, as the means formerly necessary for the conveyance of freeholds depend on principles, which still continue to exert their influence throughout the whole system of real property law, these means of conveyance and their principles must yet continue objects of the early attention of every student: of these means the most ancient is a *feoffment with livery of seisin*, which accordingly forms the subject of our present chapter.

The feudal doctrine explained in the fifth chapter, that all estates in land are holden of some lord, necessarily implies that all lands must always have some feudal holder or tenant. This feudal tenant is the freeholder, or holder of the freehold; he has the feudal possession, called the *seisin*, and so long as he is *seised*, nobody else can be. The freehold is said to be *in* him, and till it is taken out of him and given to some other, the land itself is regarded as in his custody or possession. Now this legal possession of lands — this seisin of the freehold — is a matter of great importance, and much formerly depended upon its proper transfer from one person to another; thus we have seen that, before the act for the amendment of the law of inheritance, seisin must have been acquired by every heir before he could himself become the stock of descent. The transfer or delivery of the seisin, though it accompanies the transfer of the estate of the holder of the seisin, is yet not the same thing as the transfer of his estate. For a tenant merely for life is as much a feudal holder, and consequently as much in possession, or seised, of the freehold, as a tenant in fee simple can be. If, therefore, a person seised of an estate in fee simple were to grant a lease to another for his life, the lessee must necessarily have the whole seisin given up to him, although he would not acquire the whole estate of his lessor; for an estate for life is manifestly a less estate than an estate in fee simple. In ancient times, however, possession was the great point; and, until the enactments above referred to, the conveyance of an estate of freehold was of quite a distinct character from such assurances as were made use of, when it was not intended to affect the freehold or feudal possession. For instance, we have seen that a tenant for a term of years is regarded in law as having merely a chattel interest; he has not the feudal possession or freehold in himself, but his possession, like that of a bailiff or servant, is the possession of his landlord. The consequence is, that any expressions in a deed, from which an intention can be gathered to grant the occupation of land for a certain time, have always been sufficient for a lease for a term of years however long; but a lease for a single life, which transfers the freehold, formerly required technical language to give it effect.

A feoffment with livery of seisin was then nothing more than a gift of an estate in the land with *livery*, that is, delivery of the *seisin* or feudal possession; this livery of seisin was said to be of two kinds, a *livery in deed* and a *livery in law*. Livery in deed was performed "by delivery of the ring or haspe of the doore, or by a branch or twigge of a tree, or by a turfe of land, and with these or the like words, the feoffor and feoffee both holding the deed of feoffment and the ring of the doore, haspe, branch, twigge or turfe, and the feoffer saying, 'Here I deliver you seisin and possession of this house, in the name of all the lands and tenements contained in this deed according to the forme and effect of this deed,' or by words without any ceremony or act, as the feoffor being at the house doore, or within the house, 'Here I deliver you seisin and possession of this house, in the name of seisin and possession of all the lands and tenements contained in this deed' ". The feoffee then, if it were a house, entered alone, shut the door, then opened it, and let in the others. In performing this ceremony, it was requisite that all persons who had any estate or possession in the house or land, of which seisin was delivered, should either join in or consent to making the livery, or be absent from the premises; for the object was to give the entire and undisputed possession to the feoffee. If the feoffment was made of different lands lying scattered in one and the same county, livery of seisin of any parcel, in the name of the rest, was sufficient for all, if all were in the complete possession of the same feoffor; but if they were in several counties, there must have been as many liveries as there were counties. For if the title to these lands should come to be disputed, there must have been as many trials as there were counties; and the jury of one county are not considered judges of the notoriety of a fact in another. Livery in *law* was not made *on* the land, but *in sight of it* only, the feoffor saying to the feoffee, "I give you yonder land, enter and take possession." If the feoffee entered accordingly in the lifetime of the feoffor, this was a good feoffment; but if either the feoffor or feoffee died before entry, the livery was void. This livery was good although the land lay in another county; but it required always to be made between the parties themselves, and could not be deputed to an attorney, as might livery in deed. The word *give* was the apt and technical term to be employed in a feoffment; its use arose in those times when gifts from feudal lords to their tenants were the conveyances principally employed.

In addition to the livery of seisin, it was also necessary that the estate which the feoffee was to take should be marked out, whether for his own life or for that of another person, or in tail, or in fee simple, or otherwise. This marking out of the estate is as necessary now as formerly, and it is called *limiting* the estate. If the feudal holding is transferred, the estate must necessarily be an estate of freehold; it cannot be an estate at will, or for a fixed term of years merely. Thus the land may be given to the feoffee to hold to himself simply; and the estate so limited is, as we have seen, but an estate for his life, and the feoffee is then generally called a *lessee* for his life; though when a mere life interest is intended to be limited, the land is usually expressly given to hold to the lessee "during the term of his natural life". If the land be given to the feoffee *and the heirs of his body*, he has an estate tail, and is called a *donee* in tail. And in order to confer an estate tail, it is necessary (except in a will, where greater indulgence is allowed), that words of *procreation*, such as heirs *of his body*, should be made use of; for a gift of lands to a man and his *heirs male* is an estate in fee simple, and not in fee tail, there being no words of procreation to ascertain the body out of which they shall issue; and an estate in lands descendible to collateral male heirs only, in entire exclusion of females, is unknown to the English law. If the land be given to hold to the feoffee *and his heirs*, he has an estate in fee simple, the largest estate which the law allows. In every conveyance (except by will) of an estate of inheritance, whether in fee tail or in fee simple, the word *heirs* is necessary to be used as a word of limitation to mark out the estate. Thus if a grant be made to a man *and his seed*, or to a man *and his off spring*, or to a man *and the issue of his body*, all these are insufficient to confer an estate tail, and only give an estate for life for want of the word *heirs*; so if a man purchase lands to have and to hold *to him for ever*, or to him *and his assigns for ever*, he will have but an estate for his life, and not a fee simple. Before alienation was permitted, the heirs of the tenant were the only persons, besides himself, who could enjoy the estate; and if they were not mentioned, the tenant could not hold longer than for his own life; hence the necessity of the word *heirs* to create an estate in fee tail or fee simple. At the present day, the free transfer of estates in fee simple is universally allowed; but this liberty, as we have seen, is now given by the law and not by the particular words by which an estate may happen to be created. So that, though conveyances of estates in fee simple are usually made to hold to the purchaser, *his heirs and assigns for ever*, yet the word *heirs* alone gives him a fee simple, of which the law enables him to dispose; and the remaining words, *and assigns for ever*, have at the present day no conveyancing virtue at all; but are merely declaratory of that power of alienation which the purchaser would possess without them.

The formal delivery of the seisin or feudal possession, which always took place in a feoffment, rendered it, till recently, an assurance of great power; so that, if a person should have made a feoffment to another of an estate in fee simple, or of any other estate, not warranted by his own interest in the lands, such a feoffment would have operated *by wrong*, as it is said, and would have conferred on the feoffee the whole estate limited by the feoffment along with the seisin actually delivered. Thus if a tenant for his own life should have made a feoffment of the lands for an estate in fee simple, the feoffee would not merely have acquired an estate for the life of the feoffor, but-would have become seised of an estate in fee simple by wrong; accordingly, such a feoffment by a tenant for life was regarded as a cause of forfeiture to the person entitled in reversion; such a feoffment being in fact a conveyance of his reversion, without his consent, to another person. In the same manner, feoffments made by idiots and lunatics appear to have been only voidable and not absolutely void; whereas their conveyances made by any other means are void *in toto*; for, if the seisin was actually delivered to a person, though by a lunatic or idiot, the accompanying estate must necessarily have passed to him, until he should have been deprived of it. Again, the formal delivery of the seisin in a feoffment appears to be the ground of the validity of such a conveyance of gavelkind lands, by an infant of the age of fifteen years; although a conveyance of the same lands by the infant, made by any other means, would be voidable by him, on attaining his majority. By the act to amend the law of real property, it is, however, now provided, that a feoffment shall not have any tortious operation; but a feoffment made under a custom by an infant is expressly recognized.

Down to the time of King Henry VIII. nothing more was requisite to a valid feoffment than has been already mentioned. In the reign of this king, however, an act of parliament of great importance was passed, known by the name of the Statute of Uses. And since this statute, it has now become further requisite to a feoffment, either that there should be a *consideration* for the gift, or that it should be expressed to be made, not simply *unto*, but *unto and to the* feoffee. The manner in which this result has been brought about by the Statute of Uses will be explained in the next chapter.

If proper words of gift were used in a feoffment, and witnesses were present who could afterwards prove them, it mattered not, in ancient times, whether or not they were put into writing; though writing, from its greater certainty, was generally employed. There was this difference, however, between writing in those days, and writing in our own times. In our own times, almost everybody can write; in those days very few of the landed gentry of the country were so learned as to be able to sign their own names. Accordingly, on every important occasion, when a written document was required, instead of signing their names, they affixed their seals; and this writing, thus sealed, was delivered to the party for whose benefit it was intended. Writing was not then employed for every trivial purpose, but was a matter of some solemnity; accordingly, it became a rule of law, that every writing under seal imported a consideration: — that is, that a step so solemn could not have been taken without some sufficient ground. This custom of sealing remained after the occasion for it had passed away, and writing had been generally introduced; so that, in all legal transactions, a seal was affixed to the written document, and the writing so sealed was, when delivered, called a *deed*, in Latin *factum*, a thing done; and, for a long time after writing had come into common use, a written instrument, if unsealed, had in law no superiority over mere words; nothing was in fact called a *writing*, but a document under seal. And at the present day a *deed*, or a writing sealed and delivered, still imports a consideration, and maintains in many respects a superiority in law over a mere unsealed writing. In modern practice the kind of seal made use of is not regarded, and the mere placing of the finger on a seal already made, is held to be equivalent to sealing; and the words "I deliver this as my act and deed," which are spoken at the same time, are held to be equivalent to delivery, even if the party keep the deed himself. The sealing and delivery of a deed are termed the *execution* of it. Occasionally a deed is delivered to a third person not a party to it, to be delivered up to the other party or parties, upon the performance of a condition, as the payment of money or the like. It is then said to be delivered as an *escrow* or mere writing *(scriptum)*; for it is not a perfect deed until delivered up on the performance of the condition; but when so delivered up, it operates from the time of its execution. Any alteration or rasure in or addition to a deed is presumed to have been made before its execution. And it was formerly held that any alteration, rasure or addition made in a material part of a deed, after its execution by the grantor, even though made by a stranger, would render it void, and that any alteration in a deed made by the party to whom it was delivered, though in words not material, would also render it void. But a more reasonable doctrine has lately prevailed; and it has now been held that the filling in of the date of the deed, or of the names of the occupiers of the lands conveyed, or any such addition, if consistent with the purposes of the deed, will not render it void, even though done by the party to whom it has been delivered, after its execution. If an estate has once been conveyed by a deed, of course the subsequent alteration, or even the destruction, of the deed cannot operate to reconvey the estate; and the deed, even though cancelled, may be given in evidence to show that the estate was conveyed by it whilst it was valid. But the deed having become void, no action could be brought upon any covenant contained in it.

Previously to the Stamp Act, 1870, every deed, if not charged with any *ad valorem* or other stamp duty, nor expressly exempted from all stamp duty, was liable to a stamp duty of 1*l.* 15*s.*; and if the deed, together with any schedule, receipt or other matter put or indorsed thereon or annexed thereto, contained 2160 words, or 30 common law folios of 72 words each, or upwards, it was liable to a further *progressive* duty of 10*s.* for every *entire* quantity of 1080 words, or 15 folios, over and above the first 1080 words. But the duplicate or counterpart of any deed was liable only to a stamp duty of five shillings and a *progressive* duty of half-a-crown, unless the original were liable to a less duty, in which case the duty was the same as on the original. If, however, the deed were signed or executed by any party thereto, or bore date, before or upon the 10th of October, 1850, when the former act to amend the stamp duties took effect, then the progressive duty was 1*l.* 5*s.* for every entire quantity of 1080 words beyond the first 1080. But the Stamp Act, 1870, has now consolidated and amended the provisions relating to the stamp duties. The stamp duty for a deed of any kind not described in the schedule to the act, is now only 10*s.*; and all progressive duties are abolished. The duplicate or counterpart of any deed is subject to the same duty as before, except the progressive duty.

Deeds are divided into two kinds, *Deeds poll* and *Indentures*: a deed poll being made by one party only, and an indenture being made between two or more parties. Formerly, when deeds were more concise than at present, it was usual, where a deed was made between two parties, to write two copies upon the same piece of parchment, with some word or letters of the alphabet written between them, through which the parchment was cut, often in an indented line, so as to leave half the words on one part, and half on the other, thus serving the purpose of a tally. But at length indenting only came into use; and now every deed, to which there is more than one party, is cut with an indented or waiving line at the top, and is called an *indenture*. Formerly, when a deed assumed the form of an indenture, every person who took any immediate benefit under it, was always named as one of the parties. But now, by the act to amend the law of real property it is enacted that, under an indenture, an immediate estate or interest in any tenements or hereditaments, and the benefit of a condition or covenant respecting any tenements or hereditaments, may be taken, although the taker thereof be not named a party to the same indenture; also that a deed, purporting to be an indenture, shall have the effect of an indenture, although not actually indented. A deed made by only one party is polled, or shaved even at the top, and is therefore called a *deed poll*; and, under such a deed, any person may accept a grant, though of course none but the party can make one. All deeds must be written either on paper or parchment.

So manifest are the advantages of putting down in writing matters of any permanent importance, that, as commerce and civilization advanced, writings not under seal must necessarily have come into frequent use; but, until the reign of King Charles II., the use of writing remained perfectly optional with the parties, in every case which did not require a deed under seal. In this reign, however, an act of parliament was passed, requiring the use of writing in many transactions, which previously might have taken place by mere word of mouth. This act is intituled "An Act for Prevention of Frauds and Perjuries," and is now commonly called the Statute of Frauds. It enacts, amongst other things, that all leases, estates, interests of freehold, or terms of years, or any uncertain interest, in messuages, manors, lands, tenements, or hereditaments, made or created by livery of seisin only, or by parol, and not put in writing, and signed by the parties so making or creating the same, or their agents thereunto lawfully authorized by writing, shall have the force and effect of leases or estates at will only, and no greater force and effect; any consideration for making any such parol leases or estates, or any former law or usage to the contrary notwithstanding. The only exception to this sweeping enactment is in favour of leases not exceeding three years from the making, and on which a rent of two-thirds at least of the full improved value is reserved to the landlord. In consequence of this act, it became necessary that a feoffment should be put into writing, and signed by the party making the same, or his agent lawfully authorized by writing; but a deed or writing *under seal* was not essential, if livery of seisin were duly made. But now by the act to amend the law of real property, it is provided that a feoffment, other than a feoffment made under a custom by an infant, shall be void at law, unless evidenced by deed. Where a deed is made use of, it is a matter of doubt, whether signing, as well as sealing, is absolutely necessary: previously to the Statute of Frauds, signing was not at all essential to a deed, provided it were only sealed and delivered; and the Statute of Frauds seems to be aimed at transactions by parol only, and not to be intended to affect deeds. Of this opinion is Mr. Preston. Sir William Blackstone, on the other hand, thinks signing now to be as necessary as sealing. And the Court of Queen's Bench has, if possible, added to the doubt. Mr. Preston's, however, appears to be the better opinion. However this may be, it would certainly be most unwise to raise the question by leaving any deed sealed and delivered, but not signed.

The doubt above mentioned is just of a class with many others, with which the student must expect to meet. Lying just by the side of the common highway of legal knowledge, it yet remains uncertain ground. The abundance of principles and the variety of illustrations to be found in legal text books, are apt to mislead the student into the supposition, that he has obtained a map of the whole country which lies before him. But further research will inform him that this opinion is erroneous, and that, though the ordinary paths are well beaten by author after author again going over the same ground, yet much that lies to the right hand and to the left still continues unexplored, or known only as doubtful and dangerous. The manner in which our laws are formed is the chief reason for this prevalence of uncertainty. Parliament, the great framer of the laws, seldom undertakes the task of interpreting them, a task indeed which would itself be less onerous, were more care and pains bestowed on the making of them. But, as it is, a doubt is left to stand for years, till the cause of some unlucky suitor raises the point before one of the Courts; till this happens, the judges themselves have no authority to remove it; and thus it remains a pest to society, till caught in the act of raising a lawsuit. No wonder then, when judges can do so little, that writers should avoid all doubtful points. Cases, which have been decided, are continually cited to illustrate the principles on which the decisions have proceeded; but in the absence of decision, a lawyer becomes timid, and seldom ventures to draw an inference, lest he should be charged with introducing a doubt.

To return: a feoffment, with livery of seisin, though once the usual method of conveyance, has long since ceased to be generally employed. For many years past, another method of conveyance has been resorted to, which could be made use of at any distance from the property; but as this mode derived its effect from the Statute of Uses, it will be necessary to explain that statute before proceeding further.

CHAPTER VIII
OF USES AND TRUSTS

Previously to the reign of Henry VIII., when the Statute of Uses, was passed, a simple gift of lands to a person and his heirs, accompanied by livery of seisin, was all that was necessary to convey to that person an estate in fee simple in the lands. The courts of law did not deem any consideration necessary; but if a man voluntarily gave lands to another, and put him in possession of them, they held the gift to be complete and irrevocable; just as a gift of money or goods, made without any consideration, is, and has ever been, quite beyond the power of the giver to retract it, if accompanied by delivery of possession. In law, therefore, the person to whom a gift of lands was made, and seisin delivered, was considered thenceforth to be the true owner of the lands. In equity, however, this was not: always the case; for the Court of Chancery, administering equity, held that the mere delivery of the possession or seisin by one person to another was not at all conclusive of the right of the feoffee to enjoy the lands of which he was enfeoffed. Equity was unable to take from him the title which he possessed, and could always assert in the courts of law; but equity could and did compel him to make use of that legal title, for the benefit of any other person who might have a more righteous claim to the beneficial enjoyment. Thus if a feoffment was made of lands to one person for the benefit or to the use of another, such person was bound in conscience to hold the lands to the use or for the benefit of the other accordingly; so that while the title of the person enfeoffed was good in a court of law, yet he derived no benefit from the gift, for the Court of Chancery obliged him to hold entirely for the use of the other for whose benefit the gift was made. This device was introduced into England about the close of the reign of Edward III. by the foreign ecclesiastics, who contrived by means of it to evade the statutes of mortmain, by which lands were prohibited from being given for religious purposes; for they obtained grants to persons *to the use* of the religious houses; which grants the clerical chancellors of those days held to be binding. In process of time, such feoffments to one person to the use of another became very common; for the Court of Chancery allowed the *use* of lands to be disposed of in a variety of ways, amongst others by will, in which a disposition could not then be made of the lands themselves. Sometimes persons made feoffments of lands to others to the use of themselves the feoffors; and when a person made a feoffment to a stranger, without any consideration being given, and without any declaration being made for whose use the feoffment should be, it was considered in Chancery that it must have been meant by the feoffor to be for his own use. So that though the feoffee became *in law* absolutely seised of the lands, yet *in equity* he was held to be seised of them to the use of the feoffor. The Court of Chancery paid no regard to that implied consideration, which the law affixed to every deed on account of its solemnity, but looked only to what actually passed between the parties; so that a feoffment accompanied by a deed, if no consideration actually passed, was held to be made *to the use* of the feoffor, just as a feoffment by mere parol or word of mouth. If however there was any, even the smallest, consideration given by the feoffee, such as five shillings, the presumption that the feoffment was for the use of the feoffor was rebutted, and the feoffee was held entitled to his own use.

Transactions of this kind became in time so frequent that most of the lands in the kingdom were conveyed to uses "to the utter subversion of the ancient common laws of this realm". The attention of the legislature was from time to time directed to the public inconvenience to which these uses gave rise; and after several attempts to amend them, an act of parliament was at last passed for their abolition. This act is no other than the Statute of Uses, a statute which still remains in force, and exerts at the present day a most important influence over the conveyance of real property. By this statute it was enacted, that where any person or persons shall stand seised of any lands or other hereditaments to the use, confidence or trust of any other person or persons, the persons that *have* any such use, confidence or trust (by which was meant the persons beneficially entitled) shall be deemed in lawful seisin and possession of the same lands and hereditaments for such estates as they have in the use, trust or confidence. This statute was the means of effecting a complete revolution in the system of conveyancing. It is a curious instance of the power of an act of parliament; it is in fact an enactment that what is given to A. shall, under certain circumstances, not be given to A. at all, but to somebody else. For suppose a feoffment be now made to A. and his heirs, and the seisin duly delivered to him; if the feoffment be expressed to be made to him and his heirs *to the use* of some other person, as B. and his heirs, A. (who would, before this statute, have had an estate in fee simple at law) now takes *no permanent estate*, but is made by the statute to be merely a kind of conduit pipe for conveying the estate to B. For B. (who before would have had only a use or trust in equity) shall now, *having the use*, be deemed in lawful seisin and possession; in other words, B. now takes, not only the beneficial interest, but also the estate in fee simple at law, which is wrested from A. by force of the statute. Again, suppose a feoffment to be now made simply *to A. and his heirs* without any consideration. We have seen that before the statute the feoffor would in this case have been held in equity to have the use, for want of any consideration to pass it to the feoffee; now, therefore, the feoffor, having the use, shall be deemed in lawful seisin and possession; and consequently, by such a feoffment, although livery of seisin be duly made to A., yet no permanent estate will pass to him; for the moment he obtains the estate he holds it to the use of the feoffor; and the same instant comes the statute, and gives to the feoffor, who has the use, the seisin and possession. The feoffor, therefore, instantly gets back all that he gave; and the use is said to *result* to himself. If however the feoffment be made *unto and to the use* of A. and his heirs — as, before the statute, A. would have been entitled for his own use, so now he shall be deemed in lawful seisin and possession, and an estate in fee simple will effectually pass to him accordingly. The propriety of inserting, in every feoffment, the words *to the use of*, as well as *to* the feoffee, is therefore manifest. It appears also that an estate in fee simple may be effectually conveyed to a person by making a feoffment to any other person and his heirs, to the use of or upon confidence or trust for such former person and his heirs. Thus, if a feoffment be made to A. and his heirs, to the use of B. and his heirs, an estate in fee simple will now pass to B., as effectually as if the feoffment had been made directly unto and to the use of B. and his heirs in the first instance. The words *to the use of* are now almost universally employed for such a purpose; but "upon confidence," or "upon trust for," would answer as well, since all these expressions are mentioned in the statute.

The word *trust*, however, is never employed in modern conveyancing, when it is intended to vest an estate in fee simple in any person by force of the Statute of Uses. Such an intention is always carried into effect by the employment of the word *use*; and the word *trust* is reserved to signify a holding by one person for the benefit of another similar to that, which, before the statute, was called a *use*. For, strange as it may appear, with the Statute of Uses remaining unrepealed, lands are still, as everybody knows, frequently vested in trustees, who have the seisin and possession in law, but yet have no beneficial interest, being liable to be brought to account for the rents and profits by means of the Chancery Division of the High Court of Justice. The Statute of Uses was evidently intended to abolish altogether the jurisdiction of the Court of Chancery over landed estates, by giving actual possession at law to every person beneficially entitled in equity. But this object has not been accomplished; for the Court of Chancery soon regained in a curious manner its former ascendancy, and has kept it to the present day. So that all that was ultimately effected by the Statute of Uses, was to import into the rules of law some of the then existing doctrines of the Courts of Equity, and to add three words, *to the use*, to every conveyance. Supreme Court The Supreme Court of Judicature Act, 1873, now provides for the transfer of the jurisdiction of all the Courts both of law and equity to the High Court of Justice thereby established; and it enacts that in all matters, not therein particularly mentioned, in which there is any conflict or variance between the rules of equity and the rules of the common law with reference to the same matter, the rules of equity shall prevail.

The manner in which the Court of Chancery regained its ascendancy was as follows. Soon after the passing of the Statute of Uses, a doctrine was laid down, that there could not be a use upon a use. For instance, suppose a feoffment had been made to

A. and his heirs, to the use of B. and his heirs, to the use of C. and his heirs; the doctrine was, that the use to C. and his heirs was a use upon a use, and was therefore not affected by the Statute of Uses, which could only *execute* or operate on the use to B. and his heirs. So that B. and not C. became entitled, under such a feoffment, to an estate in fee simple in the lands comprised in the feoffment. This doctrine has much of the subtlety of the scholastic logic which was then prevalent. As Mr. Watkins says, it must have surprised every one, who was not sufficiently learned to have lost his common sense. It was however adopted by the courts and is still law. Even if the first use be to the feoffee himself, in which case he takes by the common law, no subsequent use will be *executed*, and the feoffee will take the fee simple; thus, under a feoffment unto and to the use of A. and his heirs, to the use of C. and his heirs, C. takes no estate in law, for the use to him is a use upon a use; but the fee simple vests in A. to whom the use is first declared. Here then was at once an opportunity for the Court of Chancery to interfere. It was manifestly inequitable that C., the party to whom the use was last declared, should be deprived of the estate, which was intended solely for his benefit; the Court of Chancery, therefore, interposed on his behalf, and constrained the party, to whom the law had given the estate, to hold in *trust* for him to whom the use was last declared. Thus arose the modern doctrine of uses and trusts. And hence it is, that if it is now wished to vest a freehold estate in one person as trustee for another, the conveyance is made unto the trustee, or some other person (it is immaterial which), and his heirs, *to the use* of the trustee and his heirs, *in trust* for the party intended to be benefited (called *cestui que trust)* and his heirs. An estate in fee simple is thus vested in the trustee, by force of the Statute of Uses, and the entire beneficial interest is given over to the cestui que trust by the doctrines of the Court of Chancery. The estate in fee simple, which is vested in the trustee, is called the *legal estate*, being an estate, to which the trustee was entitled, only in the contemplation of a court of *law*, as distinguished from equity. The interest of the cestui que trust is called an *equitable estate*, being an estate to which he was entitled only in the contemplation of the Court of Chancery, which administered *equity*. The Supreme Court of Judicature Act, 1873, has assigned to the Chancery Division of the High Court the execution of trusts, charitable and private; but the doctrine of trusts remains the same. In the present instance, the equitable estate being limited to the cestui que trust and his heirs, he has an equitable estate in fee simple. He is the beneficial owner of the property. The trustee, by virtue of his legal estate, has the right and power to receive the rents and profits; but the cestui que trust is able, by virtue of his estate in equity, at any time to oblige his trustee to come to an account, and hand over the whole of the proceeds.

We have now arrived at a very prevalent and important kind of interest in landed property, namely, an estate in equity merely, and not at law. The owner of such an estate had no title at all in any court of law, but was obliged to have recourse exclusively to the Court of Chancery, where he found himself considered as owner, according to the equitable estate he might have had. Chancery in modern times, though in principle the same as the ancient court which first gave effect to uses, was yet widely different in the application of many of its rules. Thus we have seen that a consideration, however trifling, given by a feoffee, was sufficient to entitle him to the *use* of the lands of which he was enfeoffed. But the absence of such a consideration caused the use to remain with, or more technically to result to, the feoffor, according to the rules of Chancery in ancient times. And this doctrine has now a practical bearing on the transfer of legal estates; the ancient doctrines of Chancery having, by the Statute of Uses, become the means of determining the owner of the legal estate, whenever USES are mentioned. But the modern Court of Chancery took a wider scope, and would not withhold or grant its aid, according to the mere payment or non-payment of five shillings: thus, circumstances of fraud, mistake, or the like, may induce the Chancery Division of the High Court, which now stands in the place of the Court of Chancery, to require a grantee under a voluntary conveyance to hold merely as a trustee for the grantor; but the mere want of a valuable consideration would not now be considered a sufficient cause for its interference.

By the act to confer on the County Courts a limited jurisdiction in equity, it was enacted, amongst other things, that these courts should have and exercise all the power and authority of the High Court of Chancery in all suits for the execution of trusts in which the trust estate or fund should not exceed in amount or value the sum of five hundred pounds. This act came into operation on the first of October, 1865.

In the construction and regulation of trusts, equity is said to follow the law, that is, the Court of Chancery generally adopted the rules of law applicable to legal estates; thus, a trust for A. for his life, or for him and the heirs of his body, or for him and his heirs, will give him an equitable estate for life, in tail, or in fee simple. An equitable estate tail may also be *barred*, in the same manner as an estate tail at law, and cannot be disposed of by any other means. But the decisions of equity, though given by rule, and not at random, do not follow the law in all its ancient technicalities, but proceed on a liberal system, correspondent with the more modern origin of its power. Thus, equitable estates in tail, or in fee simple, may be conferred without the use of the words *heirs of the body*, or *heirs*, if the intention be clear: for, equity pre-eminently regards the intentions and agreements of parties; accordingly, words which at law would confer an estate tail, are sometimes construed in equity, in order to further the intention of the parties, as giving merely an estate for life, followed by separate and independent estates tail to the children of the donee. This construction is frequently adopted by equity in the case of marriage articles, where an intention to provide for the children might otherwise be defeated by vesting an estate tail in one of the parents, who could at once bar the entail, and thus deprive the children of all benefit. So if lands be directed to be sold, and the money to arise from the sale be directed to be laid out in the purchase of other land to be settled on certain persons for life or in tail, or in any other manner, such persons will be regarded in equity as already in possession of the estates they are intended to have: for, whatever is fully agreed to be done, equity considers as actually accomplished. And in the same manner if money, from whatever source arising, be directed to be laid out in the purchase of land to be settled in any manner, equity will regard the persons on whom the lands are to be settled as already in the possession of their estates. And in both the above cases the estates tail directed to be settled maybe barred, before they are actually given, by a disposition duly enrolled, of the lands which are to be sold in the one case, or of the money to be laid out in the other. Again, an equitable estate in fee simple immediately belongs to every purchaser of freehold property the moment he has signed a contract for purchase, provided the vendor has a good title; and it is understood that the whole estate of the vendor is contracted for, unless a smaller estate is expressly mentioned, the employment of the word *heirs* not being essential. If, therefore, the purchaser were to die intestate the moment after the contract, the equitable estate in fee simple, which he had just acquired, would descend to his heir at law, who would have a right (to be enforced in equity) to have the estate paid for out of the money and other personal estate of his deceased ancestor; and the vendor would be a trustee for the heir, until he should have made a conveyance of the legal estate, to which the heir would be entitled. Many other examples of equitable or trust estates in fee simple might be furnished.

An equitable estate in fee will not escheat to the lord upon failure of heirs of the *cestui que trust*; for a trust is a mere creature of equity, and not a subject of tenure. In such a case, therefore, the trustee will hold the lands discharged from the trust which has so failed; and he will accordingly have a right to receive the rents and profits without being called to account by any one. In other words, the lands will thenceforth be his own. But previously to the Naturalization Act, 1870, it was held that if lands were purchased by a natural-born subject in trust for an alien, the crown might claim the benefit of the purchase; although, if lands were directed to be sold, and the produce given to an alien, the crown had then no claim. But, as we have seen, the Naturalization Act, 1870, now provides that real and personal property of every description may be taken, acquired, held and disposed of by an alien in the same manner in all respects as by a natural-born British subject; and a title to real and personal property of every description may be derived through, from or in succession to an alien in the same manner in all respects as through, from or in succession to a natural-born British subject. In the event of high treason being committed by the *cestui que trust* of an estate in fee simple, it was the better opinion that his equitable estate would be forfeited to the crown. But, as we have seen, all forfeitures for treason are now abolished. By a statute of the present reign, both the lord's right of escheat, and the crown's right of forfeiture, had already been taken away in the case of the failure of heirs or corruption of blood of the *trustee*, except so far as he himself might have any beneficial interest in the lands of which he was seised. And now, as we have seen, on the death of a bare trustee intestate, the legal estate in fee vested in him vests in his legal personal representative from time to time.

The descent of an equitable estate on intestacy follows the rules of the descent of legal estates; and, therefore, in the case of gavelkind and borough-English lands, trusts affecting them will descend according to the descendible quality of the tenure.

Trusts or equitable estates may be created and passed from one person to another, without the use of any particular ceremony or form of words. But, by the Statute of Frauds, it is enacted, that no action shall be brought upon any agreement made upon consideration of marriage, or upon any contract or sale of lands, tenements or hereditaments, or any interest in or concerning them, unless the agreement upon which such action shall be brought, or some memorandum or note thereof, shall be in writing, and signed by the party to be charged therewith, or some other person thereunto by him lawfully authorized. It is also enacted, that all declarations or creations of trusts or confidences of any lands, tenements or hereditaments, shall be manifested and proved by some writing, signed by the party who is by law enabled to declare such trusts, or by his last will in writing; and further, that all grants and assignments of any trust or confidence shall likewise be in writing, signed by the party granting or assigning the same, or by his last will. Trusts arising or resulting from any conveyance of lands or tenements, by implication or construction of law, and trusts transferred or extinguished by an act or operation of *law*, are exempted from this statute. In the transfer of equitable estates it is usual, in practice, to adopt conveyances applicable to the legal estate; but this is never necessary. If writing is used, and duly signed, in order to satisfy the Statute of Frauds, and the intention to transfer is clear, any words will answer the purpose.

The sale of real estate by auction is now regulated by an act which renders invalid every such sale where a puffer is employed; and which requires that the particulars or conditions of sale shall state whether the sale is without reserve, or subject to a reserved price, or whether a right to bid is reserved. And if the sale is stated to be without reserve or to that effect, the seller may not employ any person to bid at the sale, and the auctioneer may not knowingly take any bidding from any such person. But where the sale is declared to be subject to a right for the seller to bid, he or any one person on his behalf may bid at the auction in such manner as he may think proper. This act also very properly abolishes a practice which had long prevailed in Courts of Chancery of opening the biddings after a sale by auction of land under their authority, if a price considerably higher were afterwards offered; so that a bonâ fide purchaser was never sure of his bargain. But now the highest bona fide bidder is to be declared and allowed the purchaser, except in the case of fraud or improper conduct in the management of the sale.

Courts of Equity, looking to the substance of contracts rather than to the letter, have been in the habit of enforcing their performance, in some cases where the time fixed has gone by, and the contract has therefore, according to the letter of the law, come to an end. The Supreme Court of Judicature Act, 1873, which transfers to the Court thereby established the jurisdiction of the superior courts both of law and equity, accordingly provides, that stipulations in contracts, as to time or otherwise, which would not, before the commencement of that act, have been deemed to be, or to have become, of the essence of such contracts in a Court of Equity, shall receive in all courts the same construction and effect as they would have theretofore received in equity.

The County Courts have now jurisdiction in equity in all suits for specific performance of, or for reforming, delivering up or cancelling of, any agreement for the sale, purchase or lease of any property, where, in the case of a sale or purchase, the purchase-money, or in case of a lease the value of the property, shall not exceed five hundred pounds.

Trust estates, besides being subject to voluntary alienation, are also liable, like estates at law, to involuntary alienation for the payment of the owner's debts. By the Statute of Frauds it was provided, that if any *cestui que trust* should die, leaving a trust in fee simple to descend to his heir, such trust should be assets by descent, and the heir should be chargeable with the obligation of his ancestors for and by reason of such assets, as fully as he might have been if the estate in law had descended to him in possession in like manner as the trust descended. And the subsequent statutes to which we have before referred, for preventing the debtor from defeating his bond creditor by his will, and for rendering the estates of all persons liable on their decease to the payment of their just debts of every kind, apply as well to equitable or trust estates as to estates at law.

The same Statute of Frauds also gave a remedy to the creditor who had obtained a *judgment* against his debtor, by providing, that it should be lawful for every sheriff or other officer to whom any writ should be directed, upon any judgment, to deliver execution unto the party in that behalf suing, of all such lands and hereditaments as any other person or persons should be seised or possessed of *in trust for him against whom execution was sued*, like as the sheriff or other officer might have done if the party against whom execution should be sued had been seised of such lands or hereditaments of such estate as they be seised of in trust for him *at the time of execution sued*. This enactment was evidently copied from a similar provision made by a statute of Henry VII., respecting lands of which any other person or persons were seised *to the use* of him against whom execution was sued; and which statute of course became inoperative when uses were, by the Statute of Uses, turned into estates at law. The construction placed upon this enactment of the Statute of Frauds was more favourable to purchasers than that placed on the statute of Edward I., by which fee simple estates at law were first rendered liable to judgment debts. For it was held that although the trustee might have been seised in trust for the debtor at the time of obtaining the judgment, yet if he had conveyed away the lands to a purchaser before execution was actually sued out on the judgment, the lands could not afterwards be taken; because the trustee was not, in the words of the statute, seised in trust for the debtor *at the time of execution sued*. The act for extending the remedies of creditors against the property of debtors, however, deprived purchasers of this advantage, in consideration perhaps of the greater facilities which it afforded in the search for judgments; for it provided, that execution might be delivered, under the writ of elegit, of all such lands and hereditaments as the person against whom execution was sued, *or any person in trust for him, should have been* seised or possessed of at the time of entering up the judgment, *or at any time afterwards*; and a remedy in equity was also given to the judgment creditor against all lands and hereditaments of or to which the debtor should at the time of entering up the judgment, or at any time afterwards, be seised, possessed or entitled for any estate or interest whatever at law or in equity. But the still more recent enactments, to which we have before referred, have greatly diminished the effect of these provisions.

Trust estates are subject to debts due to the crown in the same manner and to the same extent as estates at law. They are also equally liable to involuntary alienation on the bankruptcy of the *cestui que trust*. But, on the bankruptcy of the trustee, the legal estate in the premises of which he is trustee remains vested in him and does not pass to the trustee for his creditors; and the same rule formerly applied to cases of insolvency.

The circumstance of property being vested in trustees sometimes occasions inconvenience. A trustee may become lunatic, or may leave the country, or may refuse to convey, when required, the lands of which he is trustee; or he may die intestate without an heir, or leaving an infant heir, on whom, if he was a sole or a sole surviving trustee, other than a merely bare trustee, the lands will descend at law. In order to remedy the inconvenience thus occasioned to the persons beneficially entitled, it is provided by acts of parliament of the present reign that, in the case of a lunatic trustee, the Lord Chancellor, or the judges entrusted by the Queen's sign manual with the care of the persons and estates of lunatics, and the Chancery Division of the High Court in other cases, may make an order vesting the lands in any other person or persons; and such an order will operate as a valid conveyance of such lands accordingly. It is also provided that, whenever it is expedient to appoint a new trustee, and it is inexpedient, difficult, or impracticable to do so without the assistance of the Court, the Court may make an order appointing a new trustee or new trustees, either in substitution for or in addition to any existing trustee or trustees, or whether there be any existing trustee or not. The Court is also empowered to appoint a new trustee in the place of any trustee who shall have been convicted of felony. And upon making any order appointing a new trustee, the Court may direct that any lands subject to the trust shall vest in the person or persons who, upon the appointment, shall be the trustee or trustees for such estate as the Court shall direct; and such order will have the same effect as if the person or persons who before such order were the trustee or trustees (if any) had duly executed all proper conveyances of such lands. Property held in trust for charities may also be vested by the Court in new trustees, or in the official trustee of charity lands, without any conveyance. But every such order is now chargeable with a stamp duty of 10*s*. All the power and authority of the Court, in any of the above-mentioned matters, is now vested in the County Courts, in all proceedings in which the trust estate or fund to which the proceeding relates shall not exceed in amount or value the sum of five hundred pounds. By another act of parliament provision is made for vesting the property of congregations or societies for purposes of religious worship or education in new trustees from time to time without any conveyance. The provisions of this act have recently been extended to Literary and Scientific Institutions; and also to burial grounds. The act to facilitate the incorporation of trustees of charities for religious, educational, literary, scientific and public charitable purposes has already been referred to.

An act has also been passed which contains a general provision for the appointment of new trustees, similar to the powers for that purpose ordinarily inserted in well-drawn trust deeds. This act, which is intituled "An Act to give to Trustees, Mortgagees and others certain Powers now commonly inserted in Settlements, Mortgages and Wills," extends to instruments executed, or wills confirmed or revived by codicil executed, after the 28th of August, 1860, the date of the act. It provides that whenever any trustee shall die, or desire to be discharged from, or refuse or become unfit or incapable to act in, the trusts or powers reposed in him, the surviving or continuing trustees or trustee, or the acting executors or administrators of the last surviving or continuing trustee, or the last retiring trustee, may, if there be no person nominated for that purpose by the instrument creating the trust, or no such person able and willing to act, appoint a new trustee. And every such trustee, and also every trustee appointed by the Court, either before or after the passing of the act, is invested with the same powers as if he had been originally nominated by the instrument creating the trust. And the above-mentioned power of appointing new trustees may be exercised in cases where a trustee nominated in a will has died in the lifetime of the testator, as well as where he may have died after the testator's decease. It is now provided that a conveyance or transfer made for effectuating the appointment of a new trustee, is not to be charged with any higher duty than 10*s*.

The concurrent existence of two distinct systems of jurisprudence was a peculiar feature of English Law. On one side of Westminster Hall a man might have succeeded in his suit under circumstances in which he would undoubtedly have been defeated on the other side; for he might have had a title in equity, and not al law (being a *cestui que trust)*, or a title at law and not in equity (being merely a trustee). In the former case, though he would have succeeded in a chancery suit, he never would have thought of bringing an action at law; in the latter case he would have succeeded in an action at law; but equity would have taken care that the fruits should be reaped only by the person beneficially entitled. The equitable title was, therefore, the beneficial one, but if barely equitable, it might have occasioned the expense and delay of a chancery suit to maintain it.

A step was taken towards the amalgamation of law and equity by the Common Law Procedure Act, 1854, which conferred on the Courts of Common Law an extensive equitable jurisdiction. The plaintiff in any action, except replevin and ejectment, was allowed to claim a writ of mandamus commanding the defendant to fulfil any duty in the fulfilment of which the plaintiff was personally interested, and by the non-performance of which he might have sustained damage. In all cases of breach of contract or other injury, where the party injured was entitled to maintain and had brought an action, he was allowed to claim a writ of injunction against the repetition or continuance of such breach or injury. If the defendant would have been entitled to relief against the judgment on equitable grounds, he was allowed to plead, by way of defence to the action, the facts which entitled him to such relief; and the plaintiff might have replied, in answer to any plea of the defendant's, facts which avoided such plea on equitable grounds. But the facts pleaded were required to be such as would entitle the person pleading them to absolute and unconditional relief in the Court of Chancery, otherwise the plea would not have been allowed. The change effected was not therefore so great as might, at first sight, have been supposed. Another act of parliament conferred a common law jurisdiction upon the Court of Chancery: — the Chancery Amendment Act, 1858, empowered the Court of Chancery to award damages like a Court of

Law in all cases of injunction and specific performance; and the amount of such damages might have been assessed, or any question of fact tried, by a jury before the Court itself, or by the Court itself without a jury.

The Supreme Court of Judicature Act, 1873, to which we have already referred, has now amalgamated all the superior courts of law and equity. It provides that if any plaintiff claims to be entitled to any equitable estate or right, or to relief upon any equitable ground, against any deed, instrument or contract, or against any right, title or claim whatsoever asserted by the defendant, or to any relief founded upon a legal right which theretofore could only have been given by a court of equity, the Courts respectively, and every judge thereof, shall give to such plaintiff the same relief as ought to have been given by the Court of Chancery in a suit or other proceeding for the same or the like purpose properly instituted before the passing: of the act. It also provides that if any defendant claims to be entitled to any equitable estate or right, or to relief upon any equitable ground, against any deed, instrument or contract, or against any right, title or claim asserted by the plaintiff, or alleges any ground of equitable defence to any claim of the plaintiff, the said Courts respectively, and every judge thereof, shall give to every equitable estate, right or ground of relief so claimed, and to every equitable defence so alleged, the same effect, by way of defence against the claim of the plaintiff, as the Court of Chancery ought to have given, if the same or the like matters had been relied on by way of defence in any suit or proceeding, instituted in that Court for the same or the like purpose before the passing of the act. Provision is made for counter-claims by the defendant. Incidental equities are also to be recognized by the Courts respectively and every judge thereof. And no cause or proceeding at any time pending in the High Court of Justice, or before the Court of Appeal, is to be restrained by prohibition or injunction; but every matter of equity, on which an injunction against the prosecution of any such cause or proceeding might have been obtained, if the act had not passed, either unconditionally or on any terms or conditions, may be relied on by way of defence thereto. Proceedings, however, may be stayed as therein provided.

Subject to these provisions all legal rights are to be recognized as before. And, as far as possible, all matters in controversy between the parties are to be settled in the same action, and all multiplicity of legal proceedings concerning any of such matters is to be avoided. The act further provides, that a mandamus or an injunction may be granted by an interlocutory order of the Court, in all cases in which it shall appear to the Court to be just or convenient that such order should be made; and any such order may be made either unconditionally or upon such terms and conditions as the Court shall think just.

Trusts, however, are not abolished; and, as we have seen, the execution of trusts, charitable and private, is assigned to the Chancery Division of the Court. The beneficial title is still called the equitable title; and the legal estate may still be vested in some other person than the beneficial owner. Every purchaser of landed property has, therefore, a right to a good title both at law and in equity; and if the legal estate should be vested in a trustee, or any person other than the vendor, the concurrence of such trustee or other person must be obtained for the purpose of vesting the legal estate in the purchaser, or, if he should please, in a new trustee of his own choosing. When a person has an estate at law, and does not hold it subject to any trust, he has of course the same estate in equity, but without any occasion for resorting to its aid. To him, therefore, the doctrine of trusts does not apply: his legal title is sufficient; the law declares the nature and incidents of his estate, and equity has no ground for interference.

We shall now take leave of equity and equitable estates, and proceed, in the next chapter, to explain a modern conveyance.

CHAPTER IX
OF A MODERN CONVEYANCE

In modern times, down to the year 1841, the kind of conveyance employed, on every ordinary purchase of a freehold estate, was called a lease and release; and for every such transaction, two deeds were always required. From that time to the year 1845, the ordinary method of conveyance was a release merely, or, more accurately, a release made in pursuance of the act of parliament intituled "An Act for rendering a Release as effectual for the Conveyance of Freehold Estates as a Lease and

Release by the same Parties." The object of this act was merely to save the expense of two deeds to every purchase, by rendering the lease unnecessary.

A further alteration was then made, by the act to simplify the transfer of property, which enacted, that, after the 31st day of December, 1844, every person might convey by any deed, without livery of seisin, or a prior lease, all such freehold land as he might, before the passing of the act, have conveyed by lease and release, and every such conveyance should take effect, as if it had been made by lease and release; provided always, that every such deed should be chargeable with the same stamp duty as would have been chargeable if such conveyance had been made by lease and release.

This act, however, had not been in operation more than nine months when it was repealed by the act to amend the law of real property, which provides, that after the 1st of October, 1845, all corporeal tenements and hereditaments shall, as regards the conveyance of the immediate freehold thereof, be deemed to lie in grant as well as in livery. A simple deed of grant is therefore now sufficient to grant the freehold or feudal seisin of all lands. But as a lease and release was so long the usual method of conveyance, the nature of a conveyance by lease and release should still form a subject of the student's inquiry; and with this we will accordingly begin.

From the little that has already been said concerning a lease for years, the reader will have gathered, that the lessee is put into possession of the premises leased for a definite time, although his possession has nothing feudal in its nature, for the law still recognizes the landlord as retaining the seisin or feudal possession. Entry by the tenant was, however, in ancient times, absolutely necessary to make a complete lease; although, in accordance with feudal principles, it was not necessary that the landlord should depart at once and altogether, as he must have done in the case of a feoffment where the feudal seisin was transferred. When the tenant has thus gained a footing on the premises, under an express contract with his landlord, he became, with respect to the feudal possession, in a different position from a mere stranger; for, he was then capable of acquiring such feudal possession, without any formal livery of seisin, by a transfer or conveyance from his landlord, of all his (the landlord's) estate in the premises. Being already in possession by the act and agreement of his landlord, and under a tenancy recognized by the law, there was not the same necessity for that open delivery of the seisin to him, as there would have been to a mere stranger. In his case, indeed, livery of seisin would have been improper, for he was already in possession under his lease; and, as a delivery of the possession of the lands could not, therefore, be made to him, it was necessary that the landlord's interest should be conveyed in some other manner. Now the ancient common law always required that a transfer or gift of every kind relating to real property should be made, either by actual or symbolical delivery of the subject of the transfer, or, when this was impossible, by the delivery of a written document. But in former times, as we have seen, every writing was under seal; and a writing so sealed and delivered is in fact a deed. In this case, therefore, a deed was required for the conveyance of the landlord's interest; and such conveyance by deed, under the above circumstances, was termed a *release*. To a lease and release of this kind, it is obvious that the same objection applies as to a feoffment: the inconvenience of actually going on the premises is not obviated; for, the tenant must enter before he can receive the release. In the very early periods of our history, this kind of circuitous conveyance was, however, occasionally used. A lease was made for one, two, or three years, completed by the actual entry of the lessee for the express purpose of enabling him to receive a release of the inheritance, which was accordingly made to him a short time afterwards. The lease and release, executed in this manner, transferred the freehold of the releasor as effectually as if it had been conveyed by feoffment. But a lease and release would never have obtained the prevalence they afterwards acquired had not a method been found out of making a lease, without the necessity of actual entry by the lessee.

The Statute of Uses was the means of accomplishing this desirable object. This statute, it may be remembered, enacts, that when any person is seised of lands to the use of another, he that has the use shall be deemed in lawful seisin and possession of the lands, for the same estate as he has in the use. Now, besides a feoffment to one person to the use of another, there were, before this statute, other modes by which a use might be raised or created, or, in other words, by which a man might become seised of lands to the use of some other person. Thus — if, before the Statute of Uses, a bargain was made for the sale of an estate, and the purchase-money paid, but no feoffment was executed to the purchaser, — the Court of Chancery, in analogy to its modern doctrine on the like occasions, considered that the estate ought in conscience immediately to belong to the person who paid the money, and, therefore, held the bargainor or vendor to be immediately seised of the lands in question *to the use* of the purchaser. This proper and equitable doctrine of the Court of Chancery had rather a curious effect when the Statute of Uses came into operation; for, as by means of a contract of this kind the purchaser became entitled to the *use* of the lands, so, after the passing of the statute, he became at once entitled, on payment of his purchase-money, to the lawful seisin and possession: or rather, he was deemed really to have, by force of the statute, such seisin and possession, so far at least as it was possible to consider a man in possession, who in fact was not. It, consequently, came to pass that the seisin was thus transferred from one person to another, by a mere *bargain and sale*, that is, by a contract for sale and payment of money without the necessity of a feoffment, or even of a deed; and, moreover, an estate in fee simple at law was thus duly conveyed from one person to another without the employment of the technical word *heirs*, which before was necessary to mark out the estate of the purchaser; for, it was presumed that the purchase-money was paid for an estate in fee simple; and as the purchaser had, under his contract, such an estate in the *use*, he of course became entitled, by the very words of the statute, to the same estate in the legal seisin and possession.

The mischievous results of the statute, in this particular, were quickly perceived. The notoriety in the transfer of estates, on which the law had always laid so much stress, was at once at an end; and it was perceived to be very undesirable that so important a matter as the title to landed property should depend on a mere verbal bargain and money payment, or *bargain and sale*, as it was termed. Shortly after the passing of the Statute of Uses, it was accordingly required by another act of parliament, passed in the same year, that every bargain and sale of any estate of inheritance or freehold should be made by deed indented and enrolled, within six months (which means lunar months) from the date, in one of the courts of record at Westminster, or before the *custos rotulorum* and two justices of the peace and the clerk of the peace for the county in which the lands lay, or two of them at least, whereof the clerk of the peace should be one. A stop was thus put to the secret conveyance of estates by mere contract and payment of money. For a deed entered on the records of a Court is of course open to public inspection; and the expense of enrolment was, in some degree, a counterbalance to the inconvenience of going to the lands to give livery of seisin. It was not long, however, before a loophole was discovered in this latter statute, through which, after a few had ventured to pass, all the world soon followed. It was perceived that the act spoke only of estates *of inheritance of freehold*, and was silent as to bargains and sales for a mere term of years, which is not a freehold. A bargain and sale of lands for a year only, was not therefore affected by the act, but remained still capable of being accomplished by word of mouth and payment of money. The entry on the part of the tenant, required by the law, was supplied by the Statute of Uses; which, by its own force, placed him in legal intendment in possession for the same estate as he had in the use, that is, for the term bargained and sold to him. And as any pecuniary payment, however small, was considered sufficient to raise a use, it followed that if A., a person seised in fee simple, bargained and sold his lands to B. for one year in consideration of ten shillings paid by B. to A., B. became, in law, at once possessed of an estate in the lands for the term of one year, in the same manner as if he had actually entered on the premises under a regular lease. Here then was an opportunity of making a conveyance of the whole fee simple, without livery of seisin, entry or enrolment. When the bargain and sale for a year was made, A. had simply to release by deed to B. and his heirs his (A.'s) estate and interest in the premises, and B. became at once seised of the lands for an estate in fee simple. This bargain and sale for a year, followed by a release, is the modern conveyance by *lease and release* — a method which was first practised by Sir Francis Moore, serjeant at law, at the request, it is said, of Lord Norris, in order that some of his relations might not know what conveyance or settlement he should make of his estate; and although the efficiency of this method was at first doubted, it was, for more than two centuries, the common means of conveying lands in this country. It will be observed that the bargain and sale (or lease, as it is called) for a year derived its effect from the Statute of Uses; the release was quite independent of that statute, having existed long before, and being as ancient as the common law itself. The Statute of Uses was employed in the conveyance by lease and release only for the purpose of giving to the intended releasee, without his actually entering on the lands, such an estate as would enable him to receive the release. When this estate for one year was obtained by the lease, the Statute of Uses had performed its part, and the fee simple was conveyed to the releasee by the release alone. The release would, before the Statute of Uses, have conveyed the fee simple to the releasee, supposing him to have obtained that possession for one year, which, after the statute, was given him by the lease. After the passing of the Statute of Frauds, it became necessary that every bargain and sale of lands for a year should be put into writing, as no pecuniary rent was ever reserved, the consideration being usually five shillings, the receipt of which was acknowledged, though in fact it was never paid. And the bargain and sale, or lease for a year, was usually made by deed, though this was not absolutely necessary. It was generally dated the day before the date of the release, though executed on the same day as the release, immediately before the execution of the latter.

This cumbrous contrivance of two deeds to every purchase continued in constant use down to the year 1841, when the act was passed to which we have before referred, intituled "An Act for rendering a Release as effectual for the Conveyance of Freehold Estates as a Lease and Release by the same Parties." This act enacts that every deed or instrument of release of a freehold estate, or purporting or intended to be so, which shall be expressed to be made in pursuance of the act, shall be as effectual, and shall take effect as a conveyance to uses or otherwise, and shall operate in all respects, as if the releasing party or parties, who shall have executed the same, had also executed, in due form, a deed or instrument of bargain and sale, or lease for a year, for giving effect to such release, although no such deed or instrument of bargain and sale, or lease for a year, shall be executed. And now, by the act to amend the law of real property, a deed of grant is alone sufficient for the conveyance of all corporeal hereditaments.

The legal seisin being thus capable of being transferred by a deed of grant, there is the same necessity now as there was when a feoffment was employed, that the estate which the purchaser is to take should be marked out. If he has purchased an estate in fee simple, the conveyance must be expressed to be made to him *and his heirs*; for the construction of all conveyances, wills only excepted, is in this respect the same; and a conveyance to the purchaser simply, without these words, would merely convey to him an estate for his life, as in the case of a feoffment. In this case also, as well as in a feoffment, it is the better opinion that, in order to give permanent validity to the conveyance, it is necessary either that a consideration should be expressed in the conveyance, or that it should be made *to the use of* the purchaser as well as *unto* him: for a lease and release was formerly, and a deed of grant is now, as much an established conveyance as a feoffment; and the rule was, before the Statute of Uses, that any *conveyance*, and not a feoffment particularly, made to another without any consideration, or any declaration of uses, should be deemed to be made *to the use* of the party conveying. In order, therefore, to avoid any such construction, and so to prevent the Statute of Uses from immediately undoing all that has been done, it is usual to express, in every conveyance, that the purchaser shall hold, not only unto, but unto *and to the use of* himself and his heirs.

A conveyance might also have been made by lease and release, as well as by a feoffment, to one person and his heirs, *to the use* of some other person and his heirs; and, in this case, as in a similar feoffment, the latter person took at once the whole fee simple, the former being made, by the Statute of Uses, merely a conduit-pipe for conveying the estate to him. This extraordinary result of the Statute of Uses is continually relied on in modern conveyancing; and it may now be accomplished by a deed of grant in the same manner as it might have been before effected by a lease and release. It is found particularly advantageous as a means for avoiding a rule of law, that a man cannot make any conveyance to himself; thus if it were wished to make a conveyance of lands from A., a person solely seised, to A. and B. jointly, this operation could not, before the Statute of Uses, have been effected by less than two conveyances; for a conveyance from A. directly to A. and B. would pass the whole estate solely to B.. It would, therefore, have been requisite for A. to make a conveyance to a third person, and for such person then to reconvey to A. and B. jointly. And this was the method actually adopted, under similar circumstances, with respect to leasehold estates and personal property, which are not affected by the Statute of Uses, until an act was passed by which any person may now assign leasehold or personal property to himself jointly with another; but this act does not extend to freeholds. If the estate be freehold, A. must convey to B. and his heirs, to the use of A. and B. and their heirs; and a joint estate in fee simple will immediately vest in another to his them both. Suppose, again, a person should wish to convey a freehold estate to another, reserving to himself a life interest, — without the aid of the Statute of Uses he would be unable to accomplish this result by a single deed. But, by means of the statute, he may now make a conveyance of the property to the other and his heirs, *to the use* of himself (the conveying party) for his life, and from and immediately after his decease, *to the use* of the other and his heirs and assigns. By this means the conveying party will at once become seised of an estate only for his life, and after his decease an estate in fee simple will remain for the other.

The reader will now be in a situation to understand an ordinary purchase deed of the simplest kind, with a specimen of which he is accordingly presented: — "THIS INDENTURE made the first day of January 1846 between A. B. of Cheapside in the city of London esquire of the one part and C. D. of Lincoln's Inn in the county of Middlesex esquire of the other part WHEREAS by indentures of lease and release bearing date respectively the first and second days of January 1838 and respectively made between E. F. of the one part and the said A. B. of the other part for the consideration therein mentioned the messuage lands and hereditaments hereinafter described with the appurtenances were conveyed unto and to the use of the said A. B. his heirs and assigns for ever AND WHEREAS the said A. B. hath contracted with the said C. D. for the absolute sale to him of the inheritance in fee simple in possession of and in the said messuage lands and hereditaments with the appurtenances free from all incumbrances for the sum of one thousand pounds "NOW THIS INDENTURE WITNESSETH that in pursuance of the said contract and in consideration of the sum of one thousand pounds of lawful money of Great Britain to the said A. B. in hand paid by the said C. D. upon or before the execution of these presents (the receipt of which said sum of one thousand pounds in full for the absolute purchase of the inheritance in fee simple in possession of and in the messuage lands and hereditaments hereinbefore referred to and hereinafter described with the appurtenances he the said A. B. doth hereby acknowledge and from the same doth release the said C. D. his heirs executors administrators and assigns) He the said A. B. DOTH by these presents GRANT unto the said C. D. and his heirs ALL that messuage or tenement *[here describe the premises]* Together with all outhouses ways watercourses trees commonable rights easements and appurtenances to the said messuage lands hereditaments and premises hereby granted or any of them belonging or there with used or enjoyed And all the estate and right of the said A. B. in and to the same To HAVE AND TO HOLD the said messuage lands hereditaments and premises intended to be hereby granted with the appurtenances unto and to the use of the said C. D. his heirs and assigns for ever." [*Then follow covenants by the vendor with the purchaser for the title; that is, that he has good right to convey the premises, for their quiet enjoyment by the purchaser, and freedom from incumbrances, and that the vendor and his heirs will make all such further conveyances may be reasonably required.]* "In WITNESS whereof the said parties to these presents have hereunto set their hands and seals the day and year first above written." To the foot of the deed are appended the seals and signatures of the parties; and, on the back is endorsed a further receipt for the purchase-money, also an attestation by the witnesses, of whom desirable that there should be two, though the deed would not be void even without any. On the face of the deed will be observed the proper stamps, without which it could not formerly have been admitted as evidence. But the Common Law Procedure Act, 1854, provided that, upon payment to the proper officer of the Court of the stamp duty, and certain penalties, any deed or other document should be admissible in evidence, saving all just exceptions on other grounds. And a similar provision is contained in the Stamp Act, 1870, by which the stamp duties on deeds have now been consolidated. Purchase-deeds are now subject to *ad valorem* stamps of one-half per cent., or five shillings per fifty pounds on the amount or value of the consideration for the sale, according to the table below.

There was formerly a further progressive duty of 10*s*. for every *entire* quantity of 1080 words over and above the first 1080, unless the *ad valorem* duty was less than 10*s*., in which case the progressive duty was equal to the amount of the *ad valorem* duty. The present scale of *ad valorem* duties was first imposed by the Act to amend the Laws relating to the Inland Revenue, which was passed on the 5th of July, 1865. Before this act the table of stamp duties advanced in a slightly different manner by less minute steps. These duties again did not apply to any deed or instrument signed or executed by any party thereto, or bearing date, before or upon the 10th of October, 1850. Such a deed, unless preceded by a lease for a year, bears the same stamp duty as the lease for a year was subject to, and also, whether so preceded or not, an *ad valorem* duty according to the table stated below.

If the premises should be situate in either of the counties of Middlesex or York, or in the town and county of Kingston-upon-Hull, a memorandum will or ought to be found indorsed, to the effect that a memorial of the deed was duly registered on such a day, in such a book and page of the register, established by act of parliament, for the county of Middlesex, or the ridings of York, or the town of Kingston-upon-Hull. Under these acts, all deeds are to be adjudged fraudulent and void against any subsequent purchaser or mortgagee for valuable consideration, unless a memorial of such deeds be duly registered before the registering of the memorial of the deed under which such subsequent purchaser or mortgagee shall claim. Wills of lands in the above counties ought also to be registered, in order to prevail against subsequent purchasers or mortgagees. Conveyances of lands forming part of the great level of the fens, called Bedford Level, are also required to be registered in the Bedford Level Office; but the construction which has been put on the statute, by which such registry is required, prevents any priority of interest from being gained by priority of registration.

From the specimen before him, the reader will be struck with the stiff and formal style which characterizes legal instruments; but the formality to be found in every properly drawn deed has the advantage, that the reader who is acquainted with the usual order knows at once where to find any particular portion of the contents; and, in matters of intricacy, which must frequently occur, this facility of reference is of incalculable advantage. The framework of every deed consists but of one, two, or three simple sentences, according to the number of times that the *testatum*, or witnessing part, "Now this Indenture witnesseth," is repeated. This *testatum* is always written in large letters; and, though there is no limit to its repetition (if circumstances should require it), yet, in the majority of cases, it occurs but once or twice at most. In the example above given, it will be seen that the sentence on which the deed is framed is as follows: — "This Indenture, made on such a day between such parties, witnesseth, that for so much money A. B. doth grant certain premises unto and to the use of C. D. and his heirs." After the names of the parties have been given, an interruption occurs for the purpose of introducing the recitals; and when the whole of the introductory circumstances have been mentioned, the thread is resumed, and the deed proceeds, "Now this Indenture witnesseth." The receipt for the purchase-money is again a parenthesis; and soon after comes the description of the property, which further impedes the progress of the sentence, till it is taken up in the *habendum*, "To have and to hold," from which it uninterruptedly proceeds to the end. The contents of deeds, embracing as they do all manner of transactions between man and man, must necessarily be infinitely varied, and a simple conveyance, such as that we have given, is rare, compared with the number of those in which special circumstances occur. But in all deeds, as nearly as possible, the same order is preserved. The names of all the *parties* are invariably placed at the beginning: then follow recitals of facts relevant to the matter in hand; then a preliminary recital, stating shortly what is to be done; then, the *testatum*, containing the *operative words* of the deed, or the words which affect the transaction, of which the deed is the witness or evidence; after this, if the deed relate to property, come the *parcels* or description of the property, either at large, or by reference to some deed already recited; then, the *habendum* showing the estate to be holden: then, the *uses* and *trusts*, if any; and, lastly, such qualifying provisoes and covenants, as may be required by the special circumstances of the case. Throughout all this, not a single stop is to be found, and the sentences are so framed as to be independent of their aid; for, no one would wish the title to his estates to depend on the insertion of a comma or semicolon. The commencement of sentences, and now and then some few important words, which serve as landmarks, are rendered conspicuous by capitals: by the aid of these, the practised eye at once collects the sense; whilst, at the same time, the absence of stops renders it next to impossible materially to alter the meaning of a deed, without the forgery being discovered.

The adherence of lawyers, by common consent, to the same mode of framing their drafts has given rise to a great similarity in the outward appearance of deeds; and the eye of the reader is continually caught by the same capitals, such as "THIS INDENTURE," "AND WHEREAS," "NOW THIS INDENTURE WITNESSETH," "TO HAVE AND TO HOLD," &c. This similarity of appearance seems to have been mistaken by some for a sameness of contents, — an error for which any one but a lawyer might perhaps be pardoned. And this mistake, coupled with a laudable anxiety to save expense to the public, appears to have produced a plan for making conveyances by way of schedule. In pursuance of this plan, two acts of parliament were some time since passed, one for conveyances, the other for leases. These acts, however, as might have been expected, are very seldom employed; nor is it possible that any schedule should ever comprehend the multitude of variations to which purchase-deeds are continually liable. In the midst of this variety, the adoption, as nearly as possible, of the same framework, is a great saving of trouble, and consequently of expense; but so long as the power of alienation possessed by the public is exerciseable in such a variety of ways, and for such a multitude of purposes as is now permitted, so long will the conveyance of landed property call for the exercise of learning and skill, and so long also will it involve the expense requisite to give to such learning and skill its proper remuneration. The remuneration, however, afforded to the profession of the law has hitherto been bestowed in a manner which calls for some remark. In a country like England, where every employment is subject to the keenest competition, there can be little doubt but that, whatever method may be taken for the remuneration of professional services, the nature and quantity of the trouble incurred must, on the average and in the long run, be the actual measure of the remuneration paid. The misfortune is, that when a wrong method of remuneration is adopted, the true proportion between service and reward is necessarily obtained by indirect means, and therefore in a more troublesome, and, consequently, more expensive manner, than if a proper scale had been directly used. In the law, unfortunately, this has been the case, and there seems no good reason why any individual connected with the law should be ashamed or afraid of making it known. The labour of a lawyer is very different from that of a copyist or printer; it consists first and chiefly in acquiring a minute acquaintance with the principles of the law, then in obtaining a knowledge of the facts of any particular case which may be brought before him, and lastly, in practically applying to such case the principles he has previously learnt. But, for the last and least of these items alone has he hitherto obtained any direct remuneration; for, deeds have hitherto been paid for by the length, like printing or copying, without any regard to the principles they involved, or to the intricacy or importance of the facts to which they might relate; and, more than this, the rate of payment was fixed so low, that no man of education could afford for the sake of it, first to ascertain what sort of instrument the circumstances might require, and then to draw a deed containing the full measure of ideas of which words are capable. The payment to a solicitor for drawing a deed was fixed at one shilling for every seventy-two words, denominated a *folio*; and the fees of counsel, though paid in guineas, averaged about the same. The consequence of this false economy on the part of the public has been, that certain well known and long established lengthy forms, full of synonyms and expletives, are current among lawyers as *common forms*, and, by the aid of these, ideas are diluted to the proper remunerating strength; not that a lawyer actually inserts nonsense simply for the sake of increasing his fee; but words, sometimes unnecessary in any case, sometimes only in the particular case in which he is engaged, are suffered to remain, sanctioned by the authority of time and usage. The proper amount of verbiage to a common form is well established and understood; and whilst any attempt to exceed it is looked on as disgraceful, it is never likely to be materially diminished till a change is made in the scale of payment. The case of the medical profession is exactly parallel; for, so long as the public think that the medicine supplied is the only thing worth paying for, so long will cures ever be accompanied with the customary abundance of little bottles. In both cases, the system is bad; but the fault is not with the profession, who bear the blame, but with the public, who have fixed the scale of payment, and who, by a little more direct liberality, might save themselves a considerable amount of indirect expense. If physicians' prescriptions were paid for by their length, does any one suppose that their present conciseness would long continue? — unless indeed the rate of payment were fixed so high as to leave the average remuneration the same as at present. The acts above mentioned contained a provision that, in taxing any bill for preparing and executing any deed under the acts, the taxing officer should consider, not the length of such deed, but only the skill and labour employed and responsibility incurred in the preparation thereof. This, so far, was an effort in the right direction. And an act has now been passed to amend the law relating to the remuneration of attorneys and solicitors, by which such remuneration is now authorized, under certain restrictions, to be fixed by agreement; and which provides, that, upon any taxation of costs, the taxing officer may, in determining the remuneration, if any, to be allowed to the attorney or solicitor for his services, have regard, subject to any general rules or orders hereafter to be made, to the skill, labour and responsibility involved. But long rooted customs are hard to eradicate. The student must, therefore, make up his mind to find in legal instruments a considerable amount of verbiage; at the same time he should be careful not to confound this with that formal and orderly style which facilitates the lawyer's perusal of deeds, or with that repetition which is often necessary to exactness without the dangerous aid of stops. The form of a purchase-deed, which has been given above, is disencumbered of the usual verbiage, whilst, at the same time, it preserves the regular and orderly arrangements of its parts. A similar conveyance, by deed of grant, in the old established common forms, will be found in the Appendix. At the present day, however, these forms are often much curtailed.

To return: — A lease and release was said to be an innocent conveyance; for when, by means of the lease and the Statute of Uses, the purchaser had once been put into possession, he obtained the fee simple by the release; and a release never operates by wrong, as a feoffment occasionally did, but simply passes that which may lawfully and rightly be conveyed. The same rule is applicable to a deed of grant. Thus, if a tenant merely for his own life should, by a lease and release, or by a grant, purport to convey to another an estate in fee simple, his own life interest only would pass, and no injury would be done to the reversioner. The word *grant* is the proper and technical term to be employed in a deed of grant, but its employment is not absolutely necessary; for it has been held that other words indicating an intention to grant will answer the purpose.

In addition to a conveyance by deed of grant, other methods are occasionally employed. Thus, there may be a *bargain and sale* of an estate in fee simple, by deed duly inrolled pursuant to the statute 27 Hen. VIII. c. 16, already mentioned. The chief advantage of a bargain and sale is, that by a statute of Anne an office copy of the inrolment of a bargain and sale is made as good evidence as the original deed. In some cities and boroughs the inrolment of bargains and sales is made by the mayors or other officers. And in the counties palatine of Lancaster and Durham it may be made in the palatine courts; and so the inrolment of bargains and sales of land in the county of Cheshire might have been made in the palatine courts of that county until their abolition. Bargains and sales of lands in the county of York may be inrolled in the register of the riding in which the lands lie. When a bargain and sale is employed, the whole legal estate in fee simple passes, as we have seen, by means of the Statute of Uses, — the bargainor becoming seised to the use of the bargainee and his heirs. A bargain and sale, therefore, cannot, like a lease and release, or a grant, be made to one person to the use of another; for, the whole force of the Statute of Uses is already exhausted in transferring thc legal estate in fee simple to the bargainee; so that the use declared would be a use upon a use, void at law, though valid in equity. Similar to a bargain and sale is another method of conveyance occasionally, though very rarely, employed, namely, a *covenant to stand seised* to the use of another, in consideration of blood or marriage. In addition to these methods, there may be a conveyance by *appointment* of a use, under a *power of appointment*, of which more will be said in a future chapter. The student, indeed, can never be too careful to avoid supposing that, when he has read and understood a chapter of the present, or any other elementary work, he is therefore acquainted with all that is to be known on the subject. To place him in a position to comprehend more is all that can be attempted in a first book.

CHAPTER X
OF A WILL OF LANDS

The right of testamentary alienation of lands is a matter depending upon act of parliament. We have seen, that previously to the reign of Henry VIII. an estate in fee simple, if not disposed of in the lifetime of the owner, descended, on his death, to his heir at law. To this rule, gavelkind lands, and lands in a few favoured boroughs, formed exceptions; and the hardship of the rule was latterly somewhat mitigated by the prevalence of conveyances to *uses*; for the Court of Chancery allowed the *use* to be devised by will. But when the Statute of Uses came into operation, and all uses were turned into legal estates, the title of the heir again prevailed, and the inconvenience of the want of testamentary power then began to be felt. To remedy this inconvenience, an act of parliament, to which we have before referred, was passed six years after the enactment of the Statute of Uses. By this act, every person having any lands or hereditaments holden in socage, or in the nature of socage tenure, was enabled by his last will and testament in writing, to give and devise the same at his will and pleasure; and those who had estates in fee simple in lands held by knights' service were enabled, in the same way, to give and devise two third parts thereof. When, by the statute of 12 Car. II. c. 24 socage was made the universal tenure, all estate in fee simple became at once devisable, being all then holden by socage. This extensive power of devising lands by a mere writing unattested was soon curtailed by the Statute of Frauds, which required that all devises and bequests of any lands or tenements, devisable either by statute, or the custom of Kent, or any borough, or any other custom, should be in writing, and signed by the party so devising the same, or by some other person in his presence and by his express directions, and should be attested and subscribed in the presence of the said devisor by three or four credible witnesses, or else they should be utterly void and of none effect. And thus the law continued till the year 1837, when an act was passed for the amendment of the laws with respect to wills. By this act the original statute of Henry VIII. was repealed, except as to wills made prior to the 1st of January, 1838, and the law was altered to its present state. This act permits of the devise by will of every kind of estate and interest in real property which would otherwise devolve to the heir of the testator, or, if he became entitled by descent, to the heir of his ancestor; but enacts, that no will shall be valid, unless it shall be in writing, and signed at the foot or end thereof by the testator, or by some other person in his presence and by his direction; and such signature shall be made or acknowledged by the testator, in the presence of *two* or more witnesses, present at the same time; and such witnesses shall attest, and shall subscribe the will in the presence of the testator. One would have thought that this enactment was sufficiently clear, especially that part of it which directs the will to be signed at the foot or end thereof. Some very careless testators, and very clever judges, have, however, contrived to throw upon this clause of the act a discredit which it does not deserve. And it has accordingly been enacted, by way of explanation, that every will shall, so far only as regards the position of the signature of the testator, or of the person signing for him, be deemed to be valid, if the signature shall be so placed at, or after, or following, or under, or beside, or opposite to the end of the will, that it shall be apparent on the face of the will that the testator intended to give effect by such his signature to the writing signed as his will; and that no such will shall be affected by the circumstance that the signature shall not follow, or be immediately after, the foot or end of the will, or by the circumstance that a blank, space shall intervene between the concluding word of the will and the signature, or by the circumstance that the signature shall be placed among the words of the testimonium clause, or of the clause of attestation, or shall follow or be after or under the clause of attestation, either with or without a blank space intervening, or shall follow or be after or under or beside the names, or one of the names, of the subscribing witnesses, or by the circumstance that a signature shall be on a side or page, or other portion of the paper or papers, containing the will, whereon no clause or paragraph or disposing part of the will shall be written above the signature, or by the circumstance that there shall appear to be sufficient space on or at the bottom of the preceding side or page, or other portion of the same paper, on which the will is written, to contain the signature; and the enumeration of the above circumstances is not to restrict the generality of the above enactment. But no signature is to be operative to give effect to any disposition or direction which is underneath, or which follows it; nor shall it give effect to any disposition or direction inserted after the signature shall be made. The unlearned reader will perhaps be of opinion that there is not one of the positions above so laboriously enumerated, that might not very properly have been considered as at the foot or end of the will within the spirit and meaning of the act; except in the case of a large blank being left before the signature, apparently for the purpose of the subsequent insertion of other matter: in which case the fraud to which the will lays itself open would be a sufficient reason for holding it void.

The Statute of Frauds, it will be observed, required that the witnesses should be credible; and, on the point of credibility, the rules of law with respect to witnesses have, till recently, been very strict; for the law had so great a dread of the evil influence of the love of money, that it would not even listen to any witness who had the smallest pecuniary interest in the result of his own testimony. Hence, under the Statute of Frauds, a bequest to a witness to a will, or to the wife or husband of a witness, prevented such witness from being heard in support of the will; and, the witness being thus incredible, the will was void for want of three credible witnesses. By an act of Geo. II., a witness to whom a gift was made was rendered credible, and the gift only which was made to the witness was declared void; but the act did not extend to the case of a gift to the husband or wife of a witness; such a gift, therefore, still rendered the whole will void. Under the Wills Act, however, the incompetency of the witness at the time of the execution of the will, or at any time afterwards, is not sufficient to make the will invalid; and if any person shall attest the execution of a will, to whom, or to whose wife or husband, any beneficial interest whatsoever shall be given (except a mere charge for payment of debts), the person attesting will be a good witness; but the gift of such beneficial interest to such person, or to the wife or husband of such person, will be void. Creditors, also, are good witnesses, although the will should contain a charge for payment of debts; and the mere circumstance of being appointed executor is no objection to a witness. By more recent statutes, the rule which excluded the evidence of witnesses in courts of justice, and of parties to actions and suits, on account of interest, has been very properly abolished; and the evidence of interested persons is now received, and its value estimated according to its worth; but the Wills Act is not affected by these statutes. The courts of common law had formerly exclusive jurisdiction in questions arising on the validity of a will of real estate, whilst the ecclesiastical courts had the like exclusive jurisdiction over wills of personal estate. But an act was passed in the present reign establishing a Court of Probate, in which all wills of personal estate are now required to be proved. This act provides for the citation before the court of the heir at law of the testator and the devisees of his real estate; and such heir and devisees, when cited, will be bound by the proceedings; but this occurs only when a contest is expected or actually takes place. In all ordinary cases a will, so far as it affects real estate, does not require to be proved.

So much, then, for the power to make a will of lands, and for the formalities with which it must be accompanied. A will, it is well known, does not take effect until the decease of the testator. In the meantime, it may be revoked in various ways; as, by the marriage of either a man or a woman; though, before the Wills Act, the marriage of a man was not sufficient to revoke his will, unless he also had a child born. A will may also be revoked by burning, tearing, or otherwise destroying the same, by the testator, or by some person in his presence, and by his direction, with the intention of revoking the same. But the Wills Act enacts, that no obliteration, interlineation, or other alteration, made in any will after its execution shall have any effect (except so far as the words or effect of the will, before such alteration, shall not be apparent), unless such alteration shall be executed in the same manner as a will; but the signature of the testator, and the subscription of the witnesses, may be made in the margin, or on some other part of the will, opposite or near to such alteration, or at the foot or end of or opposite to a memorandum referring to such alteration, and written at the end, or some other part of the will. A will may also be revoked by any writing, executed in the same manner as a will, and declaring an intention to revoke, or by a subsequent will or codicil, to be executed as before. And where a codicil is added, it is considered as part of the will; and the disposition made by the will is not disturbed further than is absolutely necessary to give effect to the codicil.

The above are the only means by which a will can now be revoked; unless, of course, the testator choose afterwards to part with any of the property comprised in his will, which he is at perfect liberty to do. In this case the will is revoked, as to the property parted with, if it does not find its way back to the testator, so as to be his at the time of his death. Under the statute of Hen. VIII. a will of lands was regarded in the light of a *present conveyance*, to come into operation at a future time, namely, on the death of the testator. And if a man, having made a will of his lands, afterwards disposed of them, they would not, on returning to his possession, again become subject to his will, without a subsequent republication or revival of the will. But, under the Wills Act, no subsequent conveyance shall prevent the operation of the will, with respect to such devisable estate or interest as the testator shall have at the time of his death. In the same manner, the old statute was not considered as enabling a person to dispose by will of any lands, except such as he was possessed of at tie time of making his will: so that lands purchased after the date of the will could not be affected by any of its dispositions, but descended to the heir at law. This also is altered by the Wills Act, which enacts, that every will shall be construed, with reference to the property comprised in it, to speak and take effect as if it had been executed immediately before the death of the testator, unless a contrary intention shall appear by the will. So that every man may now dispose, by his will, of all such landed property, or real estate, as he may hereafter possess, as well as that which he now has. Again, the result of the old rule, that a will of lands was a present conveyance, was, that a general devise by a testator of the residue of his lands was, in effect, a specific disposition of such lands and such only as the testator then had, and had not left to any one else. A general residuary devisee was a devisee of the lands not otherwise left, exactly as if such lands had been given him by their names. The consequence of this was, that if any other persons, to whom lands were left, died in the lifetime of the testator, the residuary devisee had no claim to such lands, the gift of which thus failed; but the lands descended to the heir at law. This rule is altered by the act, under which, unless a contrary intention appear by the will, all real estate comprised in any devise, which shall fail by reason of the death of the devisee in the lifetime of the testator, or by reason of such devise being contrary to law, or otherwise incapable of taking effect, shall be included in the residuary devise (if any) contained in the will.

This failure of a devise, by the decease of the devisee in the testator's lifetime, is called a *lapse*; and this lapse is not prevented by the lands being given to the devisee *and his heirs*; and in the same way, before the Wills Act, a gift to the devisee and the *heirs of his body* would not carry the lands to the heir of the body of the devisee, in case of the devisee's decease in the lifetime of the testator. For, the terms *heirs* and *heirs of the body* are words of limitation merely; that is, they merely mark out the estate, which the devisee, if living at the testator's death, would have taken, — in the one case an estate in fee simple, in the other an estate tail; and the heirs are no objects of the testator's bounty, further than as connected with their ancestor. Two cases have, however, been introduced by the Wills Act, in which the devise is to remain unaffected by the decease of the devisee in the testator's lifetime. The first case is that of a devise of real estate to any person for an *estate tail*; in which case, if the devisee should die in the lifetime of the testator, leaving issue who would be inheritable under such entail, and any such issue shall be living at the death of the testator, such devise shall not lapse, but shall take effect as if the death of such person had happened immediately after the death of the testator, unless a contrary intention shall appear by the will. The other case is that of the devisee being *a child or other issue* of the testator dying in the testator's lifetime and leaving issue any of whom are living at the testator's death. In this case, unless a mere life estate shall have been left to the devisee, the devise shall not lapse, but shall take effect as in the former case.

The construction of wills is the next object of our attention. In construing wills, the Courts have always home in mind, that a testator may not have had the same opportunity of legal advice in drawing his will, as he would have had in executing a deed. And the first great maxim of construction accordingly is, that the intention of the testator ought to he observed. The decisions of the Courts, in pursuing this maxim, have given rise to a number of subsidiary rules, to be applied in making out the testator's intention; and, when doubts occur, these rules are always made use of to determine the meaning; so that the true legal construction of a will is occasionally different from that which would occur to the mind of an unprofessional reader. Certainty cannot be obtained without uniformity, nor uniformity without rule. Rules, therefore, have been found to be absolutely necessary; and the indefinite maxim of observing the intention is now largely qualified by the numerous decisions which have been made respecting all manner of doubtful points, each of which decisions forms or confirms a rule of construction, to be attended to whenever any similar difficulty occurs. It is, indeed, very questionable, whether this maxim of observing the intention, reasonable as it may appear, has been of any service to testators; and it has certainly occasioned a great deal of trouble to the Courts. Testators have imagined that the making of wills, to be so leniently interpreted, is a matter to which anybody is competent; and the consequence has been an immense amount of litigation, on all sorts of contradictory and nonsensical bequests. An intention, moreover, expressed clearly enough for ordinary apprehensions, has often been defeated by some technical rule, too stubborn to yield to the general maxim, that the intention ought to be observed. Thus, in one case, a testator declared his intention to be, that his son should not sell or dispose of his estate, for longer time than his life, and to that intent he devised the same to his son for his life, and after his decease, to the heirs of the body of his said son. The Court of King's Bench held, as the reader would no doubt expect, that the son took only an estate for his life; but this decision was reversed by the Court of Exchequer Chamber, and it is now well settled that the decision of the Court of King's Bench was erroneous. The testator unwarily made use of technical terms, which always require a technical construction. In giving the estate to the son for life, and after his decease to the heirs of his body, the testator had, in effect, given the estate to the son *and the heirs of his body*. Now such a gift is an estate tail; and one of the inseparable incidents of an estate tail is, that it may be barred in the manner already described. The son was, therefore, properly entitled, not to an estate for life only, but to an estate tail, which would at once enable him to dispose of the lands for an estate in fee simple. In contrast to this case are those to which we have before adverted, in the chapter on estates for life. In those cases, an intention to confer an estate in fee simple was defeated by a construction, which gave only an estate for life; a gift of lands or houses to a person simply, without words to limit or mark out the estate to be taken, was held to confer a mere life interest. But, in such cases, the Courts, conscious of the pure technicality of the rule, were continually striving to avert the hardship of its effect, by laying hold of the most minute variations of phrase, as matter of exception. Doubt thus took the place of direct hardship; till the legislature thought it time to interpose. A remedy is now provided by the act for the amendment of the laws with respect to wills, which enacts, that where any real estate shall be devised to any person, without any words of limitation, such devise shall be construed to pass the fee simple, or other the whole estate or interest, which the testator had power to dispose of by will, in such real estate, unless a contrary intention shall appear by the will. In these cases, therefore, the rule of law has been made to give way to the testator's intention; but the case above cited, in which an estate tail was given when a life estate only was intended, is sufficient to show, that rules still remain which give to certain phrases such a force and effect, as can be properly directed by those only who are well acquainted with their power.

Another instance of the defeat of intention arose in the case of a gift of lands to one person, "and in case he shall die without issue," then to another. The courts interpreted the words, "in case he shall die without issue," to mean "in case of his death, and of the failure of his issue;" so that the estate was to go over to the other, not only in case of the death of the former, leaving no issue *living at his decease*, but also in the event of his leaving issue, and his issue afterwards failing, by the decease of all his descendants. The courts considered that a man might properly be said to be "dead without issue," if he had died and left issue, all of whom were since deceased; quite as much as if he had died, and left no issue behind him. In accordance with this view, they held such a gift as above mentioned to be, by implication, a gift to the first person and his issue, with a remainder over, on such issue failing, to the second. This was, in fact, a gift of an estate tail to the first party; for an estate tail is just such an estate as is descendible to the issue of the party, and will cease when he has no longer heirs of his body, that is, when his issue fails. Had there been no power of barring entails, this would no doubt have been a most effectual way of fulfilling to the utmost the testator's intention. But, as we have seen, every estate tail in possession is liable to be barred, and turned into a fee simple, at the will of the owner. With this legal incident of such an estate, the courts considered that they had nothing to do; and, by this construction, they accordingly enabled the first devisee to bar the estate tail which they adjudged, him to possess, and also the remainder over to the other party. He thus was enabled at once to acquire the whole fee simple, contrary to the intention of the testator, who most probably had never heard of estates tail, or of the means of barring them. This rule of construction had been so long and firmly established, that nothing but the power of parliament could effect an alteration. This was done by the act for the amendment of the laws with respect to wills, which directs that in a will the words "die without issue," and similar expressions, shall be construed to mean a want or failure of issue in the lifetime, or at the death of the party, and not an indefinite failure of issue; unless a contrary intention shall appear by the will, by reason of such person having a prior estate tail, or of a preceding gift being, without any implication arising from such words, a gift of an estate tail to such person or issue, or otherwise.

From what has been said, it will appear that, before the above-mentioned alteration, an estate tail might have been given by will, by the mere implication, arising from the apparent intention of the testator, that the land should not go over to any one else, so long as the first devisee had any issue of his body. In the particular class of cases to which we have referred, this implication is now excluded by express enactment. But the general principle by which any kind of estates may be given by will, whenever an intention so to do is expressed, or clearly implied, still remains the same. In a deed, technical words are always required; to create an estate tail by a deed, it is necessary, as we have seen, that the word *heirs*, coupled with *words of procreation*, such as heirs *of the body*, should be made use of. So, we have seen that, to give an estate in fee simple, it is necessary, in a deed, to use the word *heirs* as a word of limitation, to limit or mark out the estate. But in a will, a devise to a person and his seed, or to him and his issue, and many other expressions, are sufficient to confer an estate tail; and a devise to a man and his *heirs male*, which, in a deed, would be held to confer a fee simple, in a will gives an estate in tail male; for the addition of the word "male," as a qualification of heirs, shows that a class of heirs, less extensive than heirs general, was intended; and the gift of an estate in tail male, to which, in a will, words of procreation are unnecessary, is the only gift which at all accords with such an intention. So, even before the enactment, directing that a devise without words of limitation should be construed to pass a fee simple, an estate in fee simple was often held to be conferred, without the use of the word *heirs*. Thus, such an estate was given by a devise to one *in fee simple*, or to him *for ever*, or to him *and his assigns for ever*, or by a devise of all the testator's *estate*, or of all his *property*, or all his *inheritance*, and by a vast number of other expressions, by which an intention to give the fee simple could be considered as expressed or implied.

The doctrine of uses and trusts applies as well to a will as to a conveyance made between living parties. Thus, a devise of lands to A. and his heirs to the use of B. and his heirs, upon certain trusts to be performed by B., will vest the legal estate in fee simple in B.; and the Court of Chancery will compel him to execute the trust; unless, indeed, he disclaim the estate, which he is at perfect liberty to do. But, if any trust or duty should be imposed upon A., it will then become a question, on the construction of the will, whether or not A. takes any *legal* estate; and, if any, to what extent. If no trust or duty is imposed on him, he is a mere conduit-pipe for conveying the legal estate to B., filling the same passive office as a person to whom a feoffment or conveyance has been made to the use of another. From a want of acquaintance on the part of testators with the Statute of Uses, great difficulties have frequently arisen in determining the nature and extent of the estates of trustees under wills. In doubtful cases, the leaning of the courts was to give to the trustees no greater estate than was absolutely necessary for the purposes of their trust. But this doctrine having frequently been found inconvenient, provision has been made in the Wills Act, that, under certain circumstances, not always to be easily explained, the fee simple shall pass to the trustees, instead of an estate determinable when the purposes of the trust shall be satisfied.

The above examples may serve as specimens of the great danger a person incurs, who ventures to commit the destination of his property to a document framed in ignorance of the rules, by which the effect of such document must be determined. The Wills Act, by the alterations above mentioned, has effected some improvement; but no act of parliament can give skill to the unpractised, or cause every body to attach the same meaning to doubtful words. The only way, therefore, to avoid doubts on the construction of wills, is to word them in proper technical language, — a task to which those only who have studied such language can be expected to be competent.

If the testator should devise land to the person who is his heir at law, it is provided by the "Act for the Amendment of the Law of Inheritance" that such heir shall be considered to have acquired the land as a devisee, and not by descent. Such heir, thus taking by *purchase*, will, therefore, become the stock of descent; and in case of his decease intestate, the lands will descend to *his* heir, and not to the heir of the testator, as they would have done had the lands *descended* on the heir. Before this act, an heir to whom lands were left by his ancestor's will was considered to take by his prior title of descent as heir, and not under the will, — unless the testator altered the estate and limited it in a manner different from that in which it would I have descended to the heir.

It is usually the practice, as is well known, for every testator to appoint an executor or executors of his will; and the executors so appointed have important powers of disposition over the personal estate of the testator. But the devise of the real estate of the testator is quite independent of the executors' assent or interference, unless the testator should either expressly or by implication have given his executors any estate in or power over the same. In modern times, however, the doctrine has been broached, that if a testator charges his real estate with the payment of his debts, such a charge gives by implication a power to his executors to sell his real estate for the payment of his debts. The author has elsewhere attempted to show that this doctrine, though recognized in several modern cases, is inconsistent with legal principles; and in this he has since been supported by the great authority of Lord St. Leonards. In consequence, however, of the difficulties to which these cases gave rise, an act has passed by which, where there is a charge of debts or legacies, the trustees in some cases and in other cases the executors of a testator are empowered to sell his real estate for the purpose of paying such debts or legacies. The act to further amend the law of property and to relieve trustees, which was passed on the 13th August,

1859, enacts, that where, by any will that shall come into operation after the passing of the act, the testator shall have charged his real estate or any specific portion thereof with the payment of his debts or of any legacy, and shall have devised the estate so charged to any trustee or trustees for the whole of his estate or interest therein, and shall not have made any express provision for the raising of such debts or legacy out of the estate, such trustee or trustees may, notwithstanding any trusts actually declared by the testator, raise such debts or legacy by sale or mortgage of the lands devised to them. And the powers thus conferred extend to all persons in whom the estate devised shall for the time being be vested by survivorship, descent or devise, and to any persons appointed to succeed to the trusteeship, either under any power in the will, or by the Court of Chancery, now represented by the Chancery Division of the High Court. But if any testator, who shall have created such a charge, shall not have devised the hereditaments charged in such terms as that his whole estate and interest therein shall become vested in any trustee or trustees, the executor or executors for the time being named in his will (if any) shall have the same power of raising the same monies as is before vested in the trustees; and such power shall from time to time devolve to the person or persons (if any) in whom the executorship shall for the time being be vested. And purchasers or mortgagees are not to be bound to inquire whether the powers thus conferred shall have been duly exercised by the persons acting in exercise thereof. But these provisions are not to prejudice or affect any sale or mortgage made or to be made in pursuance of any will coming into operation before the passing of the act; nor are they to extend to a devise to any person in fee or in tail, or for the testator's whole estate and interest, charged with debts or legacies; nor are they to affect the power of any such devisee to sell or mortgage as he or they may by law now do. In these cases the law is that the devisee may, in the exercise of his inherent right of alienation, either sell or mortgage the lands devised to him; but if legacies only are charged thereon, the purchaser or mortgagee is bound to see his money duly applied in their payment. If, however, the testator's debts are charged on the lands, then, whether there be legacies also charged or not, the practical impossibility of obliging the purchaser or mortgagee to look to the payment of so uncertain a charge exonerates him from all liability to do more than simply pay his money to the devisee on his sole receipt.

It is provided by the Registry Acts for Middlesex and Yorkshire and the town and county of Kingston-upon-Hull, that a memorial of all wills of lands in those counties shall be registered within six months after the death of every testator dying within the kingdom of Great Britain, or within three years after the death of every testator dying upon the seas or in parts beyond the seas; otherwise every such devise by will shall be adjudged fraudulent and void against any subsequent purchaser or mortgagee for valuable consideration. But the Vendor and Purchaser Act, 1874, now provides, that where the will of a testator devising lands in Middlesex or Yorkshire has not been registered within the period allowed by law in that behalf, an assurance of such land to a purchaser or mortgagee by the devisee, or by some one deriving title under him, shall, if registered before, take precedence of and prevail over, any assurance from the testator's heir at law.

CHAPTER XI
OF THE MUTUAL RIGHTS OF HUSBAND AND WIFE

The next subject of our attention will be the mutual rights in respect of lands, arising from the relation of husband and wife. In pursuing this subject, let us consider, first, the rights of the husband in respect of the lands of his wife; and, secondly, the rights of the wife in respect of the lands of her husband.

1. First, then, as to the rights of the husband in respect of the lands of his wife. By the act of marriage, the husband and wife become in law one person, and so continue during the coverture or marriage. The wife is as it were merged in her husband. Accordingly, the husband is entitled to the whole of the rents and profits which may arise from his wife's lands, and acquires a freehold estate therein, during the continuance of the coverture; and, in like manner, all the goods and personal chattels of the wife, the property in which passes by mere delivery of possession, belong solely to her husband. For, by the ancient common law, it was impossible that the wife should have any power of disposition over property for her separate benefit, independently

of her husband. In modern times, however, a more liberal doctrine has been established by the Court of Chancery, now represented by the Chancery Division of the High Court of Justice; for this court now permits property of every kind to be vested in trustees, in trust to apply the income for the sole and separate use of a woman during any coverture, present or future. Trusts of this nature are continually enforced by the court; that is, the court will oblige the trustees to hold for the sole benefit of the wife, and will prevent the husband from interfering with her in the disposal of such income; she will consequently enjoy the same absolute power of disposition over it as if she were sole or unmarried. And, if the income of property should be given directly to a woman, for her separate use, without the intervention of any trustee, the Court will compel her husband himself to hold his marital rights in such income simply as a trustee for his wife independently of himself. The limitation of property in trust for the separate use of an intended wife is one of the principal objects of a modern marriage settlement. By means of such a trust, a provision may be secured, which shall be independent of the debts and liabilities of the husband, and thus free from the risk of loss, either by reason of his commercial embarrassments, or of his extravagant expenditure. In order more completely to protect the wife, the Court allows property thus settled for the separate use of a woman to be so tied down for her own personal benefit, that she shall have no power, during her coverture, to anticipate or assign her income; for it is evident that, to place the wife's property beyond the power of her husband, is not a complete protection for her, — it must also be placed beyond the reach of his persuasion. In this particular instance, therefore, an exception has been allowed to the general rule, which forbids any restraint to be imposed on alienation. When the trust, under which property is held for the separate use of a woman during any coverture, declares that she shall not dispose of the income thereof in any mode of anticipation, every attempted disposition by her during such coverture will be deemed absolutely void.

Not only the income, but also the corpus of any property, whether real or personal, may be limited to the separate use of a married woman. Recent decisions have established that a simple gift of real estate, either with or without the intervention of trustees, for the separate use of a married woman, is sufficient to give her in equity a power to dispose of it by deed or will, without the consent or concurrence of her husband. The same rule has long been established with respect to personal estate. But where the legal estate in lands is vested in the wife, it must still be conveyed by a deed to be separately acknowledged by her, in the manner to be presently explained.

The Married Women's Property Act, 1870, now provides that where any freehold, copyhold or customary-hold property shall descend upon any woman, married after the passing of that act, as heiress or co-heiress of an intestate, the rents and profits of such property shall, subject and without prejudice to the trusts of any settlement affecting the same, belong to such woman for her separate use, and her receipts alone shall be a good discharge for the same.

Whilst provisions for the separate benefit of a married woman have thus arisen in equity, the rule of law by which husband and wife are considered as one person still continues in operation, and is occasionally productive of rather curious consequences. Thus, if lands be given to A. and B. (husband and wife), and C., a third person, and their heirs — here, had A. and B. been distinct persons, each of the three joint tenants would, as we have seen, have been entitled, as between themselves, to one-third part of the rents and profits, and would have had a power of disposition also over one-third part of the whole inheritance. But, since A. and B., being husband and wife, are only one person, they will take, under such a gift, a moiety only of the rents and profits, with a power to dispose only of one-half of the inheritance; and C., the third person, will take the other half, as joint tenant with them. Again, if lands be given to A. and B. (husband and wife) and their heirs — here, had they been separate persons, they would have become, under the gift, joint tenants in fee simple, and each would have been enabled, without the consent of the other, to dispose of an undivided moiety of the inheritance. But, as A. and B. are one, they now take, as it is said, *by entireties*; and, whilst the husband may do what he pleases with the rents and profits during the coverture, he cannot dispose of any part of the inheritance, without his wife's concurrence. Unless they both agree in making a disposition, each one of them must run the risk of gaining the whole by survivorship, or losing it by dying first. Another consequence of the unity of husband and wife is the inability of either of them to convey to the other. As a man cannot convey to himself, so he cannot convey to his wife, who is part of himself. But a man may leave lands to his wife by his will; for the married state does not deprive the husband of that disposing power which he would possess if single, and a devise by will does not take effect until after his decease. And by means of the Statute of Uses, the effect of a conveyance by a man to his wife can be produced; for a man may convey to another person to the use of his wife in the same manner as, under the statute, we have seen, a man may convey to the use of himself.

If the wife should survive her husband, her estates in fee simple will remain to herself and her heirs, after his death, unaffected by any debts which he may have incurred, or by any alienation which he may have attempted to make; for, although the wife, by marriage, is prevented from disposing of her fee simple estates, either by deed or will, yet neither can the husband, without his wife's concurrence, make any disposition of her lands to extend beyond the limits of his own interest. If, however, he should survive his wife, he will, in case he has had issue by her born alive, that may by possibility inherit the estate as her heir, become entitled to an estate for the residue of his life in such lands and tenements of his wife as she was solely seised of in fee simple, or fee tail in possession. The husband, while in the enjoyment of this estate, is called a tenant by the *curtesy* of England, or, more shortly, tenant by the curtesy. If the wife's estate should be equitable only, that is, if the lands should be vested in trustees for her and her heirs, her husband will still, on surviving, in case he has had issue which might inherit, be entitled to be tenant by the curtesy, in the same manner as if the estate were legal; for equity in this respect follows the law. But, whether legal or equitable, the estate must be a several one, or else held under a tenancy in common, and must not be one of which the wife was seised or possessed jointly with any other person or persons. The estate must also be an estate in possession; for there can be no curtesy of an estate in reversion expectant on a life interest or other estate of freehold. The husband must also have had, by his wife, issue born alive; except in the case of gavelkind lands, where the husband has a right to his curtesy, whether he has had issue or not; but, by the custom of gavelkind, curtesy extends only to a moiety of the wife's lands, and ceases if the husband marries again. The issue must also be capable of inheriting as heir to the wife. Thus, if the wife be seised of lands in tail male, the birth of a daughter only will not entitle her husband to be tenant by curtesy; for the daughter cannot by possibility inherit such an estate from her mother. And it is necessary that the wife should have acquired an actual seisin of all estates, of which it was; possible that an actual seisin could be obtained; for the husband has it in his own power to obtain for his wife an actual seisin; and it is his own fault if he has not done so. A tenancy by the curtesy is not now of very frequent occurrence; the rights of husbands in the lands of their wives are, at the present day, generally ascertained by proper settlements made previously to marriage.

By a statute of the reign of Henry VIII. power was given for all persons of full age, having an estate of inheritance in fee simple or in fee tail, in right of their wives, or jointly with their wives, to make leases, with the concurrence of their wives, of such of the lands as had been most commonly let to farm for twenty years before, for any term not exceeding twenty-one years or three lives, under the same restrictions as tenants in tail were by the same act empowered to lease. This statute, so far as it respects tenants in tail, has already been referred to. It was repealed by the act to facilitate leases and sales of settled estates; but this act has been itself repealed by the Settled Estates Act, 1877. This act now empowers every person entitled to the possession or the receipt of the rents and profits of any unsettled estate, as tenant by the curtesy, or in right of a wife who is seised in fee, to demise the same (except the principal mansion-house and the demesnes thereof, and other lands usually occupied therewith), for any term not exceeding twenty-one years in England or thirty-five years in Ireland, subject to the same restrictions as before mentioned in the case of a tenant for life. And any such demise will be valid against the wife of the person granting the same, and any person claiming through or under her. By a statute of Anne, every husband seised in right of his wife only, who, after the determination of his estate or interest, without the express consent of the persons next immediately entitled after the determination of such estate or interest, shall hold over and continue in possession of any hereditaments, shall he adjudged to be a trespasser; and the full value of the profits received during such wrongful possession may be recovered in damages against him or his executors or administrators.

Hitherto we have seen the extent of the husband's interest, and power of disposition, apart from his wife. If land should be settled in trust for the separate use of the wife, with a clause restraining alienation, we have seen that neither husband nor wife can make any disposition. But, in all other cases, the husband and wife may together make any such dispositions of the wife's interest in real estate as she could do if unmarried. The mode in which such dispositions were formerly effected was, by a *fine* duly levied in the Court of Common Pleas. We have already had occasion to advert to fines, in respect to their former operation on estates tail. They were, as we have seen, fictitious suits commenced and then compromised by leave of the Court, whereby the lands in question were acknowledged to be the right of one of the parties. Whenever a married woman was party to a fine, it was necessary that she should be examined apart from her husband, to ascertain whether she joined in the fine of her own freewill, or was compelled to it by the threats and menaces of her husband. Having this protection, a fine by husband and wife was an effectual conveyance, as well of the wife's as of the husband's interest of every kind, in the land comprised in the fine. But without a fine, no conveyance could be made of the wife's lands; thus, she could not leave them by her will, even to her husband; although, by means of the Statute of Uses, a testamentary appointment of lands, in the nature of a will, might be made by the wife in favour of her husband, in a manner to be hereafter explained. And in this respect the law still remains unaltered, although a change has been made in the machinery for effecting conveyances of the lands of married women. The cumbrous and expensive nature of fines having occasioned their abolition, provision has now been made by the act for the abolition of Fines and Recoveries, for the conveyance by deed merely of the interests of married women in real estate. Every kind of conveyance or disclaimer of freehold estates which a woman could execute if unmarried may now be made by her by a deed executed with her husband's concurrence: but the separate examination, which was before necessary in the case of a fine, is still retained; and every deed, executed under the provisions of the act, must be produced and *acknowledged* by the wife as her own act and deed, before a judge of one of the superior courts at Westminster, or of any county court, or a master in Chancery, or two commissioners, who must, before they receive the acknowledgment, examine her apart from her husband touching her knowledge of the deed, and must ascertain whether she freely and voluntarily consents thereto. A recent statute removes doubts which might arise, in consequence of any person taking the acknowledgment being an interested party. The Vendor and Purchaser Act, 1874, now provides, that when any hereditament shall be vested in a married woman as a bare trustee, she may convey the same as if she were a feme sole.

2. As to the rights of the wife in the lands of her husband. We have seen that, during the coverture, all the power is possessed by the husband, even when the lands belong to the wife, except in cases which fall within the Married Women's Property Act, 1870; and of course this is the case when they are the husband's own. After the decease of her husband, the wife however becomes, in some cases, entitled to a life interest in part of her deceased husband's lands. This interest is termed the *dower* of the wife. And by the act of parliament for the amendment of the law relating to dower, the dower of women married after the 1st of January, 1834, is placed on a different footing from that of women who were married previously. But as the old law of dower still regulates the rights of all women who were married on or before that day, it will be necessary, in the first place, to give some account of the old law before proceeding to the new.

Dower, as it existed previously to the operation of the Dower Act, was of very ancient origin, and retained an inconvenient property which accrued to it in the simple times when alienation of lands was far less frequent than at present. If at any time during the coverture the husband become solely seised of any estate of inheritance, that is fee simple or fee tail, in lands to which any issue, which the wife might have had, might by possibility have been heir, she from that time became entitled, on his decease, to have one equal third part of the same lands allotted to her, to be enjoyed by her in severally during the remainder of her life. This right having once attached to the lands, adhered to them, notwithstanding any sale or devise which the husband might make. It consequently became necessary for the husband, whenever he wished to make a valid conveyance of his lands, to obtain the concurrence of his wife, for the purpose of releasing her right to dower. This release could be effected only by means of a fine, in which the wife was separately examined. And when, as often happened, the wife's concurrence was not obtained on account of the expense involved in levying a fine, a defect in the title obviously existed so long as the wife lived. As the right to dower was paramount to the alienation of the husband, so it was quite independent of his debts, — even of those owing to the crown. It was necessary, however, that the husband should be seised of an estate of inheritance at law; for the Court of Chancery, whilst it allowed to husbands curtesy of their wives' equitable estates, withheld from wives a like privilege of dower out of the equitable estates of their husbands. The estate, moreover, must have been held in severally or in common, and not in joint tenancy; for the unity of interest which characterizes a joint tenancy forbids the intrusion into such a tenancy of the husband or wife of any deceased joint tenant; on the decease of any joint tenant, his surviving companions are already entitled, under the original gift, to the whole subject of the tenancy. The estate was also required to be an estate of inheritance in possession; although a seisin in law, obtained by the husband, was sufficient to cause his wife's right of dower to attach. In no case, also, was any issue required to be actually born; it was sufficient that the wife might have had issue who might have inherited. The dower of the widow in gavelkind lands consisted, and still consists, like the husband's curtesy, of a moiety, and continues only so long as she remains unmarried and chaste.

In order to prevent this inconvenient right from attaching on newly-purchased lands, and to enable the purchaser to make a title at a future time, without his wife's concurrence, various devices were resorted to in the framing of purchase-deeds. The old-fashioned method of barring dower was to take the conveyance to the purchaser and his heirs, to the use of the purchaser and a trustee and the heirs of the purchaser; but, as to the estate of the trustee, it was declared to be in trust only for the purchaser and his heirs. By this means the purchaser and the trustee became joint tenants for life of the legal estate, and the remainder of the inheritance belonged to the purchaser. If, therefore, the purchaser died during the life of his trustee, the latter acquired in law an estate for life by survivorship; and as the husband had never been solely seised, the wife's dower never arose; whilst the estate for life of the trustee was subject in equity to any disposition which the husband might think fit to make by his will. The husband and his trustee might also, at any time during their joint lives, make a valid conveyance to a purchaser without the wife's concurrence. The defect of the plan was, that if the trustee happened to die during the husband's life, the latter became at once solely seised of an estate in fee simple in possession; and the wife's right to dower accordingly attached. Moreover, the husband could never make any conveyance of an estate in fee simple without the concurrence of his trustee so long as he lived. This plan, therefore, gave way to another method of framing purchase-deeds, which wall be hereafter explained, and by means of which the wife's dower under the old law is effectually barred, whilst the husband alone, without the concurrence of any other person, can effectually convey the lands.

The right of dower might have been barred altogether by a *jointure*, agreed to be accepted by the intended wife previously to marriage, in lieu of dower. This jointure was either legal or equitable. A legal jointure was first authorized by the Statute of Uses, which, by turning uses into legal estates, of course render them liable to dower. Under the provisions of this statute, dower may be barred by the wife's acceptance previously to marriage, and in satisfaction of her dower, of a competent livelihood of freehold lands and tenements, to take effect in profit or possession presently after the death of the husband for the life of the wife at least. If the jointure be made after marriage, the wife may elect between her dower and her jointure. A legal jointure, however, has in modern times seldom been resorted to as a method of barring dower: when any jointure has been made, it has usually been merely of an equitable kind; for if the intended wife be of age, and a party to the settlement, she is competent, in equity, to extinguish her title to dower upon any terms to which she may think proper to agree. And if the wife should have accepted an equitable jointure, the Court of Chancery will effectually restrain her from setting up any claim to her dower. But in equity, as well as at law, the jointure, in order to be an absolute bar of dower, must be made before marriage.

With regard to women married since the 1st of January, 1834, the doctrine of jointures is of very little moment. For, by the act for the amendment of the law relating to dower, the dower of such women has been placed completely within the power of their husbands. Under the act no widow is entitled to dower out of any land which shall have been absolutely disposed of by her husband in his lifetime or by his will. And all partial estates and interests, and all charges created by any disposition or will of the husband, and all debts, incumbrances, contracts and engagements to which his lands may be liable, shall be effectual as against the right of his widow to dower. The husband may also either wholly or partially deprive his wife of her right to dower, by any declaration for that purpose made by him, by any deed, or by his will. As some small compensation for these sacrifices, the act has granted a right of dower out of lands to which the husband had a right merely without having had even a legal seisin; dower is also extended to equitable as well as legal estates of inheritance in possession, excepting of course estates in joint tenancy. The effect of the act is evidently to deprive the wife of her dower, except as against her husband's heir at law. If the husband should die intestate, and possessed of any lands, the wife's dower out of such lands is still left her for her support, — unless, indeed, the husband should have executed a declaration to the contrary. A declaration of this kind has, unfortunately, found its way, as a sort of common form, into many purchase-deeds. Its insertion seems to have arisen from a remembrance of the troublesome nature of dower under the old law, united possibly with some misapprehension of the effect of the new enactment. But, surely, if the estate be allowed to descend, the claim of the wife is at least equal to that of the heir, supposing him a descendant of the husband; and far superior, if the heir be a lineal ancestor, or remote relation. The proper method seems therefore to be, to omit any such declaration against dower, and so to leave to the widow a prospect of sharing in the lands, in case her lord shall not think proper to dispose of them.

The act to facilitate leases and sales of settled estates now empowers every person entitled to the possession or the receipt of the rents and profits of any unsettled estate as tenant in dower, to grant leases not exceeding twenty-one years, in the same manner as a tenant by the curtesy, or a tenant for life under a settlement made after that act came in force.

An action for dower, like other real actions, was formerly commenced in the Court of Common Pleas; and when real actions were abolished in the year 1833 writs for the recovery of dower were excepted. By an act of 1860 these writs were abolished, and the action was commenced by writ of summons issuing out of the Court of Common Pleas, in the same manner as the writ of summons in an ordinary action; and the proceedings were the same as in ordinary actions commenced by writ of summons. A widow's dower might also have been recovered by bill in equity. And now by the Judicature Act, 1873, the jurisdiction of the Courts of Common Pleas and Chancery has been transferred respectively to the Common Pleas and Chancery Divisions of the High Court of Justice.

PART II
OF INCORPOREAL HEREDITAMENTS

Our attention has hitherto been directed to real property of a corporeal kind. We have considered the usual estates which may be held in such property, — the mode of descent of such estates as are inheritable, — the tenure by which estates in fee simple are holden, — and the usual method of the alienation of such estates, whether in the lifetime of the owner or by his will. We have also noticed the modification in the right and manner of alienation produced by the relation of husband and wife. Besides corporeal property, we have seen that there exists also another kind of property, which, not being of a visible and tangible nature, is denominated *incorporeal*. This kind of property, though it may accompany that which is corporeal, yet does not in itself admit of actual delivery. When, therefore, it was required to be transferred as a separate subject of property, it was always conveyed, in ancient times, by writing, that is, by deed; for we have seen, that formerly all legal writings were in fact deeds. Property of an incorporeal kind was, therefore, said to lie in *grant*, whilst corporeal property was said to lie in *livery*. For the word *grant*, though it comprehends all kinds of conveyances, yet more strictly and properly taken, is a conveyance by deed only. And *lirery*, as we have seen, is the technical name for that delivery which was made of the seisin, or feudal possession, on every feoffment of lands and houses, or corporeal hereditaments. In this difference in the ancient mode of transfer accordingly lay the chief distinction between these two classes of property. But, as we have seen, the act to amend the law of real property now provides that all corporeal tenements and hereditaments shall, as regards the conveyance of the immediate freehold thereof, be deemed to lie in grant as well as in livery. There is, accordingly, now no practical difference in this respect between the two classes; and the lease for a year stamp, to which a grant of corporeal hereditaments had been previously subject, was abolished by the Stamp Act of 1850.

CHAPTER I
OF A REVERSION AND A VESTED REMAINDER

The first kind of incorporeal hereditament which we shall mention is somewhat of a mixed nature, being at one time incorporeal, at another not; and, for this reason, it is not usually classed with those hereditaments which are essentially and entirely of an incorporeal kind. But as this hereditament partakes, during its existence, very strongly of the nature and attributes of other incorporeal hereditaments, particularly in its always permitting, and generally requiring, a deed of grant for its transfer, — it is here classed with such hereditaments. It is called, according to the mode of its creation, a *reversion* or a *vested remainder*.

If a tenant in fee simple should grant to another person a lease for a term of years, or for life, or even if he should grant an estate tail, it is evident that he will not thereby dispose of all his interest; for in each case, his grantee has a less estate than himself. Accordingly, on the expiration of the term of years, or on the decease of the tenant for life, or on the decease of the donee in tail without having barred his estate tail and without issue, the remaining interest of the tenant in fee will *revert* to himself or his heirs, and he or his heir will again become tenant in fee simple in possession. The smaller estate which he has so granted is called, during its continuance, the *particular* estate, being only a part, or *particular* of the estate in fee. And, during the continuance of such particular estate, the interest of the tenant in fee simple, which still remains undisposed of — that is, his present estate, in virtue of which, he is to have again the possession at some future time — is called his *reversion*.

If at the same time with the grant of the particular estate he should also dispose of this remaining interest or *reversion*, or any part thereof, to some other person, it then changes its name, and is termed, not a *reversion*, but a *remainder*. Thus, if a grant be made by A., a tenant in fee simple, to B. for life, and after his decease to C. and his heirs, the whole fee simple of A. will be disposed of, and C.'s interest will be termed a *remainder*, expectant on the decease of B. A remainder, therefore, always has its origin in express grant: a reversion merely arises incidentally, in consequence of the grant of the particular estate. It is created simply by the law, whilst a remainder springs from the act of the parties.

1. And, first, of a reversion. If the tenant in fee simple should have made a lease merely for a term of years, his reversion is looked on, in law, precisely as a continuance of his old estate, with respect to himself and his heirs, and to all other persons but the tenant for years. The owner of the fee simple is regarded as having simply placed a bailiff on his property; and the consequence is, that, subject to the lease, the owner's rights of alienation remain unimpaired, and may be exercised in the same manner as before. The feudal possession or *seisin* has not been parted with. And a conveyance of the reversion may, therefore, be made by a feoffment, with livery of *seisin*, made with the consent of the tenant for years. But, if this mode of or by deed of transfer should not be thought eligible, a grant by deed will be equally efficacious. For the estate of the grantor is strictly incorporeal, the tenant for years having the actual possession of the lands: so long, therefore, as such actual possession continues, the estate in fee simple is strictly an incorporeal reversion, which, together with the *seisin* or feudal possession, may be conveyed by deed of grant. But, if the tenant in fee simple should have made a lease for life he must have parted with his *seisin* to the tenant for life; for, an estate for life is an estate of freehold, and such tenant for life will, therefore, during his life, continue to be the freeholder, or holder of the feudal seisin. No feoffment can consequently be made by the tenant in fee simple; for he has no seisin of which to make livery. His reversion is but a fragment of his old estate, and remains purely incorporeal, until, by the dropping of the life of the grantee, it shall again become an estate in possession. Till then, that is, so long as it remains a reversion expectant on an estate of freehold, it can only be conveyed, like all other incorporeal hereditaments when apart from what is corporeal, by a deed of grant.

We have before mentioned, that, in the case of a lease for life or years, a tenure is created between the parties, the lessee becoming tenant to the lessor. To this tenure are usually incident two things, *fealty* and *rent*. The oath of fealty is now never exacted; but the rent, which may be reserved, is of practical importance. This rent is called in law *rent service* in order to distinguish it from other kinds of rent, to be spoken of hereafter, which have nothing to do with the services anciently rendered by a tenant to his lord. It consists, usually, but not necessarily, of money; for, it may be rendered in corn, or in anything else. Thus, an annual rent of one peppercorn is sometimes reserved to be paid, when demanded, in cases where it is wished that lands should be holden rent free, and yet that the landlord should be able at any time to obtain from his tenant an acknowledgment of his tenancy. To the reservation of a rent service, a deed was formerly not absolutely necessary. For, although the rent is an incorporeal hereditament, yet the law considered that the same ceremony, by which the nature and duration of the estate were fixed and evidenced, was sufficient also to ascertain the rent to be paid for it. But, by the act to amend the law of real property, it is provided, that a lease, required by law to be in writing, of any tenements or hereditaments shall be void at law, unless made by deed. In every case, therefore, where the Statute of Frauds has required leases to be in writing, they must now be made by deed. But, according to the exception in that statute, where the lease does not exceed three years from the making, a rent of two-thirds of the full improved value, or more, may still be reserved by parol merely. Rent service, when created, is considered to be issuing out of every part of the land in respect of which it is paid: one part of the land is as much subject to it as another. For the recovery of rent service, the well known remedy is by *distress* and sale of the goods of the tenant, or any other person, found on any part of the premises. This remedy for the recovery of rent service belongs to the landlord of common right, without any express agreement. In modern times it has been extended and facilitated by various acts of parliament.

In addition to the remedy by distress, there is usually contained in leases a condition of re-entry, empowering the landlord, in default of payment of the rent for a certain time, to re-enter on the premises and hold them as of his former estate. When such a condition is inserted, the estate of the tenant, whether for life or years, becomes determinable on such re-entry. In former times, before any entry could be made under a proviso or condition for re-entry on non-payment of rent, the landlord was required to make a demand, upon the premises, of the precise rent due, at a convenient time before sunset of the last day when the rent could be paid according to the condition; thus, if the proviso were for re-entry on non-payment of the rent by the space of thirty days, the demand must have been made on the evening of the thirtieth day. But now, if half a year's rent is due, and no sufficient distress is found on the premises, the landlord may recover the premises, at the expiration of the period limited by the proviso for re-entry, by action of ejectment, without any formal demand or entry; but all proceedings are to cease on payment by the tenant of all arrears and costs, at any time before the trial. Formerly also the tenant might, at an indefinite time after he was ejected, have filed his bill in the Court of Chancery, and he would have been relieved by that Court from the forfeiture he had incurred, on his payment to his landlord of all arrears and costs. But by a statute of the present reign, the right of the tenant, apply for relief in equity was restricted to six calendar months next after the execution of the judgment on the ejectment; and by a more recent statute, the same relief was allowed to be given by the Courts of Law. In ancient times, also, the benefit of a condition of re-entry could belong only to the landlord and his heirs; for the law would not allow of the transfer of a mere conditional right to put an end to the estate of another. A right of re-entry was conned in the same light as a right to bring an action for money due; which right in ancient times was not assignable. This doctrine sometimes occasioned considerable inconvenience; and in the reign of Henry VIII. it was found to press hardly on the grantees from the crown of the lands of the dissolved monasteries. For these grantees were of course unable to take advantage of the conditions of re-entry, which the monks had inserted in the leases of their tenants. A parliamentary remedy was, therefore, applied for the benefit of the favourites of the crown; and the opportunity was taken for making the same provision for the public at large. A statute was accordingly passed, which enacts, that as well the grantees of the crown as all other persons being grantees or assignees, their heirs, executors, successors, and assigns, shall have the like advantages against the lessees, by entry for non-payment of rent, or for doing of waste, or other forfeiture as the lessors or grantors themselves, or their heirs or successors, might at any time have had or enjoyed; and this statute is still in force. There exist also further means for the recovery of rent in certain actions at law, which the landlord may bring against his tenant for obtaining payment.

Rent service, being incident to the reversion, passes by a grant of such reversion without the necessity of any express mention of the rent. Formerly no grant could be made of any reversion without the consent of the tenant, expressed by what was called his *attornment* to his new landlord. It was thought reasonable that a tenant should not have a new landlord imposed upon him without his consent; for, in early times, the relation of lord and tenant was of a much more personal nature than it is at present. The tenant, therefore, was able to prevent his lord. from making a conveyance to any person whom he did not choose to accept as a landlord; for he could refuse to attorn tenant to the purchaser, and without attornment the grant was invalid. The landlord, however, had it always in his power to convey his reversion by the expensive process of a *fine* duly levied in the Court of Common Pleas; for this method of conveyance, being judicial in its nature, was carried into effect without the tenant's concurrence; and the attornment of the tenant, which for many purposes was desirable, could in such case be compelled. It can easily be imagined, that a doctrine such as this was found inconvenient when the rent paid by the tenant became the only service of any benefit rendered to the landlord. The necessity of attornment to the validity of the grant of a reversion was accordingly abolished by a statute passed in the reign of Queen Anne. But the statute very properly provides, that no tenant shall be prejudiced or damaged by payment of his rent to the grantor, or by breach of any condition for nonpayment of rent, before notice of the grant shall be given to him by the grantee. And by a further statute, any attornment which may be made by tenants without their landlords' consent, to strangers claiming title to the estate of their landlords, is rendered null and void. Nothing, therefore, is now necessary for the valid conveyance of any rent service, but a grant by deed of the reversion, to which such rent is incident. When the conveyance is made to the tenant himself, it is called a *release*.

The doctrine, that rent service, being incident to the reversion, always follows such reversion, formerly gave rise to the curious and unpleasant consequence of the rent being sometimes lost when the reversion was destroyed. For it is possible, under certain circumstances, that an estate may be destroyed and cease to exist. For instance, suppose A. to have been a tenant of lands for a term of years, and B. to have been his undertenant for a less term of years at a certain rent; this rent was an incident of A.'s reversion, that is, of the term of years belonging to A. If, then, A.'s term should by any means have been destroyed, the rent paid to him by B. would, as an incident of such term, have been destroyed also. Now, by the rules of law, a conveyance of the immediate fee simple to A. would at once have destroyed his term, — it not being possible that the term of years and the estate in fee simple should subsist together. In legal language the term of years would have been *merged* in the larger estate in fee simple; and the term being merged and gone, it followed as a necessary consequence, that all its incidents, of which B.'s rent was one, ceased also. This unpleasant result was some time since provided for and obviated with respect to leases surrendered in order to be renewed, — the owners of the new leases being invested with the same right to the rent of undertenants, and the same remedy for recovery thereof, as if the original leases had been kept, on foot. But in all other cases the inconvenience continued, until a remedy was provided by the act to simplify the transfer of property. This act, however, was shortly afterwards repealed by the act to amend the law of real property, which provides, in a more efficient though somewhat crabbed clause, that, when the reversion expectant on a lease, made either before or after the passing of the act, of any tenements or hereditaments of any tenure, shall after the 1st of October, 1845, be surrendered or merge, the estate, which shall for the time being confer, as against the tenant under the same lease, the nest vested right to the same tenements or hereditaments, shall, to the extent and for the purpose of preserving such incidents to and obligations on the same reversion as but for the surrender or merger thereof would have subsisted, be deemed the reversion expectant on the same lease.

2. A remainder chiefly differs from a reversion in this, — that between the owner of the particular estate and the owner of the remainder (called the remainderman) no tenure exists. They both derive their estates from the same source, the grant of the owner in fee simple; and one of them has no more right to be lord than the other. But as all estates must be holden of some

person, — in the case of a grant of a particular estate with a remainder in fee simple, — the particular tenant and the remainderman both hold their estates of the same chief lord as their grantor held before. It consequently follows, that no rent service is incident to a remainder, as it usually is to a reversion; for rent service is an incident of tenure, and in this case no tenure exists. The other point of difference between a reversion and a remainder we have already noticed, namely, that a reversion arises necessarily from the grant of the particular estate, being simply that part of the estate of the grantor which remains undisposed of, but a remainder is always itself created by an express grant.

We have seen that the powers of alienation possessed by a tenant in fee simple enable him to make a lease for a term of years, or for life, or a gift in tail, as well as to grant an estate in fee simple. But these powers are not simply in the alternative, for he may exercise all these powers of alienation at one and the same moment; provided, of course, that his grantees come in one at a time, in some prescribed order, the one waiting for liberty to enter until the estate of the other is determined. In such a case the ordinary mode of conveyance is alone made use of; and until the passing of the act to amend the law of real property, if a feoffment should have been employed, there would have been no occasion for a *deed* to limit or mark out the estates of those who could not have immediate possession. The seisin would have been delivered to the first person who was to have possession; and if such person was to have been only a tenant for a term of years, such seisin would have immediately vested in the prescribed owner of the first estate of freehold, whose bailiff the tenant for years is accounted to be. From such first freeholder, on the determination of his estate, the seisin, by whatever means vested in him, will devolve on the other grantees of freehold estates in the order in which their estates are limited to come into possession. So long as a regular order is thus laid down, in which the possession of the lands may devolve, it matters not how many kinds of estates are granted, or on how many persons the same estate is bestowed. Thus a grant may be made at once to fifty different people separately for their lives. In such case the grantee for life who is first to have the possession is the particular tenant to whom, on a feoffment, seisin would be delivered, and all the rest are remaindermen; whilst the reversion in fee simple, expectant on the decease of them all, remains with the grantor. The second grantee for life has a remainder expectant on the decease of the first, and will be entitled to possession on the determination of the estate of the first, either by his decease, or in case of his forfeiture, or otherwise. The third grantee must wait till the estate both of the first and second shall have determined; and so of the rest. The mode in which such a set of estates would be marked out is as follows: — To A. for his life, and after his decease to B. for his. life, and after his decease to C. for his life, and so on. This method of limitation is quite sufficient for the purpose, although it by no means expresses all that is meant. The estates of B. and C. and the rest are intended to be as immediately and effectually vested in them, as the estate of A.; so that if A. were to forfeit his estate, B. would have an immediate right to the possession: and so again C. would have a right to enter, whenever the estates both of A. and B. might determine. But, owing to the necessary infirmity of language, all this cannot be expressed in the limitations of every ordinary deed. The words "and after his decease" are, therefore, considered a sufficient expression of an intention to confer a vested remainder after an estate for life. In the case we have selected of numerous estates, every one given only for the life of each grantee, it is manifest that very many of the grantees can derive no benefit; and should the first grantee survive all the others, and not forfeit his estate, not one of them will take anything. Nevertheless, each one of these grantees has an estate for life in remainder, immediately *vested* in him; and each of these remainders is capable of being transferred, both at law and in equity, by a deed of grant, in the same manner as a reversion. In the same way, a grant may be made of a term of years to one person, an estate for life to another, an estate in tail to a third, and last of all an estate in fee simple to a fourth; and these grantees may be entitled to possession in any prescribed order, except as to the grantee of the estate in fee simple, who must necessarily come last; for his estate, if not literally interminable, yet carries with it an interminable power of alienation, which would keep all the other grantees for ever out of possession. But the estate tail may come first into possession, then the estate for life, and then the term of years; or the order may be reversed, and the term of years come first, then the estate for life, then the estate tail, and lastly the estate in fee simple, which, as we have said, must wait for possession till all the others shall have been determined. When a remainder comes after an estate tail, it is liable to be barred by the tenant in tail, as we have already seen. This risk it must run. But, if any estate, be it ever so small, is always ready, from its commencement to its end, to come into possession the moment the prior estates, be they what they may, happen to determine, — it is then a *vested remainder*, and recognized in law as an estate grantable by deed. It would be an estate in possession, were it not that other estates have a prior claim; and their priority alone postpones, or perhaps may entirely prevent, possession being taken by the remainderman. The gift is immediate; but the enjoyment must necessarily depend on the determination of the estates of those who have a prior right to the possession.

In all the cases which we have as yet considered, each of the remainders has belonged to a different person. No one person has had more than one estate. A., B. and C. may each have had estates for life; or the one may have had a term of years, the other an estate for life, and the last a remainder in tail or in fee simple. But no one of them has as yet had more than one estate. It is possible, however, that one person may have, under certain circumstances, more than one estate in the same land at the same time, — one of his estates being in possession, and the other in remainder, or perhaps all of them being remainders. The limitation of a remainder in tail, or in fee simple to a person who has already an estate of freehold, as for life, is governed by a rule of law, known by the name of the rule in *Shelley's case*, — so called from a celebrated case in Lord Coke's time, in which the subject was much discussed, — although the rule itself is of very ancient date. As this rule is generally supposed to be highly technical, and founded on principles not easily to be perceived, it may be well to proceed gradually in the attempt to explain it.

We have already seen, that, in ancient times, the feudal holding of an estate granted to a vassal continued only for his life. And from the earliest times to the present day a grant or conveyance of lands, made by any instrument (a will only excepted), to A. B. simply, without further words, will give him an estate for his life, and no longer. If the grant was anciently made to him and his heirs, his heir, on his death, became entitled; and it was not in the power of the ancestor to prevent the descent of his estate accordingly. He could not sell it without the consent of his lord; much less could he then devise it by his will. The ownership of an estate in fee simple was then but little more advantageous than the possession of a life interest at the present day. The powers of alienation belonging to such ownership, together with the liabilities to which it is subject, have almost all been of slow and gradual growth, as has already been pointed out in different parts of the preceding chapters. A tenant in fee simple was, accordingly, a person who held to him and his heirs; that is, the land was given to him to hold for his life, and to his heirs, to hold after his decease. It cannot, therefore, be wondered at, that a gift, expressly in these terms, "To A. for his life, and after his decease to his heirs," should have been anciently regarded as identical with a gift to A. and his heirs, that is, a gift in fee simple. Nor, if such was the law formerly, can it be matter of surprise that the same rule should have continued to prevail up to the present time. Such indeed has been the case. Notwithstanding the vast power of alienation now possessed by a tenant in fee simple, and the great liability of such an estate to involuntary alienation for the purpose of satisfying the debts of the present tenant, the same rule still holds; and a grant to A. for his life, and after his decease to his heirs, will now convey to him an estate in fee simple, with all its incidents; and in the same manner a grant to A. for his life, and after his decease to the heirs of his body, will now convey to him an estate tail as effectually as a grant to him and the heirs of his body. In these cases, therefore, as well as in ordinary limitations to A. and his heirs, or to A. and the heirs of his body, the words *heirs*, and *heirs of his body*, are said to be *words of limitation*; that is, words which limit or mark out the estate to be taken by the grantee. At the present day, when the heir is perhaps the last person likely to get the estate, these words of limitation are regarded simply *as* formal means of conferring powers and privileges on the grantee — as mere technicalities, and nothing more. But, in ancient times, these same words of limitation really meant what they said, and gave the estate to the heirs, or the heirs of the body of the grantee, after his decease, according to the letter of the gift. The circumstance, that a man's estate was to go to his heir, was the very thing which, afterwards, enabled him to convey to another an estate in fee simple. And the circumstance, that it was to go to the heir of his body, was that which alone enabled him, in after times, to bar an estate tail and dispose of the lands entailed by means of a common recovery.

Having proceeded thus far, we have already mastered the first branch of the rule in *Shelley's case*, namely, that which relates to estates in possession. This part of the rule is, in fact, a mere enunciation of the proposition already explained, that when the ancestor, by any gift or conveyance, takes an estate for life, and in the same gift or conveyance, an estate is immediately limited to his heirs in fee or in tail, the words "the heirs" are words of limitation of the estate of the ancestor. Suppose, however, that it should anciently have been wished to interpose between the enjoyment of the lands by the ancestor and the enjoyment by the heir, the possession of some other party for some limited estate, as for his own life. Thus, let the estate have been given to A. and his heirs, but with a vested estate to B. for his own life, to take effect in possession next after the decease of A., — thus suspending the enjoyment of the lands by the heir of A., until after the determination of the life estate of B. In such a case it is evident that B, would have had a vested estate for his life, in remainder, expectant on the decease of A.; and the manner in which such remainder would have been limited would, as we have seen, have been to A. for his life, and after his decease to B. for his life. The only question then remaining would be as to the mode of expressing the rest of the intention, — namely, that, subject to B.'s life estate, A. should have an estate in fee simple. To this case the same reasoning applies, as we have already made use of in the case of an estate to A. for his life, and after his decease to his heirs. For an estate in fee simple is an estate, by its very terms, to a man and his heirs. But, in the present case, A. would have already had *his* estate given him by the first limitation to himself for his life; nothing, therefore, would remain but to give the estate to his heirs, in order to complete the fee simple. The last remainder would, therefore, be to the heirs of A.; and the limitations would run thus: "To A. for his life, and after his decease to B. for his life, and after his decease to the heirs of A." The heir, in this case, would not have taken any estate independently of his ancestor, any more than in the common limitation to A. and his heirs: the heir would have claimed the estate only by its descent from his ancestor, who had previously enjoyed it during his life; and the interposition of the estate of B. would have merely postponed that enjoyment by the heir, which would otherwise have been immediate. But we have seen that the very circumstance of a man's having an estate which is to go to his heir will now give him a power of alienation either by deed or will, and enable him altogether to defeat his heir's expectations. And, in a case like the present, the same privilege will now be enjoyed by A.; for, whilst he cannot by any means defeat the vested remainder belonging to B. for his life, he may, subject to B.'s life interest, dispose of the whole fee simple at his own discretion. A. therefore will now have in these lands, so long as B. lives, two estates, one in possession and the other in remainder. In possession A. has, with regard to B., an estate only for his own life. In remainder, expectant on the decease of B., he has, in consequence of his life interest being followed by a limitation to his heirs, a complete estate in fee simple. The right of B. to the possession, after A.'s decease, is the only thing which keeps the estate apart, and divides it, as it were, in two. If, therefore, B. should die during A.'s life, A. will be tenant for his own life, with an immediate remainder to his heirs; in other words, he will be tenant to himself and his heirs, and will enjoy, without any interruption, all the privileges belonging to a tenant in fee simple.

By parity of reasoning a similar result would follow, if the remainder were to the heirs of the body of A., or for an estate in tail, instead of an estate in fee simple. The limitation to the heirs of the body of A. would coalesce, as it is said, with his life estate, and give him an estate tail in remainder, expectant on the decease of B.; and if B. were to die during his lifetime, A. would become a complete tenant in tail in possession.

The example we have chosen, of an intermediate estate to B. for life, is founded on a principle evidently applicable to any number of intermediate estates, interposed between the enjoyment of the ancestor and that of his heir. Nor is it at all necessary that all these estates should be for life only; for some of them may be larger estates, as estates in tail. For instance, suppose lands given to A. for his life, and after his decease to B. and the heirs of his body, and in default of such issue (which is the method of expressing a remainder after an estate tail), to the heirs of A. In this case A. will have an estate for life in possession, with an estate in fee simple in remainder, expectant on the determination of B.'s estate tail. An important case of this hind arose in the reign of Edward III. Lands, were given to one John de Sutton for his life, the remainder, after his decease, to John his son, and Eline, the wife of John the son, and the heirs of their bodies; and in default of such issue, to the right heirs of John the father. John the father died first; then, John and Eline entered into possession. John the son then died, and afterwards Eline his wife, without leaving any heir of her body. R., another son, and heir at law of John de Sutton, the father, then entered. And it was decided by all the justices that he was liable to pay a *relief* to the chief lord of the fee, on account of the descent of the lands to himself from John the father. Thorpe, who seems to have been a judge, thus explained the reason of the decision: — "You are in as heir to your father, and your brother [father?] had the freehold before; at which time, if John his son and Eline had died [without issue] in his lifetime, he would have been tenant in fee simple."

The same principles will apply where the first estate is an estate in tail, instead of an estate for life. Thus, suppose lands to be given to A. and the heirs male of his body begotten, and in default of such issue, to the heirs female of his body begotten. Here, in default of male heirs of the body of A., the heirs female will inherit from their ancestor the estate in tail female, which by the gift had vested in him. There is no need to repeat the estate which the ancestor enjoys for his life, and to limit the lands, in default of heirs male, *to him* and to the heirs female of his body begotten. This part of his estate in tail female has been already given to him in limiting the estate in tail male. The heirs female, being mentioned in the gift, will be supposed to take the lands as heirs, that is, by descent from their ancestor, in whom an estate in tail female must consequently be vested in his lifetime. For, the same rule, founded on the same principle; will apply in every instance; and this rule is no other than the rule in *Shelley's case*, which lays it down for law, that when the ancestor, by any gift or conveyance, takes an estate of freehold, and, in the same gift or conveyance, an estate is limited, *either mediately or immediately*, to his heirs in fee or in tail, the words "the heirs" are words of limitation of the estate of the ancestor. The heir, if he should take any interest, must take as heir by descent from his ancestor; for he is not constituted, by the words of the gift or conveyance, a *purchaser* of any separate and independent estate for himself.

The rule, it will be observed, requires that an estate of freehold merely should be taken by the ancestor, and not necessarily an estate for the whole of his own life or in tail. In the examples we have given, the ancestor has had an estate at least for his own life, and the enjoyment of the lands by other parties has postponed the enjoyment by his heirs. But the ancestor himself, as well as his heirs, may be deprived of possession for a time; and yet an estate in fee simple or fee tail may be effectually vested in the ancestor, subject to such deprivation. For instance, suppose lands to be given to A., a widow, during her life, provided she continue a widow and unmarried, and after her marriage, to B. and his heirs during her life, and after her decease, to her heirs. Here, A. has an estate in fee simple, subject to the remainder to B. for her life, expectant on the event of her marrying again. For to apply to this case the same reasoning as to the former ones, A. has still an estate to her and to her heirs. She has the freehold or feudal possession, and after her decease, her heirs are to have the same. It matters not to them that a stranger may take it for a while. The terms of the gift declare that what was once enjoyed by the ancestor shall afterwards be enjoyed by the heirs of such ancestor. These very terms then make an estate in fee simple, with all its incidental powers of alienation, controlled only by the rights of B. in respect of the estate conferred on him by the same gift.

But if the ancestor should take no estate of freehold under the gift, but the land should be granted only to his heirs, a very different effect would be produced. In such a case a most material part of the definition of an estate in fee simple would be wanting. For an estate in fee simple is an estate given to a man and his heirs, and not merely to the heirs of a man. The ancestor, to whose heirs the lands were granted, would accordingly take no estate or interest by reason of the gift to his heirs. But the gift, if it should ever take effect, would be a future contingent estate for the person who, at the ancestor's decease, should answer the description of heir to his freehold estates. The gift would accordingly fall within the class of future estates, of which an explanation is endeavoured to be given in the next chapter.

CHAPTER II
OF A CONTINGENT REMAINDER

Hitherto we have observed a very extensive power of alienation possessed by a tenant in fee simple. He may make an immediate grant, not of one estate merely, or two, but of as many as he may please, provided he ascertain the order in which his grantees are to take possession. This power of alienation, it will be observed, may in some degree render less easy the alienation of the land at a future time; for, it is plain that no sale can in future be made of an unincumbered estate in fee simple in the lands, unless every owner of each of these estates will concur in the sale, and convey his individual interest, whether he be the particular tenant, or the owner of any one of the estates in remainder. But if all these owners should concur, a valid conveyance of an estate in fee simple can at any time be made. The exercise of the power of alienation, in the creation of vested remainders, does not, therefore, withdraw the land for a moment from that constant liability to complete alienation, which it has been the sound policy of modern law as much as possible to encourage.

But, great as is the power thus possessed, the law has granted to a tenant in fee simple, and to every other owner to the extent of his estate, a greater power still. For, it enables him, under certain restrictions, to grant estates to commence in interest, and not in possession merely, at a future time. So that during the period which may elapse before the commencement of such estates, the land may be withdrawn from its former liability to complete alienation, and be tied up for the benefit of those who may become the owners of such future estates. The power of alienation is thus allowed to be exercised in some degree to its own destruction. For, till such future estates come into existence, they may have no owners to convey them. Of these future estates there are two kinds, a contingent remainder, and an executory interest. The former is allowed to be created by any mode of conveyance. The latter can arise only by the instrumentality of a will, or of a *use* executed, or made into an estate by the Statute of Uses. The nature of an executory interest will be explained in the next chapter. The present will be devoted to contingent remainders, which, though abolished by the act to simplify the transfer of property, were revived the next session by the act to amend the law of real property, by which the former act, so far as it abolished contingent remainders, was repealed as from the time of its taking effect.

The simplicity of the common law allowed of the creation of no other estates than particular estates, followed by the vested remainders, which have already occupied our attention. A contingent remainder — a remainder not vested, and which never might vest, — was long regarded as illegal. Down to the reign of Henry VI. not one instance is to be found of a contingent remainder being held valid. The early authorities on the contrary are rather opposed to such a conclusion. And, at a later period, the authority of Littleton is express, that every remainder, which beginneth by a deed, must be *in* him to whom it is limited, before livery of seisin is made to him who is to have the immediate freehold. It appears, however, to have been adjudged, in the reign of Henry VI, that if land be given to a man for his life, with remainder to the right heirs of another *who is living*, and who afterwards dies, and then the tenant for life dies, the heir of the stranger shall have this land; and yet it was said that, at the time of the grant, the remainder was in a manner void. This decision ultimately prevailed. And the same case is accordingly put by Perkins, who lays it down, that if land be leased to A. for life, the remainder to the right heirs of J. S., who is alive at the time of the lease, this remainder is good, because there is one named in the lease (namely, A. the lessee for life), who may take immediately in the beginning of the lease. This appears to have been the first instance in which a contingent remainder was allowed. In this case J. S. takes no estate at all; A. has a life interest: and, so long as J. S. is living, the remainder in fee does not vest in any person under the gift; for, the maxim is *nemo est hœres viventis*, and J. S. being alive, there is no such person living as his heir. Here, accordingly, is a future estate, which will have no existence until the decease of J. S.; if however J. S. should die in the lifetime of A., and if he should leave an heir, such heir will then acquire a vested remainder in fee simple, expectant on A.'s life interest. But, until these contingencies happen or fail, the limitation to the right heirs of J. S. confers no present estate on any one, but merely gives rise to the prospect of a future estate, and creates an interest of that kind which is known as a *contingent remainder*.

The gift to the *heirs* of J. S. has been determined to be sufficient to confer an estate in fee simple on the person who may be his heir, without any additional limitation to the heirs of such heir. If, however the gift be made after the 31st of December, 1833, or by the will of a testator who shall have died after that day, the land will descend, on the decease of the heir intestate, not to *his* heir, but to the next heir of J. S., in the same manner as if J. S. had been first entitled to the estate.

When contingent remainders began to be allowed, a question arose, which is yet scarcely settled, what becomes of the inheritance, in such a case as this, during the life of J. S.? A., the tenant for life, has but a life interest; J. S. has nothing, and his heir is not yet in existence. The ancient doctrine, that the remainder must vest at once or not at all, had been broken in upon; but the judges could not make up their minds also to infringe on the corresponding rule, that the fee simple must, on every feoffment which confers an estate in fee, at once depart out of the feoffor. They, therefore, sagely reconciled the rule which they left standing to the contingent remainders which they had determined to introduce, by affirming that, during the contingency, the inheritance was either in abeyance, or *in gremio legis* or else *in nubibus*. Modern lawyers, however, venture to assert, that what the grantor has not disposed of must remain in him, and cannot pass from him until there exists some grantee to receive it. And when the gift is by way of use under the Statute of Uses, there is no doubt that, until the contingency occurs, the use, and with it the inheritance, result to the grantor. So, in the case of a will, the inheritance, until the contingency happens, descends to the heir of the testator.

But whatever difficulties may have beset the departure from ancient rules, the necessities of society required that future estates, to vest in unborn or unascertained persons, should under certain circumstances be allowed. And, in the time of Lord Coke, the validity of a gift in remainder, to become vested on some future contingency, was well established. Since his day the doctrine of contingent remainders has gradually become settled; so that, notwithstanding the uncertainty still remaining with regard to one or two points, the whole system now presents a beautiful specimen of an endless variety of complex cases, all reducible to a few plain and simple principles. To this desirable end the masterly treatise of Mr. Fearne on this subject has mainly contributed.

Let us now obtain an accurate notion of what a contingent remainder is, and, afterwards, consider the rules which are required to be observed in its creation. We have already said, that a contingent remainder is a future estate. As distinguished from an executory interest, to be hereafter spoken of, it is a future estate, which waits for and depends on the determination of the estates which precede it. But, as distinguished from a vested remainder, it is an estate in remainder, which is *not* ready, from its commencement to its end, to come into possession at any moment when the prior estates may happen to determine. For, if any contingent remainder should, at any time, become thus ready to come into immediate possession, whenever the prior estates may determine, it will then be contingent no longer, but will at once become a vested remainder. For example, suppose that a gift be made to A., a bachelor, for his life, and after the determination of that estate, by forfeiture or otherwise in his lifetime, to B. and his heirs during the life of A., and after the decease of A., to the eldest son of A. and the heirs of the body of such son. Here we have two remainders, one of which is vested, and the other contingent. The estate of B. is vested. Why? Because, though it he but a small estate, yet it is ready from the first, and, so long as it lasts, continues ready to come into possession, whenever A.'s estate may happen to determine. There may be very little doubt but that A. will commit no forfeiture, but will hold the estate as long as he lives. But, if his estate should determine the moment after the grant, or at any time *whilst B.'s estate lasts*, there is B. quite ready to take possession. B.'s estate, therefore, is vested. But the estate tail to the eldest son of A. is plainly contingent. For A., being a bachelor, has no son; and, if he should die without one, the estate tail in remainder will *not* be ready to come into possession immediately on the determination of the particular estates of A. and B. Indeed, in this case, there will be no estate tail at all. But if A. should marry and have a son, the estate tail will at once become a vested remainder; for, so long as it lasts, that is, so long as the son or any of the son's issue may live, the estate tail is ready to come into immediate possession whenever the prior estates may determine, whether by A.'s death, or by B.'s forfeiture, supposing him to have got possession. It will be observed that here there is an estate, which, at the time of the grant, is future in interest, as well as in possession; and till the son is born, or rather till he comes of age, the lands are tied up, and placed beyond the power of complete alienation. This example of a contingent remainder is here given as by far the most usual, being that which occurs every day in the settlement of landed estates.

The rules which are required for the creation of a contingent remainder may be reduced to two; of which the first and principal is well established; but the latter has occasioned a good deal of controversy. The first of these rules is, that the seisin, or feudal possession, must never be without an owner; and this rule is sometimes expressed as follows, that every contingent remainder of an estate of freehold must, have a particular estate of freehold to support it. The ancient law regarded the feudal possession of lands as a matter the transfer of which ought to be notorious; and it accordingly forbad the conveyance of any estate of freehold by any other means than an immediate delivery of the seisin, accompanied by words, either written or openly spoken, by which the owner of the feudal possession might at any time thereafter be known to all the neighbourhood. If, on the occasion of any feoffment, such feudal possession was not at once parted with, it remained for ever with the grantor. Thus a feoffment, or any other conveyance of a freehold, made to-day to A., to hold from to-morrow, would be absolutely void, as involving a contradiction. For if A. is not to have the seisin till to-morrow, it must not be given him till then. So, if, on any conveyance, the feudal possession were given to accompany any estate or estates less than an estate in fee simple, the moment such estates, or the last of them, determined, such feudal possession would again revert to the grantor, in right of his old estate, and could not be again parted with by him, without a fresh conveyance of the freehold. Accordingly, suppose a feoffment to be made to A. for his life, and after his decease and one day, to B. and his heirs. Here, the moment that A.'s estate determines by his death, the feudal possession, which is not to belong to B. till one day afterwards, reverts to the feoffor, and cannot be taken out of him without a new feoffment. The consequence is, that the gift of the future estate, intended to be made to B., is absolutely void. Had it been held good, the feudal possession would have been for one day without any owner; or, in other words, there would have been a so-called remainder of an estate of freehold, without a particular estate of freehold to support it. Let us now take the case we have before referred to, of an estate to A., a bachelor, for his life, and after his decease to his eldest son in tail. In this case it is evident, that the moment A.'s estate determines by his death, his son, if living, must necessarily be ready at once to take the feudal possession, in respect of his estate tail. The only case in which the feudal possession could, under such a limitation, ever be without an owner, at the time of A.'s decease, would be that of the mother being then *enceinte* of the son. In such a case the feudal possession would be evidently without an owner, until the birth of the son; and such posthumous son would accordingly lose his estate, were it not for a special provision which has been made in his favour. In the reign of William III. an act of parliament was passed, to enable posthumous children to take estates, as if born in their father's lifetime. And the law now considers every child *en ventre sa mere* as actually born, for the purpose of taking any benefit to which, if born, it would be entitled.

As a corollary to the rule above laid down, arises another proposition, frequently itself laid down as a distinct rule, namely, that every contingent remainder must vest, or become an actual estate, during the continuance of the particular estate which supports it, or *eo instanti* that such particular estate determines; otherwise such contingent remainder will fail altogether, and can never become an actual estate at all. Thus, suppose lands to be given to A. for his life, and after his decease to such son of A. as shall first attain the age of twenty-four years. As a contingent remainder the estate to the son is well created; for the feudal seisin is not necessarily left without an owner after A.'s decease. If, therefore, A. should, at his decease, have a son who should then be twenty-four years of age or more, such son will at once take the feudal possession by reason of the estate in remainder which vested in him the moment he attained that age. In this case the contingent remainder has vested during the continuance of the particular estate. But if there should be no son, or if the son should not have attained the prescribed age at his father's death, the remainder will fail altogether. For the feudal possession will then, immediately on the father's decease, revert, for want of another owner, to the person who made the gift in right of his reversion. And, having once reverted, it cannot now belong to the son, without the grant to him of some fresh estate by means of some other conveyance. An exception to this rule has now been made by the act to amend the law as to contingent remainders. This act provides that every contingent remainder created by any instrument executed after the passing of the act, or by any will or codicil revived or republished by any will or codicil executed after that date, in tenements or hereditaments of any tenure, which would have been valid as a springing or shifting use or executory devise or other limitation, had it not had a sufficient estate to support it as a contingent remainder, shall, in the event of the particular estate determining before the contingent remainder vests, be capable of taking effect in all respects as if the contingent remainder had originally been created as a springing or shifting use or executory devise or other executory limitation. It will be found in the next chapter, which treats of an executory interest, that there are some future limitations, which are valid by way of springing or shifting use in a deed or executory devise in a will, without being preceded by any particular estate of freehold. This subject will accordingly be resumed in the next chapter.

A contingent remainder cannot be made to vest on any event which is illegal, or *contra bonos mores*. Accordingly, no such remainder can be given to a child who may be hereafter born out of wedlock. But this can scarcely be said to be a rule for the creation of contingent remainders. It is rather a part of the general policy of the law in its discouragement of vice. In the reports of Lord Coke, however, a rule is laid down of which it may be useful to take some notice, namely, that the event on which a remainder is to depend must be a common possibility, and not a double possibility, or a possibility *on* a possibility, which the law will not allow. This rule, though professed to be founded on former precedents, is not to be found in any of the cases to which Lord Coke refers, in none of which do either of the expressions "possibility on a possibility," or "double possibility," occur. It appears to owe its origin to the mischievous scholastic logic which was then rife in our courts of law, and of which Lord Coke had so high an opinion that he deemed a knowledge of it necessary to a complete lawyer. The doctrine is indeed expressly introduced on the authority of logic: — "as the logician saith, '*potentia est duplex, remota et propinqua*' ". This logic, so soon afterwards demolished by Lord Bacon, appears to have left behind it many traces of its existence in our law; and perhaps it would be found that some of those artificial and technical rules which have most annoyed the judges of modern times owe their origin to this antiquated system of endless distinctions without solid differences. To show how little of practical benefit could ever be derived from the distinction between a common and a double possibility, let us take one of Lord Coke's examples of each. He tells us that the chance that a man and a woman, both married *to different persons*, shall themselves marry one another, is but a common possibility. But the chance that a married man shall have a son named Geoffrey is stated to be a double or remote possibility. Whereas it is evident that the latter event is at least quite as likely to happen as the former. And if the son were to get an estate from being named Geoffrey, as in the case put, there can be very little doubt but that Geoffrey would be the name given to the first son who might be born. Respect to the memory of Lord Coke has long kept on foot in our law books the rule that a possibility on a possibility is not allowed by law in the creation of contingent remainders. But the authority of this rule has long been declining, and a very learned judge, now deceased, declared plainly that it was abolished.

But although the doctrine of Lord Coke, that there can be no possibility on a possibility, has ceased to govern the creation of contingent remainders, there is yet a rule by which these remainders are restrained within due bounds, and prevented from keeping the lands, which are subject to them, for too long a period beyond the reach of alienation. This rule is the second rule, to which we have referred, and is as follows: — that an estate cannot be given to an unborn person for life, *followed by any estate to any child of such unborn person*; for in such a case the estate given to the child of the unborn person is void. This rule is apparently derived from the old doctrine which prohibited double possibilities. It may not be sufficient to restrain every kind of settlement which ingenuity might suggest; but it is directly opposed to the great motive which usually induces attempts at a perpetuity, namely, the desire of keeping an estate in the same family; and it has accordingly been hitherto found sufficient. An attempt has been made, with much ability, to explain away this rule as merely an instance of the rule by which, as we shall hereafter see, executory interests are restrained. But this rule is more stringent than that which confines executory interests; and if there were no other restraint on the creation of contingent remainders than the rule by which executory interests are confined, landed property might in many cases be tied up for at least a generation further than is now possible.

The opinion which so generally prevails, that every man may make what disposition he pleases of his own estate, — an opinion countenanced by the loose description sometimes given by lawyers on an estate in fee simple, — has not unfrequently given rise to attempts made by testators to settle their property on future generations beyond the bounds allowed by law; thus lands have been given by will to the unborn son of some living person for his life, and after the decease of such unborn son, to *his* sons in tail. This last limitation to the sons of the unborn son in tail, we have observed, is void. The courts of law, however, have been so indulgent to the ignorance of testators, that, in the case of a will, they have endeavoured to carry the intention of the testator into effect, *as nearly as can possibly be done*, without infringing the rule of law; they, accordingly, take the liberty of altering his will to what they presume he would have done had he been acquainted with the rule which prohibits the son of any unborn son from being, in such circumstances, the object of a gift. This, in French Law, is called the *cy pres* doctrine. From what has already been said, it will be apparent that the utmost that can be legally accomplished towards securing an estate in a family is to give to the unborn sons of a living person estates in tail: such estates, if not barred, will descend on the next generation; but the risk of the entails being barred cannot, by any means, be prevented. The courts, therefore, when they meet with such a disposition as above described, instead of confining the unborn son of the living person to the mere life estate given him by the terms of the will, and annulling the subsequent limitations to his offspring, give to such son an estate in tail, so as to afford to his issue a chance of inheriting should the entail remain unbarred. But this doctrine, being rather a stretch of judicial authority, is only applied where the estates given by the will to the children of the unborn child are estates in tail, and not where they are estates for life, or in fee simple. If, however, the estates be in tail, the rule equally applies, whether the estates tail be given to the sons successively according to seniority, or to all the children equally as tenants in common.

Though a contingent remainder is an estate which, if it arise, must arise at a future time, and will then belong to some future owner, yet the contingency may be of such a kind, that the future expectant owner may either in possession or in interest, till A.'s be now living. For instance, suppose that a conveyance be made to A. for his life, and if C. be living at his decease, then to B. and his heirs. Here is a contingent remainder, of which the future expectant owner, B., may be now living. The estate of B. is not a present vested estate, kept out of possession only by A.'s prior right thereto. But it is a future estate not to commence, either in possession or in interest, till A.'s decease. It is not such an estate as, according to our definition of a vested remainder, is always ready to come into possession whenever A.'s estate may end; for, if A. should die after C., B. or his heirs can take nothing. Still B., though he has no estate during A.'s life, has yet plainly a chance of obtaining one, in case C. should survive. This chance in law is called a *possibility*; and a possibility of this kind was long looked upon in much the same light as a condition of re-entry was regarded, having been inalienable at law, and not to be conveyed to another by deed of grant. A fine alone, before fines were abolished, could effectually have barred a contingent remainder. It might, however, have been released; that is to say, B. might, by deed of release, have given up his interest for the benefit of the reversioner, in the same manner as if the contingent remainder to him and his heirs had never been limited; for the law, whilst it tolerated conditions of re-entry and contingent remainders, always gladly permitted such rights to be got rid of by release, for the sake of preserving unimpaired such vested estates as might happen to be subsisting. A contingent remainder was also devisable by will under the old statutes, and is so under the present act for the amendment of the laws with respect to wills. And it was the rule in equity, that an assignment intended to be made of a possibility for a valuable consideration should be decreed to be carried into effect. But the act to amend the law real of real property now enacts, that a contingent interest, and a possibility coupled with an interest, in any tenements or hereditaments of any tenure, whether the object of the gift or limitation of such interest or possibility be or be not ascertained, may be disposed of by deed. But every such disposition, if made by a married woman, must be made conformably to the provisions of the act for the abolition of fines and recoveries.

The circumstance of a contingent remainder having been so long inalienable at law was a curious relict of the ancient feudal system. This system, the fountain of our jurisprudence as to landed property, was strongly opposed to alienation. Its policy was to unite the lord and tenant by ties of mutual interest and affection; and nothing could so effectually defeat this end as a constant change in the parties sustaining that relation. The proper method, therefore, of explaining our laws, is not to set out with the notion that every subject of property may be aliened at pleasure; and then to endeavour to explain why certain kinds of property cannot be aliened, or can be aliened only in some modified manner. The law itself began in another way. When, and in what manner, different kinds of property gradually became subject to different modes of alienation is the matter to be explained; and this explanation we have endeavoured, in proceeding, as far as possible to give. But, as to such interests as remained inalienable, the reason of their being so was, that they had not been altered, but remained as they were. The statute of *Quia emptores* expressly permitted the alienation of lands and tenements, — an alienation which usage had already authorized; and ever since this statute, the ownership of an *estate* in lands (an estate tail excepted) has involved in it an undoubted power of conferring on another person the same, or, perhaps more strictly, a similar estate. But a contingent remainder is no estate, it is merely a chance of having one; and the reason why it so long remained inalienable at law was simply because it had never been thought worth while to make it alienable.

One of the most remarkable incidents of a contingent remaindor was its liability to destruction, by the sudden determination of the particular estate upon which it depended. This liability has now been removed by the act to amend the law of real property: it was, in effect, no more than a strict application of the general rule, required to be observed in the creation of contingent remainders, that the freehold must never be left without an owner. For if, after the determination of the particular estate, the contingent remainder might still, at some future time, have become a vested estate, the freehold would, until such time, have remained undisposed of, contrary to the principles of the law before explained. Thus, suppose lands to have been given to A., a bachelor, for his life, and after his decease to his eldest son and the heirs of his body, and, in default of such issue, to B. and his heirs. In this case A. would have had a vested estate for his life in possession. There would have been a contingent remainder in tail to his eldest son, which would have become a vested estate tail in such son the moment he was born, or rather begotten; and B. would have had a vested estate in fee simple in remainder. Now suppose that, before A. had any son, the particular estate for life belonging to A., which supported the contingent remainder to his eldest son, should suddenly have determined during A.'s life, B.'s estate would then have become an estate in fee simple in possession. There must be some owner of the freehold; and B., being next entitled, would have taken possession. When his estate once became an estate in possession, the prior remainder to the eldest son of A. was for ever excluded. For, by the terms of the gift, if the estate of the eldest son was to come into possession at all, it must have come in before the estate of B. A forfeiture by A. of his life estate, before the birth of a son, would therefore at once have destroyed the contingent remainder by letting into possession the subsequent estate of B..

The determination of the estate of A. was, however, in order to effect the destruction of the contingent remainder, required to be such a determination as would put an end to his right to the freehold or feudal possession. Thus, if A. had been forcibly ejected from the lands, his right of entry would still have been sufficient to preserve the contingent remainder; and, if he should have died whilst so out of possession, the contingent remainder might still have taken effect. For, so long as A.'s feudal possession, or his right thereto, continues, so long, in the eye of the law, does his estate last.

It is a rule of law, that "whenever a greater estate and a less coincide and meet in one and the same person, without any intermediate estate, the less is immediately annihilated; or, in the law phrase, is said to be merged, that is, sunk or drowned in the greater". From the operation of this rule, an estate tail is preserved by the effect of the statute *De donis*. Thus, the same person may have, at the same time, an estate tail, and also the immediate remainder or reversion in fee simple expectant on the determination of such estate tail by failure of his own issue. But with regard to other estates, the larger will swallow up the smaller; and the intervention of a contingent remainder which, while contingent, is not an estate, will not prevent the application of the rule. Accordingly, if in the case above given A. should have purchased B.'s remainder in fee, and should have obtained a conveyance of it to himself, before the birth of a son, the contingent remainder to his son would have been destroyed. For, in such a case, A. would have had an estate for his own life, and also, by his purchase, an immediate vested estate in fee simple in remainder expectant on his own decease; there being, therefore, no vested estate intervening, a merger would have taken place of the life estate in the remainder in fee. The possession of the estate in fee simple would have been accelerated and would have immediately taken place, and thus a destruction would have been effected of the contingent remainder, which could never afterwards have become a vested estate; for, were it to have become vested, it must have taken possession subsequently to the remainder in fee simple; but this it could not do, both by the terms of the gift, and also by the very nature of a remainder in fee simple, which can never have a remainder after it. In the same manner the sale by A. to B. of the life estate of A., called in law a *surrender* of the life estate, before the birth of a son, would nave accelerated the possession of the remainder in fee simple, by giving to B. an uninterrupted estate in fee simple in possession; and the contingent remainder would consequently have been destroyed. The same effect would have been produced by A. and B. both conveying their estates to a third person, C., before the birth of a son of A. The only estates then existing in the land would have been the life estate of A. and the remainder in fee of B. C., therefore, by acquiring both these estates, would have obtained an estate in fee simple in possession, on which no remainder could depend. But now, the act to amend the law of real property has altered the law in all these cases; for, whilst the principles of law on which they proceeded have not been expressly abolished, it is nevertheless enacted, that a contingent remainder shall be, and if created before the passing of the act shall be deemed to have been, capable of taking effect, notwithstanding the determination by forfeiture, surrender or merger of any preceding estate of freehold, in the same manner in all respects as if such determination had not happened. This act, it will be observed, applies only to the three cases of forfeiture, surrender or merger of the particular estate. If, at the time when the particular estate would naturally have expired, the contingent remainder be not ready to come into immediate possession, it will still fail as before, except in the cases provided for by the recent act to amend the law as to contingent remainders.

The disastrous consequences which would have resulted from the destruction of the contingent remainder, in such a case as that we have just given, were obviated in practice by means of the interposition of a vested estate between the estates of A. and B. We have seen that an estate for the life of A., to take effect in possession after the determination, by forfeiture or otherwise, of A.'s life interest, is not a contingent, but a vested estate in remainder. It is a present existing estate, always ready, so long as it lasts, to come into possession the moment the prior estate determines. The plan, therefore, adopted for the preservation of contingent remainders to the children of a tenant for life was to give an estate, after the determination by any means of the tenant's life interest, to certain persons and their heirs during his life, as trustees for preserving the contingent remainders; for which purpose they were to enter on the premises, should occasion require; but should such entry be necessary, they were nevertheless to permit the tenant for life to receive the rents and profits during the rest of his life. These trustees were prevented by the Court of Chancery from parting with their estate, or in any way aiding the destruction of the contingent remainders which their estate supported. And, so long as their estate continued, it is evident that there existed, prior to the birth of any son, three vested estates in the land; namely, the estate of A. the tenant for life, the estate in remainder of the trustees during his life, and the estate in fee simple in remainder, belonging, in the case we have supposed, to B. and his heirs. This vested estate of the trustees, interposed between the estates of A. and B., prevented their union, and consequently prevented the remainder in fee simple from ever coming into possession, so long as the estate of the trustees endured, that is, if they were faithful to their trust, so long as A. lived.

Provision was thus made for the keeping up of the feudal possession until a son was born to take it; and the destruction of the contingent remainder in his favour was accordingly prevented. But now that contingent remainders can no longer be destroyed, of course there will be no occasion for trustees to preserve them.

The following extract from a modern settlement, of a date previous to the act to amend the law of real property, will explain the plan which used to be adopted. The lands were conveyed to the trustees and their heirs, to the uses declared by the settlement; by which conveyance the trustees took no permanent estate at all, as has been explained in the Chapter on Uses and Trusts, but the seisin was at once transferred to those to whose use estates were limited. Some of these estates were as follows: — "To the use of the said A. and his assigns for and during the term of his natural life without impeachment of waste and from and immediately after the determination of that estate by forfeiture or otherwise in the lifetime of the said A. To the use of the said *(trustees)* their heirs and assigns during the life of the said A. In trust to preserve the contingent uses and estates hereinafter limited from being defeated or destroyed and for that purpose to make entries and bring actions as occasion may require. But nevertheless to permit the said A. and his assigns to receive the rents issues and profits of the said lands hereditaments and premises during his life And from and immediately after the decease of the said A. To the use of the first son of the said A. and of the heirs of the body of such first son lawfully issuing and in default of such issue. To the use of the second third fourth fifth and all and every other son and sons of the said A. severally successively and in remainder one after another as they shall be in seniority of age and priority of birth and of the several and respective heirs of the body and bodies of all and every such son and sons lawfully issuing the elder of such sons and the heirs of his body issuing being always to be preferred to and to take before the younger of such sons and the heirs of his and their body and respective bodies issuing. And in default of such issue" &c. Then follow the other remainders.

In a former part of this volume we have spoken of equitable or trust estates. In these cases, the whole estate at law belongs to trustees, who are accountable in equity to their *cestuis que trust*, the beneficial owners. As equity follows the law in the limitation of its estates, so it permits an equitable or trust estate to be disposed of by way of particular estate and remainder, in the same manner as an estate at law. Contingent remainders may also be limited of trust estates. But between such contingent remainders, and contingent remainders of estates at law, there was always this difference, that whilst the latter were destructible, the former were not. The destruction of a contingent remainder of an estate at law depended, as we have seen, on the ancient feudal rule, which required a continuous and ascertained possession of every piece of land to be vested in some freeholder. But in the case of trust estates, the feudal possession remains with the trustee. And, as the destruction of contingent remainders at law defeated, when it happened, the intention of those who created them, equity did not so far follow the law as to introduce into its system a similar destruction of contingent remainders of trust estates. It rather compelled the trustees continually to observe the intention of those whose wishes they had undertaken to execute. Accordingly, if a conveyance had been made unto *and to the use of* A. and his heirs, in trust for B. for life, and after his decease in trust for his first and other sons successively in tail, — here the whole legal estate would have been vested in A., and no act that B. could have done, nor any event which might have happened to his equitable estate, before its natural termination, could have destroyed the contingent remainder directed to be held by A. or his heirs in trust for the eldest son.

It may be proper to mention in this place, that an act has been passed for granting duties on succession to property on the death of any person dying after the 19th of May, 1853, the time appointed for the commencement of the act. These duties are as follows: — where the successor is the lineal issue or lineal ancestor of the predecessor, the duty is at the rate of one per cent. on the value of the succession; if a brother or sister, or a descendant of a brother or sister, three per cent.; if a brother or sister of the father or mother, or a descendant of such a brother or sister, five per cent.; if a brother or sister of the grandfather or grandmother of the predecessor, or a descendant of such a brother or sister, six per cent.; and if the successor shall be in any other degree of collateral consanguinity to the predecessor, or shall be a stranger in blood to him, the duty is ten per cent.. Every past or future disposition of property, by reason whereof any person has or shall become beneficially entitled to any property or the income thereof upon the death of any person dying after the 19th of May, 1853, either immediately or after any interval, either certainly or contingently, and either originally or by way of substitutive limitation, and every devolution by law of any beneficial interest in property, or the income thereof, upon the death of any person dying after that day, to any other person in possession or expectancy, is deemed to have conferred, or to confer, on the person entitled by reason of any such disposition or devolution "a succession;" and the term "successor" denotes the person so entitled; and the term "predecessor" denotes the settlor, testator, obligor, ancestor, or other person from whom the interest of the successor is or shall be derived. The interest, however, of a successor to real property is considered to be of the value of an annuity equal to the annual value of such property during his life, or for any less period during which he may be entitled; and every such annuity is to be valued, for the purposes of the act, according to tables set forth in the schedule to the act; and the duty is to be paid by eight equal half-yearly instalments, the first to be paid at the end of twelve months after the successor shall have become entitled to the beneficial enjoyment of the property; and the seven following instalments are to be paid at half-yearly intervals of six months each, to be computed from the day on which the first instalment shall have become due. But if the successor shall die before all such instalments shall have become due, then any instalments not due at his decease shall cease to be payable; except in the case of a successor who shall have been competent to dispose by will of a continuing interest in such property, in which case the instalments unpaid at his death shall be a continuing charge on such interest in exoneration of his other property, and shall be payable by the owner for the time being of such interest.

CHAPTER III
OF AN EXECUTORY INTEREST

Contingent remainders are future estates, which, as we have seen, were, until recently, continually liable, in law, until they actually existed *as estates*, to be destroyed altogether, — executory interests, on the other hand, are future estates, which in their nature are indestructible. They arise, when their time comes, as of their own inherent strength; they depend not for protection on any prior estates, but on the contrary, they themselves often put an end to any prior estates which may be subsisting. Let us consider, first, the means by which these future estates may be created; and secondly, the time fixed by the law, within which they must arise, and beyond which they cannot be made to commence.

Section I
Of the Means by which Executory Interests may be created

1. Executory interests may now be created in two ways — under the Statute of Uses, and by will.

Executory interests created under the Statute of Uses are called *springing or shifting uses*. We have seen that, previously to the passing of this statute, the *use* of land was under the sole jurisdiction of the Court of Chancery as trusts are now. In the exercise of this jurisdiction it would seem that the Court of Chancery, rather than disappoint the intentions of parties, gave validity to such interests of a future or executory nature, as were occasionally created in the disposition of the use. For instance, if a feoffment had been made to A. and his heirs, to the use of B. and his heirs from to-morrow, the Court would, it seems, have enforced the use in favour of B., notwithstanding that, by the rules of law, the estate of B. would have been void. Here we have an instance of an executory interest in the shape of a springing use, giving to B. a future estate arising on the morrow of its own strength, depending on no prior estate, and therefore not liable to be destroyed by its prop falling. When the Statute of Uses was passed, the Jurisdiction of the Court of Chancery over uses was at once annihilated. But uses in becoming, by virtue of the statute, estates at law, brought with them into the courts of law many of the attributes, which they had before possessed while subjects of the Court of Chancery. Amongst others which remained untouched, was this capability of being disposed of in such a way as to create executory interests. The legal seisin or possession of lands became then, for the first time, disposable without the observance of the formalities previously required;

and, amongst the dispositions allowed, were these executory interests, in which the legal seisin is shifted about from one person to another, at the mercy of the springing uses, to which the seisin has been indissolubly united by the act of parliament; accordingly it now happens that, by means of uses, the legal seisin or possession of lands may be shifted from one person to another in an endless variety of ways. We have seen, that a conveyance to B. and his heirs to hold from to-morrow, is absolutely void. But by means of shifting uses, the desired result may be accomplished; for, an estate may be conveyed to A. and his heirs, to the use of the conveying party and his heirs until to-morrow, and then to the use of B. and his heirs. A very common instance of such a shifting use occurs in an ordinary marriage settlement of lands. Supposing A. to be the settlor, the lands are then conveyed by him, by the after the settlement executed a day or two before the marriage, to the trustees (say B. and C. and their heirs) "to the use of A. and his heirs until the intended marriage shall be solemnized, and from and immediately after the solemnization thereof," to the uses agreed on; for example, to the use of D., the intended husband, and his assigns for his life, and so on. Here B. and C. take no permanent estate at all, as we have already seen. A. continues, as he was, a tenant in fee simple until the marriage; and, if the marriage should never happen, his estate in fee simple will continue with him untouched. But, the moment the marriage takes place, — without any further thought or care of the parties, the seisin or possession of the lands shifts away from A. to vest in D., the intended husband, for his life, according to the disposition made by the settlement. After the execution of the settlement, and until the marriage takes place, the interest of all the parties, except the settlor, is future, and contingent also on the event of the marriage. But the life estate of D., the intended husband, is not an interest of the kind called a contingent remainder. For, the estate which precedes it, namely, that of A., is an estate in fee simple, after which no remainder can be limited. The use to D. for his life springs up on the marriage taking place, and puts an end at once and for ever to the estate in fee simple which belonged to A. Here, then, is the destruction of one estate, and the substitution of another. The possession of A. is wrested from him by the use to D., instead of *D.'s* estate waiting till A.'s possession is over, as it must have done had it been merely a remainder. Another instance of the application of a shifting use occurs in those cases in which it is wished that any person who shall become entitled under the settlement should take the name and arms of the settlor. In such a case, the intention of the settlor is enforced by means of a shifting clause, under which, if the party for the time being entitled should refuse or neglect, within a definite time, to assume the name and bear the arms, the lands will shift away from him, and vest in the person nest entitled in remainder.

From the above examples, an idea may be formed of the shifts and devices which can now be effected in settlements of land, by means of springing and shifting uses. By means of a use, a future estate may be made to spring up with certainty at a given time. It may be thought, therefore, that contingent remainders, having until recently been destructible, would never have been made use of in modern conveyancing, but that every thing would have been made to assume the shape of an executory interest. This, however, is not the case. For, in many instances, future estates are necessarily required to wait for the regular expiration of those which precede them; and, when this is the case, no art or device can prevent such estates from being what they are, contingent remainders. The only thing that could formerly be done, was to take care for their preservation, by means of trustees for that purpose. For, the law, having been acquainted with remainders long before uses were introduced into it, will never construe any limitation to be a springing or shifting use, which by any fair interpretation, can be regarded as a remainder, whether vested or contingent.

The establishment of shifting and contingent uses occasioned great difficulties to the early lawyers, in consequence of the supposed necessity that there should, at the time of the happening of the contingency on which the use was to shift, be some person seised to the use then intended to take effect. If a conveyance were made to B. and his heirs, to the use of A. and his heirs until a marriage or other event, and afterwards to the use of C. and his heirs, it was said that the use was executed in A. and his heirs by the statute, and that as this use was co-extensive with the seisin of B., B. could have no actual seisin remaining in him. The event now happens. Who is seised to the use of C.? In answer to this question it was held that the original seisin reverts back to B., and that on the event happening he becomes seised to the use of C. And to support this doctrine it was further held that meantime a possibility of seisin, or *scintilla juris*, remained vested in B. But this doctrine, though strenuously maintained in theory, was never attended to in practice. And in modern times the opinion contended for by Lord St. Leonards was generally adopted, that in fact no scintilla whatever remained in B., but that he was, by force of the statute, immediately divested of all estate, and that the uses thenceforward took effect as legal estates according to their limitations, by relation to the original seisin momentarily vested in B.

And a final blow to the doctrine has now been given by an act of parliament, which provides that where by any instrument any hereditaments have been or shall be limited to uses, all uses thereunder, whether expressed or implied by law, and whether immediate or future, or contingent or executory, or to be declared under any power therein contained, shall take effect when and as they arise, by force of and by relation to the estate and seisin originally vested in the person seised to the uses; and the continued existence in him or elsewhere of any seisin to uses or scintilla juris shall not be deemed necessary for the support of, or to give effect to future or contingent or executory uses; nor shall any such seisin to uses or scintilla juris be deemed to be suspended, or to remain or to subsist in him or elsewhere.

One of the most convenient and useful applications of springing uses occurs in the case of *powers*, which are methods of causing a use, with its accompanying estate, to spring up at the will of any given person: — Thus, lands may be conveyed to A. and his heirs to such uses as B. shall, by any deed or by his will, appoint, and in default of and until any such appointment, to the use of 0. and his heirs, or to any other uses. These uses will accordingly confer vested estates on C., or the parties having them, subject to be divested or destroyed at any time by B.'s exercising his *power* of appointment. Here B., though not owner of the property, has yet the power, at any time, at once to dispose of it, by executing a deed; and if he should please to appoint it to the use of himself and his heirs, he is at perfect liberty so to do; or, by virtue of his power, he may dispose of it by his will. This power of appointment is evidently a privilege of great value; and it is accordingly provided by the Bankruptcy Act, 1869, that the trustee for the creditors of any person becoming bankrupt may exercise, for the benefit of his creditors, all powers (except the right of nomination to a vacant ecclesiastical benefice) which might have been exercised by the bankrupt for his own benefit at the commencement of his bankruptcy or during its continuance. If, however, in the case above mentioned, B. should not become bankrupt, and should die without having made any appointment by deed or will, C.'s estate, having escaped destruction, will no longer be in danger. In such a case a liability was until recently incurred by the estate of C. in respect of the debts of B. secured by any judgment, decree, order, or rule of any court of law or equity. These judgment debts, by an act of parliament, to which reference has before been made, were made binding on all lands over which the debtor should, at the time of the judgment, or at any time afterwards, have any disposing power, which he might, without the assent of any other person, exercise for his own benefit. Before this act was passed, nothing but an appointment by B. or his assignees, in exercise of his power, could have defeated or prejudiced the estate of C. And now, by the act to which we have before referred for amending the law relating to future judgments, no judgment entered up after the 29th of July, 1864, the date of the act, can affect any land of whatever tenure, until such land shall have been actually delivered in execution by virtue of a writ of elegit, or other lawful authority, in pursuance of such judgment.

Suppose, however, that B. should exercise his power, and appoint the lands by deed, to the use of D. and his heirs. In this case, the execution by B. of the instrument required by the power, is the event on which the use is to spring up, and to destroy the estate already existing. The moment, therefore, that B. has duly executed his power of appointment over the use, in favour of D. and his heirs, D. has an estate in fee simple in possession vested in him, by virtue of the Statute of Uses, in respect of the *use* so appointed in his favour; and the previously existing estate of C. is thenceforth completely at an end. The power of disposition exercised by B. extends, it will be observed, only to the use of the lands; and the fee simple is vested in the appointee, solely by virtue of the operation of the Statute of Uses, which always instantly annexes the legal estate to the use. If, therefore, B. were to make an appointment of the lands, in pursuance of his power, to D. and his heirs, *to the use of E. and his heirs*, D. would still have the use, which is all that B. has to dispose of; and the use to E. would be a use upon a use, which, as we have seen, *is* not executed, or made into a legal estate, by the Statute of Uses. E., therefore, would obtain no estate at law: although the Court would, in accordance with the expressed intention, consider him beneficially entitled, and would treat him as the owner of an equitable estate in fee simple, obliging D. to hold his legal estate merely as a trustee for E. and his heirs.

In the exercise of a power it is absolutely necessary that the terms of the power, and all the formalities required by it, should be strictly complied with. If the power should require a *deed* only, a *will* will not do; or, if a *will* only, then it cannot be exercised by a *deed*, or by any other act, to take effect in the lifetime of the person exercising the power. So, if the power is to be exercised by a deed attested by *two* witnesses, then a deed attested by *one* witness only will be insufficient. This strict compliance with the terms of the power was carried to a great length by the courts of law; so much so, that where a power was required to be exercised by a writing *under hand and seal attested by witnesses*, the exercise of the power was held to be invalid if the witnesses did not sign a written attestation of the signature of the deed, as well as of the sealing. The decision of this point was rather a surprise upon the profession, who had been accustomed to attest deeds by an indorsement, in the words "sealed and delivered by the within-named B. in the presence of," instead of wording the attestation, as in such a case this decision required, "*Signed*, sealed and delivered," &c. In order, therefore, to render valid the many deeds which by this decision were rendered nugatory, an act of parliament was passed by which the defect thus arising was cured, as to all deeds and instruments, intended to exercise powers which were executed prior to the 30th of July, 1814, the day of the passing of the act. But as the act had no prospective operation, the words "*signed*, sealed and delivered" were still necessary to be used in the attestation, in all cases where the power was to be exercised by writing under *hand* and *seal*, *attested by* witnesses. It is, however, now provided that a deed executed after the 13th of August, 1859 in the presence of and attested by two or more witnesses in the manner in which deeds are ordinarily executed and attested, shall, so far as respects the execution and attestation thereof, be a valid execution of a power of appointment by deed or by any instrument in writing not testamentary; notwithstanding it shall have been expressly required that a deed or instrument in writing made in exercise of such power should be executed or attested with some additional or other form of execution or attestation, or solemnity. Provided always, that this provision shall not operate to defeat any direction in the instrument creating the power that the consent of any particular person shall be necessary to a valid execution, or that any act shall be performed, in order to give validity to any appointment having no relation to the mode of executing and attesting the instrument; and nothing contained in the act is to prevent the donee of a power from executing it conformably to the power by writing, or otherwise than by an instrument executed and attested as an ordinary deed; and to any such execution of a power this provision is not to extend.

This strict construction adopted by the courts of law, in the case of instruments exercising powers, is in some degree counterbalanced by the practice which prevailed in the Court of Chancery to give relief in certain cases, when a power had been defectively exercised — a relief still afforded by the High Court of Justice, now that the Court of Chancery has been abolished. If the courts of law have gone to the very limit of strictness, for the benefit of the persons entitled in default of appointment, the Court of Chancery, on the other hand, appears to have overstepped the proper boundaries of its Jurisdiction in favour of the appointee. For, if the intended appointee be a purchaser from the person intending to exercise the power, or a creditor of such person, or his wife, or his child, or if the appointment be for a charitable purpose, — in any of these cases, equity will aid the defective execution of the power; in other words, the Court will compel the person in possession of the estate, and who was to hold it until the power was duly exercised, to give it up on an undue execution of such power. It is certainly hard that, for want of a little caution, a purchaser should lose his purchase or a creditor his security, or that a wife or child should be unprovided for; but it may well be doubted whether it be truly equitable, for their sakes, to deprive the person in possession; for the lands were originally given to him to hold until the happening of an event (the execution of the power), which, if the power be *not* duly executed, has in fact never taken place.

The above remarks equally apply to the exercise of a power by will. Formerly, every execution of a power to appoint by will was obliged to be effected by a will conformed, in the number of its witnesses and other circumstances of its execution, to the requisitions of the power. But the act for the amendment of the laws with respect to wills requires that all wills should be executed and attested in the same uniform way; and it accordingly enacts, that no appointment made by will in exercise of any power shall be valid, unless the same be executed in the manner required by the act: and that every will executed in the manner thereby required shall, so far as respects the execution and attestation thereof, be a valid execution of a power of appointment by will, notwithstanding it shall have been expressly required that a will made in exercise of such power should be executed with some additional or other form of execution or solemnity.

These powers of appointment, viewed in regard to the individuals who are to exercise them, are a species of dominion over property, quite distinct from that free right of alienation which has now become inseparably annexed to every estate, except an estate tail, to which a modified right of alienation only belongs. As alienation by means of powers of appointment is of a less ancient date than the right of alienation annexed to ownership, so it is free from some of the incumbrances by which that right is still clogged. Thus a man may exercise a power of appointment in favour of himself or of his wife; although, as we have seen, a man cannot directly convey, by virtue of his ownership, either to himself or to his wife. So we have seen that a married woman could not formerly convey her estates without a *fine*, levied by her husband and herself, in which she was separately examined; and now, no conveyance of her estates can be made without a deed, in which her husband must concur, and which must be separately acknowledged by her to be her own act and deed. But a power of appointment either by deed or will may be given to any woman; and whether given to her when married or when single, she may exercise such a power without the consent of any husband to whom she may then or thereafter be married; and the power may be exercised in favour of her husband, or of any one else. The act of parliament to which we have before referred, for enabling infants to make binding settlements on their marriage, with the sanction of the Court of Chancery, extends to property over which the infant has any power of appointment, unless it be expressly declared that the power shall not be exercised by an infant. But the act provides, that in case any appointment under a power of appointment, or any disentailing assurance, shall have been executed by any *infant tenant in tail* under the act, and such infant shall afterwards die under age, such appointment or disentailing assurance shall thereupon become absolutely void.

The power to dispose of property independently of any ownership, though established for some three centuries, is at the present day frequently unknown to those to whom such a power may belong. This ignorance has often given rise to difficulties and the disappointment of intention in consequence of the execution of powers by instruments of an informal nature, particularly by wills, too often drawn by the parties themselves. A testator would, in general terms, give all his estate or all his property; and because over some of it he had only a power of appointment, and not any actual ownership, his intention, till lately, was defeated. For such a general devise was no execution of his power of appointment, but operated only on the property that was his own. He ought to have given not only all that he had, but also all of which he had any power to dispose. The act for the amendment of the laws with respect to wills has now provided a remedy for such cases, by enacting that a general devise of the real estate of a testator shall be construed to include any real estate which he may have power to appoint in any manner he may think proper, and shall operate as an execution of such power, unless a contrary intention shall appear by the will.

A power of appointment may sometimes belong to a person concurrently with the ordinary power of alienation arising from the ownership of an estate in the lands. Thus lands may be limited to such uses as A. shall appoint, and in default of and until appointment to the use of A. and his heirs. And in such a case A. may dispose of the lands either by exercise of his power, *or* by conveyance of his estate. If he exercises his power the estate limited to him in default of appointment is thenceforth defeated and destroyed; and, on the other hand, if he conveys his estate, his power is thenceforward *extinguished*, and cannot be exercised by him in derogation of his own conveyance. So if, instead of conveying his whole estate, he should convey only a partial interest, his power would be *suspended* as to such interest, although in other respects it would remain in force; that is, he may still exercise his power, so only that he do not defeat his own grant. When the same object may be accomplished either by an exercise of the power, or by a conveyance of the estate, care should be taken to express clearly by which of the two methods the instrument employed is intended to operate. Under such circumstances it is very usual first to exercise the power, and afterwards to convey the estate by *way of further assurance only*; in which case, if the power is valid and subsisting, the subsequent conveyance is of course inoperative; but if the power should by any means have been suspended or extinguished, then the conveyance takes effect.

The doctrine of powers, together with that of vested remainders, is brought into very frequent operation by the usual form of modern purchase deeds, whenever the purchaser was married on or before the first of January, 1834, or whenever, as sometimes happens, it is wished to render unnecessary any evidence that he was not so married. We have seen that the dower of such women as were married on or before the first day of January, 1834, still remains subject to the ancient law; and the inconvenience of taking the conveyance to the purchaser jointly with a trustee, for the purpose of barring dower, has also been pointed *out*. The modern method of effecting this object, and at the same time of conferring on the purchaser full power of disposition over the land, without the concurrence of any other person, is as follows: A general power of appointment by deed is in the first place given to the purchaser, by means of which he is enabled to dispose of the lands for any estate at any time during his life. In default of and until appointment, the land is then given to the purchaser for his life, and, after the determination of his life interest by any means in his lifetime, a remainder (which, as we have seen, is vested) is limited to a trustee and his heirs during the purchaser's life. This remainder is then followed by an ultimate remainder to the heirs and assigns of the purchaser for ever, or, which is the same thing, to the purchaser, his heirs and assigns for ever. These limitations are sufficient to prevent the wife's right of dower from attaching. For the purchaser has not, at any time during his life, an estate of inheritance in possession, out of which estate only a wife can claim dower: he has during his life only a life interest, together with a remainder in fee simple expectant on his own decease. The intermediate vested estate of the trustee prevents, during the whole of the purchaser's lifetime, any union of this life estate and remainder. The limitation to the heirs of the purchaser gives him, according to the rule in Shelley's case, all the powers of disposition incident to ownership: though subject, as we have seen, to the estate intervening between the limitation to the purchaser and that to his heirs. But the estate in the trustee lasts only during the purchaser's life, and during his life may at any time be defeated by an exercise of his power. A form of these *uses to bar dower*, as they are called, will be found in the Appendix. As the estate of the husband under these uses is partly legal and partly equitable, the wife, if married after the 1st of January, 1834, will not be barred of her dower by these limitations; and if the deed is of a date previous to that day, even an express declaration contained in the deed that such was the intent of the uses will not be sufficient.

Besides these general powers of appointment, there exist also powers of a special kind. Thus the *estate* which is to arise on the exercise of the power of appointment may be of a certain limited duration and nature: of this an example frequently occurs in the power of leasing which is given to every tenant for life under a properly drawn settlement. We have seen that until recently a tenant for life, by virtue of his ownership, had no power to make any disposition of the property to take effect after his decease. He could not, therefore, grant a lease for any certain term of years, but only contingently on his living so long; and even now he must apply to the Chancery Division of the High Court, unless he claims under a settlement made on or after the 1st of November, 1856, and wishes only to make a lease not exceeding twenty-one years. But if his life estate should be limited to him in the settlement by way of *use*, as is now always done, a power may be conferred on him of leasing the land for any term of years, and under whatever restrictions may be thought advisable. On the exercise of this power, a use will arise to the tenant for the term of years, and with it an estate, for the term granted by the lease, quite independently of the continuance of the life of the tenant for life. But if the lease attempted to be granted should exceed the duration authorized by the power, or in any other respect infringe on the restrictions imposed, it would be void altogether as an exercise of the power, and might, until the passing of the act next mentioned, have been set aside by any person having the remainder or reversion, on the decease of the tenant for life. But an act of parliament of the present reign now provides, that such a lease, if made bonâ fide, and if the lessee have entered thereunder, shall be considered in equity as a contract for a grant, at the request of the lessee, of a valid lease under the power, to the like purport and effect as such invalid lease, save so far as any variation may be necessary in order to comply with the terms of the power. But in case the reversioner is able and willing, during the continuance of the lessee's possession, to confirm the lease without variation, the lessee is bound to accept a confirmation accordingly; and such confirmation may be by memorandum or note in writing, signed by the persons confirming and accepting respectively, or some other persons by them respectively thereunto lawfully authorized. And the acceptance of rent by the reversioner will be deemed a confirmation of the lease as against him, if upon or before such acceptance any receipt, memorandum or note in writing, confirming such lease, is signed by the person accepting such rent, or some other person by him thereunto lawfully authorized. There is a further provision, that where a lease, granted in the intended exercise of any such power of leasing, is invalid by reason that, at the time of the granting thereof, the person granting the same could not lawfully grant such lease, but the estate of such person in the hereditaments comprised in such lease shall have continued after the time when such or the like lease might have been granted by him in the lawful exercise of such power, then and in every such case such lease shall take effect and be as valid as if the same had been granted at such last-mentioned time; and all the provisions of the act shall apply to every such lease. This enactment is valuable in the case, which sometimes happens, of a power to grant leases in possession being attempted to be exercised by a lease to commence a few days after its date. If the lessor should live till the day appointed for the commencement of the lease, the lease, which before the act would have been invalid, is rendered valid by this enactment.

Another instance of a special power occurs in the case of the power of sale and exchange usually inserted in settlements of real estate. This power provides that it shall be lawful for the trustees of the settlement, with the consent of the tenant for life in possession under the settlement, and sometimes also at their own discretion during the minority of the tenant in possession, to sell or exchange the settled lands, and for that purpose to revoke the uses of the settlement as to the lands sold or exchanged, and to appoint such other uses in their stead as may be necessary to effectuate the transaction proposed. But it is provided that the money to arise from any such sale, or which may be received for equality of exchange, shall be laid out in the purchase of other lands; and that such lands, and also the lands which may be received in exchange, shall be settled by the trustees to the then subsisting uses of the settlement. It is further provided that, until a proper purchase can be found, the money may be invested in the funds or on mortgage, and the income paid to the person who would have been entitled to the rents, if lands had been purchased and settled. The object of this power is to keep up the settlement, and at the same time to facilitate the acquisition of lands which for any reason may be more desirable, in lieu of any of the settled lands which it may be expedient to part with. The direction to lay out the money in the purchase of other lands makes the money, even before it is laid out, real estate in the contemplation of equity; and though no land should ever be purchased, the parties entitled under the settlement will take in equity precisely the same estates in the investments of the money, as they would have taken in any lands which might have been purchased therewith. The power given to the trustees to revoke the uses of the settlement and appoint new uses, enables them, by virtue of the Statute of Uses, to give the purchaser of the settled property a valid estate in fee simple, provided only that the requisitions of the power are complied with. And a recent enactment enables the Court to relieve a bona fide purchaser under such a power, in case the tenant for life, or any other party to the transaction, shall by mistake have been allowed to receive for his own benefit a portion of the purchase-money, as the value of the timber or other articles. Previously to this statute, the Courts of Equity had not considered themselves authorized to give relief in such a case. And a more recent enactment embodies in the settlement the usual provisions, whenever it is expressly declared therein that trustees or other persons therein named or indicated shall have a power of sale either generally or in any particular event, or a power of exchange. But no sale or exchange under this act, and no purchase of hereditaments out of money received on any such sale or exchange, shall be made without the consent of the person appointed by the settlement to consent, or if no such person be appointed, then of the person entitled in possession to the receipt of the rents, if there be such a person under no disability. But this is not to be taken to require any consent where it appears from the settlement to have been intended that such sale, exchange or purchase should be made without any consent. And none of the powers of the act are to take effect or be exercisable if the settlement declares that they shall not take effect; and where there is no such declaration, then if any variations or limitations of any of such powers are contained in the settlement, the same shall be exercisable or take effect subject to such variations or limitations. Of this act it has been remarked by a great authority, that the option of declaring that the act shall not take effect "will probably be frequently acted upon, more particularly owing to the latter portion of the section; for nothing can be more difficult, not to say dangerous, than an attempt to amalgamate the powers in a settlement and the powers in the act, or to engraft the latter on the former. Where the settlement is purposely silent as to the powers conferred by the act, and the settlor approves of and chooses to rely upon them, the only inconvenience will be that the settlement itself will not inform the persons claiming under it of the powers vested in them, but it will be necessary to refer to the act for the powers conferred by it."

It was decided, in a recent case, that the ordinary power of sale and exchange contained in settlements does not authorize the trustees to sell the lands with a reservation of the minerals. In consequence of this decision, which took the profession rather by surprise, an act was passed which confirms all sales, exchanges, partitions and enfranchisements theretofore made, in intended exercise of any trust or power, of land with an exception or reservation of minerals, or of the minerals separately from the residue of the land. And it is provided that for the future every trustee and other person authorized to dispose of land by way of sale, exchange, partition or enfranchisement, may, with the sanction of the Court of Chancery, now represented by the

Chancery Division of the High Court, to be obtained on petition in a summary way, dispose of the land without the minerals, or of the minerals without the land, unless forbidden so to do by the instrument creating the trust or power.

Other kinds of special powers occur where the *persons* who are to take estates under the powers are limited to a certain class. Powers to jointure a wife, and to appoint estates amongst children, are the most usual powers of this nature. When powers are thus given in favour of particular objects, the estates which arise from the exercise of the power take effect precisely as if such estates had been inserted in the settlement by which the power was given. Each estate, as it arises under the power, takes its place in the settlement in the same manner as it would have done had it been originally limited to the appointee, without the intervention of any power; and, if it would have been invalid in the original settlement, it will be equally invalid as the offspring of the power.

It is provided, by the Succession Duty Act, 1853, that where any person shall have a general power of appointment, under any disposition of property taking effect upon the death of any person, he shall, in the event of his making any appointment thereunder, be deemed to be entitled, at the time of his exercising such power, to the property thereby appointed, as a succession derived from the donor of the power; and where any person shall have a limited power of appointment, under a disposition taking effect upon any such death, any person taking any property by the exercise of such power shall be deemed to take the same as a succession derived from the person creating the power as predecessor. But where the donee of a general power of appointment shall become chargeable with duty, in respect of the property appointed by him under such power, he shall be allowed to deduct from the duty so payable any duty he may have already paid in respect of any limited interest taken by him in such property.

Powers may, generally speaking, be destroyed or extinguished by deed of release made by the donee or owner of the power to any person having any estate of freehold in the land; "for it would be strange and unreasonable that a thing, which is created by the act of the parties, should not by their act, with their mutual consent, be dissolved again". The exceptions to this rule appear to be all reducible to the simple principle, that if the duty of the donee of the power may require him to exercise it at any future time, then he cannot extinguish it by release. By the act for the abolition of fines and recoveries, it is provided, that every married woman may, with the concurrence of her husband, by deed to be acknowledged by her as her act and deed according to the provisions of the act, release or extinguish any power which may be vested in or limited or reserved to her, in regard to any lands of any tenure, or any money subject to be invested in the purchase of lands, or in regard to any estate in any lands of any tenure, or in any such money as aforesaid, as fully and effectually as she could do if she were a feme sole. Our notice of powers must here conclude.

On a subject so vast, much must necessarily remain unsaid. The masterly treatise of Sir Edward Sugden (afterwards Lord St. Leonards), and the accurate work of Mr. Chance on Powers, will supply the student with all the further information he may require.

2. An executory interest may also be created by will. Before the passing of the Statute of Uses, wills were employed only in the devising of uses, under the protection of the Court of Chancery, except in some few cities and boroughs where the legal estate in lands might be devised by special custom. In giving effect to these customary devises, the courts, in very early times, showed great indulgence to testators; and perhaps the first instance of the creation of an executory interest occurred in directions given by testators, that their executors should sell their tenements. Such directions were allowed by law in customary devises; and in such cases it is evident that the sale by the executors operated as the execution of a power to dispose of that in which they themselves had no kind of ownership. For executors, as such, have nothing to do with freeholds. Here, therefore, was a future estate or executory interest created; the fee simple was shifted away from the heir of the testator, to whom it had descended, and became vested in the purchaser, on the event of the sale of the tenement to him. The Court of Chancery also, in permitting the devise of the *use* of such lands as were not themselves devisable, allowed of the creation of executory interests by will, as well as in transactions between living persons. And in particular directions given by persons having others seised of lands to their use, that such lands should be sold by their execu-

tors, were not only permitted by the Court of Chancery, but were also recognized by the legislature. For, by a statute of the reign of Henry VIII. of a date previous to the Statute of Uses, it is provided, that in such cases, where part of the executors refuse to take the administration of the will, and the residue accept the charge of the same will, then all bargains and sales of the lands so willed to be sold by the executors, made by him or them only of the said executors that so doth accept the charge of the will, shall be as effectual as if all the residue of the executors, so refusing, had joined with him or them in the making of the bargain and sale.

But, as we have seen, the passing of the Statute of Uses abolished for a time all wills of uses, until the Statute of Wills restored them. When wills were restored, the uses, of which they had been accustomed to dispose, had been all turned into estates at law; and such estates then generally came, for the first time, within the operation of testamentary instruments. Under these circumstances, the Courts of law, in interpreting wills, adopted the same lenient construction which had formerly been employed by themselves in the interpretation of customary devises, and also by the Court of Chancery in the construction of devises of the ancient use. The statute which, in the case of wills of *uses*, had given validity to sales made by the executors accepting the charge of the will, was extended, in its construction, to directions (now authorized to be made) for the sale by the executors of the *legal estate*, and also to cases where the legal estate was devised to the executors to be sold. Future estates at law were also allowed to be created by will, and were invested with the same important attribute of indestructibility which belongs to all executory interests. These future estates were called *executory devises*, and in some respects they appear to have been more favourably interpreted than shifting uses contained in deeds, though, generally speaking, their attributes are the same. To take a common instance: a man may, by his will, devise lands to his son A., an infant, and his heirs; but in case A. should die under the age of twenty-one years, then to B. and his heirs. In this case A. has an estate in fee simple in possession, subject to an executory interest in favour of B. If A. should not die under age, his estate in fee simple will continue with him unimpaired. But if he should die under that age, nothing can prevent the estate of B.

from immediately arising, and coming into possession, and displacing for ever the estate of A. and his heirs. Precisely the same effect might have been produced by a conveyance to uses. A conveyance to C. and his heirs, to the use of A. and his heirs, but in case A. should die under age, then to the use of B. and his heirs, would have effected the same result. Not so, however, a direct conveyance independently of the Statute of Uses. A conveyance directly to A. and his heirs would vest in him an estate in fee simple, after which no limitation could follow. In such a case, therefore, a direction that, if A. should die under age, the land should belong to B. and his heirs, would fail to operate on the legal seisin; and the estate in fee simple of A. would, in case of his decease under age, still descend, without any interruption, to his heir at law.

A good illustration of the difference between a contingent remainder and an executory devise occurs in the case of a devise of lands by will to A. for life, with remainder in fee to such son of B. as shall first attain the age of twenty-one years. In this case the limitation to the son of B. is either a contingent remainder or an executory devise, according as A., the tenant for life, may or may not survive the testator. If A. should survive the testator, there will be an estate of freehold subsisting in the premises, for the determination of which the limitation to the son of B. must wait, before it can take effect in possession. This limitation is, therefore, a remainder; and, as it depends on the contingency of B. having a son who may attain twenty-one, it is a contingent remainder. But if A. should die in the lifetime of the testator, the will would start, on the testator's death, with a simple limitation to such son of B. as shall first attain the age of twenty-one years. This limitation has not to wait for the determination of any prior estate of freehold; but it arises of itself on the event of a son of B. attaining the age of twenty-one years; and it displaces, when it takes effect, the estate in fee simple, which, not being otherwise disposed of, descends, immediately on the death of the testator, to his heir-at-law. It is, therefore, in this case, not a contingent remainder, but an executory devise. Under the law as it stood before the passing of the act to amend the law as to contingent remainders, if A. survived the testator, but died before any son of B. attained twenty-one, the limitation failed for want of an estate of freehold to support it: whereas if A. died in the lifetime of the testator, it was not liable to any failure. It was to remedy the hardship occasioned by the failure of such a limitation as this, when it occurred in the shape of a contingent remainder, that the act above mentioned was framed. And, as we have seen, the act provides that such a remainder as this shall, in the event of the particular estate determining before the contingent remainder vests, be capable of taking effect in all respects as if the contingent remainder had originally been created as a springing or shifting use or executory devise, or other executory limitation. The force of the words "or other executory limitation" is not very apparent.

The alienation of an executory interest, before its becoming an actually vested estate, was formerly subject to the same rules as governed the alienation of contingent remainders. But by the act to amend the law of real property, all executory interests may now be disposed of by deed. Accordingly, to take our previous example, if a man should leave lands, by his will, to A. and his heirs, but in case A. should die under age, then to B. and his heirs, — B. may by deed, during A.'s minority, dispose of his expectancy to another person, who, should A. die under age, will at once stand in the place of B. and obtain the fee simple. But before the act, this could not have been done; B. might indeed have sold his expectancy; but *after* the event (the decease of A. under age), B. must have executed a conveyance of the legal estate to the purchaser; for, until the event, B. had no *estate* to convey.

In order to facilitate the payment of debts out of real estate, it is provided, by modern acts of parliament, that when lands are by law, or by the will of their owner, liable to the payment of his debts, and are by the will vested in any person by way of executory devise, the first executory devisee, even though an infant, may convey the whole fee simple in order to carry into effect any decree for the sale or mortgage of the estate for payment of such debts. And this provision, so far as it relates to a sale, has been extended to the case of the lands having descended to the heir subject to an executory devise over in favour of a person or persons not existing or not ascertained.

Section II
Of the Time within which Executory Interests must arise

Secondly, as to the time within which an executory estate or interest must arise. It is evident that some limit must be fixed; for if an unlimited time were allowed for the creation of these future and indestructible estates, the alienation of lands might be henceforward for ever prevented by the innumerable future estates which the caprice or vanity of some owners would prompt them to create. A limit has, therefore, been fixed on for the creation of executory interests; and every executory interest which might, under any circumstances, transgress this limit, is void altogether. With regard to future estates of a destructible kind, namely, contingent remainders, we have seen that a limit to their creation is contained in the maxim, that no remainder can be given to the unborn child of a living person for his life, followed by a remainder to any of the issue of such unborn person: — the latter of such remainders being absolutely void. This maxim, it is evident, in effect, forbids the tying up of lands for a longer period than can elapse until the unborn child of some living person shall come of age; that is, for the life of a party now in being, and for twenty-one years after, — with a further period of a few months during gestation, supposing the child should be of posthumous birth. In analogy, therefore, to the restriction thus imposed on the creation of contingent remainders, the law has fixed the following limit to the creation of executory interests; — it will allow any executory estate to commence within the period of any fixed number of now existing lives, and an additional term of twenty-one years; allowing further for the period of gestation, should gestation actually exist. This additional term of twenty-one years may be independent or not of the minority of any person to be entitled; and if no lives are fixed on, then the term of twenty-one years only is allowed. But every executory estate which might, in any event, transgress this limit, will from its commencement be absolutely void. For instance, a gift to the first son of A., a living person, who shall attain the age of twenty-four years, is a void gift. For if A. were to die, leaving a son a few months old, the estate of the son would arise, under such a gift, at a time exceeding the period of twenty-one years from the expiration of the life of A., which, in this case, is the life fixed on. But a gift to the first son of A. who shall attain the age of twenty-one years will be valid, as necessarily falling within the allowed period. When a gift is infected with the vice of its possibly exceeding the prescribed limit, it is at once and altogether void both at law and in equity. And even if, in its actual event, it should fall greatly within such limit, yet it is still as absolutely void as if the event had occurred which would have taken it beyond the boundary. If, however, the executory limitation should be in defeazance of, or immediately preceded by, an estate tail, then, as the estate tail and all subsequent estates may be barred by the tenant in tail, the remoteness of the event on which the executory limitation is to arise will not affect its validity.

It will be observed that the act to amend the law as to contingent remainders applies only to a contingent remainder which would have been valid as a springing or shifting use or executory devise or other limitation, had it not had a sufficient estate to support it as a contingent remainder. A gift to the first son of B. who shall attain the age of twenty-one years is valid as a springing or shifting use or executory devise, when not preceded by an estate of freehold to turn it into a contingent remainder. But according to the rule above laid down, a gift to the first son of B. who shall attain the age of twenty-four years is void for remoteness, when not preceded by a particular estate of freehold. When so preceded it is, as we have seen, a good contingent remainder; but if the preceding estate which supports it should determine naturally before any son of B. should attain twenty-four, then this remainder will still fail, and can derive no support from the recent act.

In addition to the limit already mentioned, a further restriction has been imposed by a modern act of parliament, on attempts to accumulate the income of property for the benefit of some future owner. This act was occasioned by the extraordinary will of the late Mr. Thellusson, who directed the income of his property to be accumulated during the lives of all his children, grandchildren and great-grandchildren *who were living at the time of his death*, for the benefit of some future descendants to be living at the decease of the survivor; thus keeping strictly within the rule which allowed any number of existing lives to be taken as the period for an executory interest. To prevent the repetition of such a cruel absurdity, the act forbids the accumulation of income for any longer term than the life of the grantor or settlor, *or* twenty-one years from the death of any such grantor, settlor, devisor or testator, *or* during the minority of any person living, or in *ventre sa mère* at the death of the grantor, devisor or testator, *or* during the minority only of any person who, under the settlement or will, would for the time being, if of full age, be entitled to the income so directed to be accumulated. But the act does not extend to any provision for payment of debts, or for raising portions for children, or to any direction touching the produce of timber or wood. Any direction to accumulate income, which may exceed the period thus allowed, is valid to the extent of the time allowed by the act, but void so far as this time may be exceeded. And if the direction to accumulate should exceed the limits allowed by law for the creation of executory interests, it will be void altogether, independently of the above act.

CHAPTER IV
OF HEREDITAMENTS PURELY INCORPOREAL

We now come to the consideration of incorporeal hereditaments, usually so called, which, unlike a reversion, a remainder, or an executory interest, are ever of an incorporeal nature, and never assume a corporeal shape. Of these purely incorporeal hereditaments there are three kinds, namely, first, such as are *appendant* to corporeal hereditaments; secondly, such as are *appurtenant*; both of which kinds of incorporeal hereditaments are transferred simply by the conveyance, by whatever means, of the corporeal hereditaments to which they may belong; and, thirdly, such as are *in gross*, or exist as separate and independent subjects of property, and which are accordingly said to lie in grant, and have always required a deed for their transfer. But almost all purely incorporeal hereditaments may exist in both the above modes, being at one time appendant or appurtenant to corporeal property, and at another time separate and distinct from it.

1. Of incorporeal hereditaments which are *appendant* to such as are corporeal, the first we shall consider is a seignory or lordship. In a previous part of our work we have noticed the ori-

gin of manors. Of such of the lands belonging to a manor as the lord granted out in fee simple to his free tenants, nothing remained to him but his seignory or lordship. By the grant of an estate in fee simple, he necessarily parted with the feudal possession. Thenceforth his interest, accordingly, became incorporeal in its nature. But he had no reversion; for no reversion can remain, as we have already seen, after an estate in fee simple. The grantee, however, became his tenant, did to him fealty, and paid to him his rent-service, if any were agreed for. This simply having a free tenant in fee simple was called a seignory. To this seignory the rent and fealty were incident, and the seignory itself was attached or appendant to the manor of the lord, who had made the grant; whilst the land granted out was said to be holden of the manor. Very many grants were thus made, until the passing of the statute of *Quia emptores* put an end to these creations of tenancies in fee simple, by directing that on every such conveyance the feoffee should hold of the same chief lord as his feoffor held before. But such tenancies in fee simple as were then already subsisting were left untouched, and they still remain in all cases in which freehold lands are holden of any manor. The incidents of such a tenancy, so far as respects the tenant, have been explained in the chapter on the tenure of an estate in fee simple. The correlative rights belonging to the lord form the incidents of his seignory. The seignory, with all its incidents, is an appendage to the manor of the lord, and a conveyance of the manor simply, without mentioning its appendant seignories, will accordingly comprise the seignories, together with all rents incident to them. In ancient times it was necessary that the tenants should attorn to the feoffee of the manor, before the rents and services could effectually pass to him. For, in this respect, the owner of a seignory was in the same position as the owner of a reversion. But the same statute which abolished attornment in the one case abolished it also in the other. No attornment, therefore, is now required.

Other kinds of appendant incorporeal hereditaments are rights of *common*, such as *common of turbary*, or a right of cutting turf in another person's land; *common of piscary*, or a right of fishing in another's water; and *common of pasture*, which is the most usual, being a right of depasturing cattle on the land of another. The rights of common now usually met with are of two kinds; one where the tenants of a manor possess rights of common over the wastes of the manor, which belong to the lord of the manor, subject to such rights; and the other, where the several owners of strips of land, composing together a common field, have at certain seasons a right to put in cattle to range over the whole. The inclosure of commons, so frequent of late years, has rendered much less usual than formerly the right of common possessed by tenants of manors over the lord's wastes. These inclosures were formerly effected by private acts of parliament, obtained for the purpose of each particular inclosure, subject to the provisions of the general inclosure act, which contained general regulations applicable to all. But by an act of parliament of the present reign commissioners were appointed, styled the Inclosure Commissioners for England and Wales, under whose sanction inclosures were more readily effected, several local inclosures being comprised in one act. The same commissioners were also invested with powers for facilitating the drainage of lands. But by a recent act provision has been made for the improvement, protection and management of commons near the metropolis, by means of schemes for the purpose, to be certified by the Inclosure Commissioners and confirmed by act of parliament. And an important act has now been passed for facilitating the regulation and improvement of commons, and for amending the acts relating to the inclosure of commons. The short title of this act is "The Commons Act, 1876." This act contains provisions, not only for the inclosure of commons, but also for their regulation and improvement when uninclosed. And if any common is situate within six miles of any town having a population of not less than five thousand inhabitants, it is called a suburban common, and as such is subjected to special regulations for the benefit of the inhabitants of such town. Improved provisions have also been made for the allotment of field gardens for the poor, and of recreation grounds. The rights of common possessed by owners of land in common fields, however useful in ancient time, are now found greatly to interfere with the modern practice of husbandry; and acts have accordingly been passed to facilitate the exchange and separate inclosure of lands in such common fields. Under the provisions of these acts, each owner may now obtain a separate parcel of land, discharged from all rights of common belonging to any other person. The rights of common above spoken of, being appendant to the lands in respect of which they are exercised, belong to the lands of common right, by force of the common law alone, and not by virtue of any grant, express or implied. And any conveyance of the lands to which such rights belong will comprise such rights of common also. Another kind of appendant incorporeal hereditament is an advowson appendant to a manor. But on this head we shall reserve our observations till we speak of the now more frequent subject of conveyance, an advowson *in gross*, or an advowson unappended to any thing corporeal.

In connection with the subject of commons, it may be mentioned that strips of waste land between an inclosure and a highway, and also the soil of the highway to the middle of the road, presumptively belong to the owner of the inclosure. And a conveyance of the inclosure, even by reference to a plan which does not comprise the highway, will carry with it the soil as far as one-half the road. But if the strips of waste land communicate so closely to a common as in fact to form part of it, they will then belong to the lord of the manor, as the owner of the common. Where a public way is foundrous, as such ways frequently were in former times, the public have by the common law a right to travel over the adjoining lands, and to break through the fences for that purpose. It is said that in former times the landowners, to prevent their fences being broken and their crops spoiled when the roads were out of repair, set back their hedges, leaving strips of waste at the side of the road, along which the public might travel without going over the lands under cultivation. Hence such strips are presumed to belong to the owners of the lands adjoining. Where lands adjoin a river, the soil of one-half of the river to the middle of the stream is presumed to belong to the owner of the adjoining lands. But if it be a tidal river, the soil up to high water mark appears presumptively to belong to the Crown. The Crown is also presumptively entitled to the sea-shore up to high water mark of medium tides; although grants of parts of the sea-shore have not unfrequently been made to subjects; and such grants may be presumed by proof of long continued and uninterrupted acts of ownership. A sudden irruption of the sea gives the Crown no title to the lands thrown under water, although when the sea makes gradual encroachments, the right of the owner of the land encroached on is as gradually transferred to the Crown.

And in the same manner when the sea gradually retires, the right of the Crown is as gradually transferred to the owner of the land adjoining the coast. But a sudden dereliction of the sea does not deprive the Crown of its title to the soil.

2. Incorporeal hereditaments *appurtenant* to corporeal hereditaments are not very often met with. They consist of such incorporeal hereditaments as are not naturally and originally appendant to corporeal hereditaments, but have been annexed to them, either by some express deed of grant or by *prescription* from long enjoyment. Rights of common and rights of way or passage over the property of another person are the principal kinds of incorporeal hereditaments usually found appurtenant to lands. When thus annexed, they will pass by a conveyance of the lands to which they have been annexed, without mention of the appurtenances; although these words, "with the appurtenances," are usually inserted in conveyances, for the purpose of distinctly showing an intention to comprise such incorporeal hereditaments of this nature as may belong to the lands. But if such rights of common or of way, though usually enjoyed with the lands, should not be strictly appurtenant to them, a conveyance of the lands merely, with their appurtenances, without mentioning the rights of common or way, will not be sufficient to comprise them. It is, therefore, usual in conveyances to insert at the end of the "parcels" or description of the property a number of "general words," in which are comprised, not only all rights of way and common, &c., which may belong to the premises, but also such as may be therewith used or enjoyed.

3. Such incorporeal hereditaments as stand separate and alone are generally distinguished from those which are appendant or appurtenant, by the appellation *in gross*. Of these the first we may mention is a seignory *in gross*, which is a seignory that has been severed from the demesne lands of the manor, to which it was anciently appendant. It has now become quite unconnected with anything corporeal, and, existing as a separate subject of transfer, it must be conveyed by deed of grant.

The next kind of separate incorporeal hereditament is a rent seck, *(redditus siccus,)* a dry or barren rent, so called, because no distress could formerly be made for it. This kind of rent forms a good example of the antipathy of the ancient law to any inroad on the then prevailing system of tenures. If a landlord granted his seignory, or his reversion, the rent service, which was incident to it, passed at the same time. But if he should have attempted to convey his rent, independently of the seignory or reversion to which it was incident, the grant would have been effectual to deprive himself of the rent, but not to enable his grantee to distrain for it. It would have been a *rent seck*. Rent seck also occasionally arose from grants being made of rent charges, to be hereafter explained, without any clause of distress. But now, by an act of Geo. II. a remedy by distress is given for rent seck, in the same manner as for rent reserved upon lease.

Another important kind of separate incorporeal hereditament is a rent charge, which arises on a grant by one person to another, of an annual sum of money, payable out of certain lands in which the grantor may have any estate. The rent charge cannot, of course, continue longer than the estate of the grantor; but, supposing the grantor to be seised in fee simple, he may make a grant of a rent charge for any estate he pleases, giving to the grantee a rent charge for a term of years, or for his life, or in tail, or in fee simple. For this purpose a *deed* is absolutely necessary; for a rent charge, being a separate incorporeal hereditament, cannot, according to the general rule, be created or transferred in any other way, unless indeed it be given by will. The creation of a rent charge or annuity, for any life or lives, or for any term of years or greater estate determinable on any life or lives, was also, until recently, required, under certain circumstances, to be attended with the inrolment, in the Court of Chancery, of a memorial of certain particulars. These annuities were frequently granted by needy persons to money lenders, in consideration of the payment of a sum of money, for which the annuity or rent charge served the purpose of an exorbitant rate of interest. In order, therefore, to check these proceedings by giving them publicity, it was provided that, as to all such annuities, granted for pecuniary consideration or money's worth, (unless secured on lands of equal or greater annual value than the annuity, and of which the grantor was seised in fee simple, or fee tail in possession,) a memorial stating the date of the instrument, the names of the parties and witnesses, the persons for whose lives the annuity was granted, the person by whom the same was to be beneficially received, the pecuniary consideration for granting the same, and the annual sum to be paid, should, within thirty days after the execution of the deed, be inrolled in the Court of Chancery; otherwise the same should be null and void to all intents and purposes. But as these annuities were only granted for the sake of evading the Usury Laws, the same statute which has repealed those laws has also repealed the statutes by which memorials of such annuities were required to be inrolled. A subsequent statute, however, provides, that any annuity or rent charge granted after the 26th of April, 1855, the date of the passing of the act, otherwise than by marriage settlement or will, for a life or lives, or for any estate determinable on a life or lives, shall not affect any lands, tenements or hereditaments, as to purchasers, mortgagees, or creditors, until the particulars mentioned in the act are registered in the Court of Common Pleas, now the Common Pleas Division of the High Court, where they are entered in alphabetical order by the name of the person whose estate is intended to be affected. A search for annuities is accordingly made in this registry on every purchase of lands, in addition to the searches for judgments, crown debts, executions and lis pendens.

In settlements where rent charges are often given by way of pin-money and jointure, they are usually created under a provision for the purpose contained in the Statute of Uses. The statute directs that, where any persons shall stand seised of any lands, tenements, or hereditaments, in fee simple or otherwise, *to the use and intent* that some other person or persons shall have yearly to them and their heirs, or to them and their assigns, for term of life or years or some other special time, any annual rent, in every such case the same persons, their heirs and assigns, *that have such use* to have any such rent shall be adjudged and deemed in possession and seisin of the same rent of such estate as they had in the use of the rent; and they may destrain for non-payment of the rent in their own names. From this enactment it follows, that if a conveyance of lands be now made to A. and his heirs, — *to the use* and intent that B. and his assigns may, during his life, thereout receive a rent charge, — B. will be entitled to the rent charge, in the same manner as if a grant of the rent charge had been duly made to him by deed. The above enactment, it will be seen, is similar to the prior clause of the Statute of Uses relating to uses of estates, and is merely a carrying out of the same design, which was to render every use, then cognizable only in Chancery, an estate or interest within the jurisdiction of the courts of law. But in this case also, as well as in the former, the end of the statute has been defeated. For a conveyance of land to A. and his heirs, *to the use* that B. and his heirs may receive a rent charge, *in trust* for C. and his heirs, will now be laid hold of under the equitable doctrines of the Court of Chancery, for C.'s benefit, in the same manner as a trust of an estate in the land itself. The statute vests the *legal estate* in the rent in B.; and C. takes nothing in a court of law, because the trust for him would be a use upon a use. But C. has the entire beneficial interest; for he is possessed of the rent charge for an *equitable estate* in fee simple.

In ancient times it was necessary, on every grant of a rent charge, to give an express power to the grantee to distrain on the premises out of which the rent charge was to issue. If this power were omitted, the rent was merely a *rent seck*. Rent service, being an incident of tenure, might be distrained for by common right; but rent charges were matters the enforcement of which was left to depend solely on the agreement of the parties. But since a power of distress has been attached by parliament to rents seck, as well as to rents service, an express power of distress is not necessary for the security of a rent charge. Such a power, however, is usually granted in express terms. In addition to the clause of distress, it is also usual, as a further security, to give to the grantee a power to enter on the premises after default has been made in payment for a certain number of days, and to receive the rents and profits until all the arrears of the rent charge, together with all expenses, have been duly paid.

Incorporeal hereditaments are the subjects of estates analogous to those which may be holden in corporeal hereditaments. If therefore a rent charge should be granted for the life of the grantee, he will possess an estate for life in the rent charge. Supposing that he should alienate this life estate to another party, without mentioning in the deed of grant the heirs of such party, the law formerly held that, in the event of the decease of the second grantee in the lifetime of the former, the rent charge became extinct for the benefit of the owner of the lands out of which it issued. The former grantee was not entitled because he had parted with his estate; the second grantee was dead, and his heirs were not entitled because they were not named in the grant. Under similar circumstances, we have seen that, in the case of a grant of corporeal hereditaments, the first person that might happen to enter upon the premises after the decease of the second grantee had formerly a right to hold possession during the remainder of the life of the former. But rents and other incorporeal hereditaments are not in their nature the subjects of occupancy; they do not lie exposed to be taken possession of by the first passer-by. It was accordingly thought that the statutes, which provided a remedy in the case of lands and other corporeal hereditaments, were not applicable to the case of a rent charge, but that it became extinct as before mentioned. By a modern decision, however, the construction of these statutes was extended to this case also; and now the act for the amendment of the laws with respect to wills, by which these statutes have been repealed, permits every person to dispose by will of estates *pur autre vie*, whether there shall or shall not be any special occupant thereof, and whether the same shall be a corporeal or an incorporeal hereditament; and in case there shall be no special occupant, the estate, whether corporeal or incorporeal, shall go to the executor or administrator of the party; and coming to him, either by reason of a special occupancy, or by virtue of the act, it shall be applied and distributed in the same manner as the personal estate of the testator or intestate.

A grant of an estate tail in a rent charge scarcely ever occurs in practice. But grants of rent charges for estates in fee simple are not uncommon, especially in the towns of Liverpool and Manchester, where it is the usual practice to dispose of an estate in fee simple in lands for building purposes in consideration of a rent charge in fee simple by way of ground rent, to be granted out of the premises to the original owner. These transactions are accomplished by a conveyance from the vendor to the purchaser and his heirs, *to the use* that the vendor and his heirs may thereout receive the rent charge agreed on, and *to the further use* that, if it be not paid within so many days, the vendor and his heirs may distrain, and *to the further use* that, in case of non-payment within so many more days, the vendor and his heirs may enter and hold possession till all arrears and expenses are paid; and subject to the rent charge, and to the powers and remedies for securing payment thereof, *to the me* of the purchaser, his heirs and assigns for ever. The purchaser thus acquires an estate in fee simple in the lands, subject to a perpetual rent charge payable to the vendor, his heirs and assigns. It should, however, be carefully borne in mind, that transactions of this hind are very different from those grants of fee simple estates which were made in ancient times by lords of manors, and from which quit or chief rents have arisen. These latter rents are rents incident to tenure, and may be distrained for of common right without any express clause for the purpose. But as we have seen, since the passing of the statute of *Quia emptores* it has not been lawful for any person to create a tenure in fee simple. The modern rents of which we are now speaking, are accordingly mere rent charges, and in ancient days would have required express clauses of distress to make them secure. They were formerly considered in law as *against common right*, that is, as repugnant to the feudal policy, which encouraged such rents only as were incident to tenure. A rent charge was accordingly regarded as a thing entire and indivisible, unlike rent service, which was capable of apportionment. And from this property of a rent charge, the law, in its hostility to such charges, drew the following conclusion: that if any part of the land, out of which a rent charge issued, were released from the charge by the owner of the rent, either by an express deed of release, or virtually by his purchasing part of the land, all the rest of the land should enjoy the same benefit and be released also. If, however, any portion of the land charged should descend to the owner of the rent as heir at law, the rent would not thereby have been extinguished, as in the case of a purchase, but would have been apportioned according to the value of the land; because such portion of the land came to the owner of the rent, not by his own act, but by the course of law. But it is now provided, that the release from a rent charge of part of the hereditaments charged therewith shall not extinguish the whole rent charge, but shall operate only to bar the right to recover any part of the rent charge out of the hereditaments released; without prejudice, nevertheless, to the rights of all persons interested in the hereditaments remaining unreleased and not concurring in or confirming the release. A recent statute empowers the Inclosure Commissioners to apportion rents of every kind on the application of any persons interested in the lands and in the rent.

The Bankruptcy Act, 1870, provides for the disclaimer by the trustee for the creditors of any property that is not readily saleable, by reason of its binding the possessor thereof to the performance of any onerous act, or to the payment of any sum of money. But he cannot disclaim, if an application in writing has been made to him by any person interested in the property, requiring him to decide whether he will disclaim or not, and he has for a period of not less than twenty-eight days after the receipt of such application, or such further time as may be allowed by the Court, declined or neglected to give notice whether he disclaims the same or not.

The rent charges of which we are speaking are usually further secured by a covenant for payment, entered into by the purchaser in the deed by which they are granted. In order to exonerate the executors or administrators of such a purchaser from perpetual liability under this covenant, it is now provided that where an executor or administrator, liable as such to the rent or covenants contained in any conveyance on chief rent or rent charge, or agreement for such conveyance, granted to or made with the testator or intestate whose estate is being administered, shall have satisfied all then subsisting liabilities, and shall have set apart a sufficient fund to answer any future claim that may be made in respect of any fixed and ascertained sum agreed to be laid out on the property (although the period for laying out the same may not have arrived), and shall have conveyed the property, or assigned the agreement to a purchaser, he may distribute the residuary personal estate of the deceased without appropriating any part thereof to meet any future liability under such conveyance or agreement. But this is not to prejudice the right of the grantor or those claiming under him to follow the assets of the deceased into the hands of the persons amongst whom such assets may have been distributed.

Although rent-charges and other self-existing incorporeal hereditaments of the like nature are no favourites with the law, yet, whenever it meets with them, it applies to them, as far as possible, the same rules to which corporeal hereditaments are subject. Thus, we have seen that the estates which may be held in the one are analogous to those which exist in the other. So estates in fee simple, both in the one and in the other, may be aliened by the owner, either in his lifetime or by his will, to one person or to several as joint tenants or tenants in common, and, on his intestacy, will descend to the same heir at law. But in one respect the analogy fails. Land is essentially the subject of *ten-*

ure; it may belong to a lord, but be holden by his tenant, by whom again it may be sub-let to another; and so long as rent is rent service, a mere incident arising out of the estate of the payer, and belonging to the estate of the receiver, so long may it accompany, as accessory, its principal, the estate to which it belongs. But the receipt of a rent charge is accessory or incident to no other hereditament. True a rent charge springs from and is therefore in a manner connected with the land on which it is charged; but the receiver and owner of a rent charge has no shadow of interest beyond the annual payment, and in the abstract right to this payment his estate in the rent consists. Such an estate therefore cannot be subject to any tenure. The owner of an estate in a rent charge consequently owes no fealty to any lord, neither can he be subject, in respect of his estate, to any rent as rent service; nor, from the nature of the property, could any distress be made for such rent service if it were reserved. So, if the owner of an estate in fee simple in a rent charge should die intestate, and without leaving any heirs, his estate cannot escheat to his lord, for he has none. It will simply cease to exist, and the lands out of which it was payable will thenceforth be discharged from its payment.

Another kind of separate incorporeal hereditament which occasionally occurs is a right of common *in gross*. This is, as the name implies, a right of common over lands belonging to another person, possessed by a man, not as appendant or appurtenant to the ownership of any lands of his own, but as an independent subject of property. Such a right of common has therefore always required a deed for its transfer.

Another important kind of separate incorporeal hereditament is an advowson in gross. An advowson is a perpetual right of presentation to an ecclesiastical benefice. The owner of the advowson is termed the patron of the benefice; but, as such, he has no property or interest in the glebe or tithes, which belong to the incumbent. As patron he simply enjoys a right of nomination from time to time, as the living becomes vacant. And this right he exercises by a *presentation* to the bishop of some duly qualified clerk or clergyman, whom the bishop is accordingly bound to *institute* to the benefice, and to cause him to be *inducted* into it. When the advowson belongs to the bishop, the forms of presentation and institution are supplied by an act called *collation*. In some rare cases of advowsons *donative*, the patron's deed of donation is alone sufficient. And by the Stamp Act, 1870, every appointment, whether by way of donation, presentation or nomination, and admission, collation or institution to or licence to hold any ecclesiastical benefice, dignity or promotion, or any perpetual curacy, is subject to an ad valorem duty according to the subjoined table. Where the patron is entitled to the advowson as his private property, he is empowered by an act of parliament of the reign of George IV. to present any clerk under a previous agreement with him for his resignation in favour of any one person named, or in favour of one of two persons, each of them being by blood or marriage an uncle, son, grandson, brother, nephew, or grand-nephew of the patron, or one of the patrons beneficially entitled. One part of the instrument by which the engagement is made must be deposited within two calendar months in the office of the registrar of the diocese, and the resignation must refer to the engagement, and state the name of the person for whose benefit it is made.

Advowsons are principally of two kinds, — advowsons of rectories, and advowsons of vicarages. The history of advowsons of rectories is in many respects similar to that of rents and of rights of common. In the very early ages of our history advowsons of rectories appear to have been almost always appendant to some manor. The advowson was part of the manorial property of the lord, who built the church and endowed it with the glebe and most part of the tithes. The seignories in respect of which he received his rents were another part of his manor, and the remainder principally consisted of the demesne and waste lands, over the latter of which we have seen that his tenants enjoyed rights of common as appendant to their estates. The incorporeal part of the property, both of the lord and his tenants, was thus strictly appendant or incident to that part which was corporeal; and any conveyance of the corporeal part naturally and necessarily carried with it that part which was incorporeal, unless it were expressly excepted. But, as society advanced, this simple state of things became subject to many innovations, and in various cases the incorporeal portions of property became severed from the corporeal parts, to which they had previously belonged. Thus we have seen that the seignory of lands was occasionally severed from the corporeal part of the manor, becoming a seignory in gross. So rent was sometimes granted independently of the lordship or reversion to which it had been incident, by which means it at once became an independent incorporeal hereditament, under the name of a *rent seck*. Or a rent might have been granted to some other person than the lord, under the name of a *rent charge*. In the same way a *right of common* might have been granted to some other person than a tenant of the manor, by means of which grant a separate incorporeal hereditament would have arisen, as a *common in gross*, belonging to the grantee. In like manner there exist at the present day two kinds of advowsons of rectories; an advowson *appendant* to a manor, and an advowson *in gross*, which is a distinct subject of property, unconnected with any thing corporeal. Advowsons in gross appear to have chiefly had their origin from the severance of advowsons appendant from the manors to which they had belonged; and any advowson now appendant to a manor, may at any time be severed from it, either by a conveyance of the manor, with an express exception of the advowson, or by a grant of the advowson alone independently of the manor. And when once severed from its manor, and made an independent incorporeal hereditament, an advowson can never become appendant again. So long as an advowson is appendant to a manor, a conveyance of the manor, even by feoffment, and without mentioning the appurtenances belonging to the manor, will be sufficient to comprise the advowson. But when severed, it must be conveyed, like any other separate incorporeal hereditament, by a deed of grant.

The advowsons of rectories were not unfrequently granted by the lords of manors in ancient times to monastic houses, bishoprics and other spiritual corporations. When this was the case the spiritual patrons thus constituted considered themselves to be the most fit persons to be rectors of the parish, so far as the receipt of the tithes and other profits of the rectory was concerned; and they left the duties of the cure to be performed by some poor priest as their vicar or deputy. In order to remedy the abuses thus occasioned, it was provided by statutes of Richard II., and Henry IV., that the vicar should be sufficiently endowed wherever any rectory was thus *appropriated*. This was the origin of vicarages, the advowsons of which belonged in the first instance to the spiritual owners of the appropriate rectories as appendant to such rectories; but many of these advowsons have since, by severance from the rectories, been turned into advowsons in gross. And such advowsons of vicarages can only be conveyed by deed, like advowsons of rectories under similar circumstances.

The sale of an advowson will not include the right to the *next presentation*, unless made when the church is full; that is, before the right to present has actually arisen by the death, resignation or deprivation of the former incumbent. For the present right to present is regarded as a personal duty of too sacred a character to be bought and sold; and the sale of such a right would fall within the offence of *simony*, — *so* called from Simon Magus, — an offence which consists in the buying or selling of holy orders, or of an ecclesiastical benefice. But, before a vacancy has actually occurred, the next presentation, or right of presenting at the next vacancy, may be sold, either together with, or independently of, the future presentations of which the advowson is composed, and this is frequently done. No spiritual person, however, may sell or assign any patronage or presentation belonging to him by virtue of any dignity or spiritual office held by him, any such sale and assignment being void. And a clergyman is prohibited by a statute of Anne from procuring preferment for himself by the purchase of a next presentation; but this statute does not prevent the purchase by a clergyman of an estate in fee or even for life in an advowson, with a view of presenting himself to the living. When the next presentation is sold, independently of the rest of the advowson, it is considered as mere personal property, property, and will devolve, in ease of the decease of the purchaser before he has exercised his right, on his executors, and cannot descend to his heir at law. The advowson itself, it need scarcely be remarked, will descend, on the decease of its owner intestate, to his heir. The law attributes to it, in common with other separate incorporeal hereditaments, as nearly as possible the same incidents as appertain to the corporeal property to which it once belonged.

Tithes are another species of separate incorporeal hereditaments, also of an ecclesiastical or spiritual kind. In the early ages of our history, and indeed down to the time of Henry VIII., tithes were exclusively the property of the Church, belonging to the incumbent of the parish, unless they had got into the hands of some monastery, or community of spiritual persons. They never belonged to any layman until the time of the dissolution of monasteries by King Henry VIII. But this monarch having procured acts of parliament for the dissolution of the monasteries and the confiscation of their property, also obtained by the same acts a confirmation of all grants made or to be made by his letters-patent of any of the property of the monasteries. These grants were many of them made to laymen, and comprised the tithes which the monasteries had possessed, as well as their landed estates. Tithes thus came for the first time into lay hands as a new species of property. As the grants had been made to the grantees and their heirs, or to them and the heirs of their bodies, or for term of life or years, the tithes so granted evidently became hereditaments in which estates might be holden, similar to those already known to be held in other hereditaments of a separate incorporeal nature; and a necessity at once arose of a law to determine the nature and attributes of these estates, How such estates might be conveyed, arid how they should descend, were questions of great importance. The former question was soon settled by an act of parliament, which directed recoveries, fines and conveyances to be made of tithes in lay hands, according as had been used for assurances of lands, tenements, and other hereditaments. And the analogy of the descent of estates in other hereditaments was followed in tracing the descent of estates of inheritance in tithes. But as tithes, being of a spiritual origin, are a distinct inheritance from the lands out of which they issue, they have not been considered as affected by any particular custom of descent, such as that of gavelkind or borough-English, to which the lands may be subject, but in all cases they descend according to the course of the common law. From this separate nature of the land and tithe, it also follows that the ownership of both by the same person will not have the effect of merging the one in the other. They exist as distinct subjects of property; and a conveyance of the land with its appurtenances, without mentioning the tithes, will leave the tithes in the hands of the conveying party. The acts which have been passed for the commutation of tithes affect tithes in the hands of laymen, as well as those possessed by the clergy. Under these acts a rent charge, varying with the price of corn, has been substituted all over the kingdom for the inconvenient system of taking tithes, in kind: and in these acts provision has been properly made for the *merger* of the tithes or rent charge in the land, by which the tithes or rent charge may at once be made to cease, whenever both land and tithes or rent charge belong to the same person.

There are other species of incorporeal hereditaments which are scarcely worth particular notice in a work so elementary as the present, especially considering the short notice that has necessarily here been taken of the more important kinds of such property. Thus, *titles of honour*, in themselves an important kind of incorporeal hereditament, are yet, on account of their inalienable nature, of but little interest to the conveyancer. The same remark also applies to *offices* or places of business and profit. No outline can embrace every feature. Many subjects, which have here occupied but a single paragraph, are of themselves sufficient to fill a volume. Reference to the different works on the separate subjects here treated of must necessarily be made by those who are desirous of full and particular information.

PART III
OF COPYHOLDS

Our present subject is one peculiarly connected with those olden times of English history to which we have had occasion to make so frequent reference. Everything relating to copyholds reminds us of the baron of old, with his little territory, in which he was king. Estates in copyhold are, however, essentially distinct, both in their origin and in their nature, from those freehold estates which have hitherto occupied our attention. Copyhold lands are lands holden by *copy* of court roll; that is, the muniments of the title to such lands are *copies* of the *roll* or book in which an account is kept of the proceedings in the *Court* of the manor to which the lands belong. For all copyhold lands belong to, and are parcel of, some manor. An estate in copyhold is not a freehold; but, in construction of law, merely an estate *at the will of the lord* of the manor, at whose will copyhold estates are expressed to be holden. Copyholds are also said to be holden *according to the custom* of the manor to which they belong, for custom is the life of copyholds.

In former days a baron or great lord, becoming possessed of a tract of land, granted part of it to freemen for estates in fee simple, giving rise to the tenure of such estates as we have seen in the chapter on Tenure. Part of the land he reserved to himself, forming the demesnes of the manor, properly so called: other parts of the land he granted out to his villeins or slaves, permitting them, as an act of pure grace and favour, to enjoy such lands at his pleasure; but sometimes enjoining, in return for such favour, the performance of certain agricultural services, such as ploughing the demesne, carting the manure, and other servile works. Such lands as remained, generally the poorest, were the waste lands of the manor, over which rights of common were enjoyed by the tenants. Thus arose a manor, of which the tenants formed two classes, the freeholders and the villeins. For each of these classes a separate Court was held: for the freeholders, a Court Baron; for the villeins another, since called a Customary Court. In the former Court the suitors were the judges; in the latter the lord only, or his steward. In some manors the villeins were allowed life interests; but the grants were not extended so as to admit any of their issue in a mode similar to that in which the heirs of freemen became entitled on their ancestors' decease. Hence arose copyholds for lives. In other manors a greater degree of liberality was shown by the lords; and, on the decease of a tenant, the lord permitted his eldest son, or sometimes all the sons, or sometimes the youngest, and afterwards other relations, to succeed him by way of heirship; for which privilege, however, the payment of a fine was usually required on the admittance of the heir to the tenancy. Frequently the course of descent of estates of freehold was chosen as the model for such inheritances; but, in many cases, dispositions the most capricious were adopted by the lord, and in time became the custom of the manor. Thus arose copyholds of inheritance. Again, if a villein wished to part with his own parcel of land to some other of his fellows, the lord would allow him to *surrender* or yield up again the land, and then, on payment of a fine, would indulgently *admit* as his tenant, on the same terms, the other, to whose use the surrender had been made. Thus arose the method, now prevalent, of conveying copyholds by *surrender* into the hands of the lord to the use of the alienee, and the subsequent *admittance* of the latter. But by long custom and continued indulgence, that which at first was a pure favour gradually grew up into a right. The will of the lord, which had originated the custom, came at last to be controlled by it.

The rise of the copyholder from a state of uncertainty to certainty of tenure appears to have been very gradual. Britton, who wrote in the reign of Edward I., thus describes this tenure under the name of villeinage: "Villeinage is to hold part of the demesnes of any lord entrusted to hold at his will by villein services to improve for the advantage of the lord." And he adds that, "In manors of ancient demesne there were pure villeins of blood and of tenure, who might be ousted of their tenements at the will of their lord". In the reign of Edward III., however, a case occurred in which the entry of a lord on his copyholder was adjudged lawful, *because he did not do his services*, by which he broke the custom of the manor, which seems to show that the lord could not, at the time, have ejected his tenant without cause. And in the reign of Edward IV. the judges gave to copyholders a certainty of tenure, by allowing to them an action of trespass on ejection by their lords without just cause. "Now," says Sir Edward Coke, "copyholders stand upon a sure ground; now they weigh not their lord's displeasure; they shake not at every sudden blast of wind; they eat, drink and sleep securely; only having a special care of the main chance, namely, to perform carefully what duties and services soever their tenure doth exact and custom doth require; then let lord frown, the copyholder cares not, knowing himself safe." A copyholder has, accordingly, now as good a title as a freeholder; in some respects a better; for all the transactions relating to the conveyance of copyholds are entered in the court rolls of the manor, and thus a record is preserved of the title of all the tenants.

In pursuing our subject, let us now follow the same course as we have adopted with regard to freeholds, and consider, first, the estates which may be holden in copyhold lands; and, secondly, the modes of their alienation.

CHAPTER I
OF ESTATES IN COPYHOLDS

With regard to the estates which may be holden in copyholds, in strict legal intendment a copyholder can have but one estate; and that is an estate at will, the smallest estate known to the law, being determinable at the will of either party. For though custom has now rendered copyholders independent of the will of their lords, yet all copyholds, properly so called, are still expressly stated, in the court rolls of manors, to be holden at the will of the lord; and, more than this, estates in copyholds are still liable to some of the incidents of a mere estate at will. We have seen that, in ancient times, the law laid great stress on the feudal possession, or *seisin*, of lands, and that this possession could only be had by the holder of an estate of freehold, that is, an estate sufficiently important to belong to a free man. Now copyholders in ancient times belonged to the class of villeins or bondsmen, and held at the will of the lord lands of which the lord himself was alone feudally possessed. In other words, the lands held by the copyholders still remained part and parcel of the lord's manor; and the freehold of these lands still continued vested in the lord; and this is the case at the present day with regard to all copyholds. The lord of the manor is actually seised of all the lands in the possession of his copyhold tenants. He has not a mere incorporeal seignory over these as he has over his freehold tenants, or those who hold of him lands, once part of the manor, but which were anciently granted to freemen and their heirs. Of all the copyholds he is the feudal possessor; and the seisin he thus has is not without its substantial advantages. The lord having a legal estate in fee simple in the copyhold lands, possesses all the rights incident to such an estate, controlled only by the custom of the manor, which is now the tenant's safeguard. Thus he possesses a right to all *mines* and *minerals* under the lands, and also to all *timber* growing on the surface, even though planted by the tenant. These rights, however, are somewhat interfered with by the rights which custom has given to the copyhold tenants; for the lord cannot come upon the lands to open his mines, or to cut his timber, without the copyholder's leave. And hence it is that timber is so seldom to be seen upon lands subject to copyhold tenure. Again, if a copyholder should grant a lease of his copyhold lands, beyond the term of a year, without his lord's consent, such a lease would be a cause of forfeiture to the lord, unless it were authorized by a special custom of the manor. For such an act would be imposing on the lord a tenant of his own lands, without the authority of custom; and custom alone is the life of all copyhold assurances. So a copyholder cannot commit any waste, either voluntary, by opening mines, cutting down timber or pulling down buildings, or permissive, by neglecting to repair. For the land, with all that is under it or on it, belongs to the lord: the tenant has nothing but a customary right to enjoy the occupation; and if he should in any way exceed this right, a cause of forfeiture to his lord would at once accrue.

A peculiar species of copyhold tenure prevails in the north of England, and is to be found also in other parts of the kingdom, particularly within manors of the tenure of ancient demesne; namely, a tenure by copy of court roll, but not expressed to be at the will of the lord. The lands held by this tenure are denominated customary freeholds. This tenure has been the subject of a great deal of learned discussion; but the Courts of Law have now decided that, as to these lands, as well as to pure copyholds, the freehold is in the lord, and not in the tenant. If a conjecture may be hazarded on so doubtful a subject, it would seem that these customary freeholds were originally held at the will of the lords, as well as those proper copyholds in which the will is still expressed as the condition of tenure; but that these tenants early acquired, by their lord's indulgence, a right to hold their lands on performance of certain fixed services as the condition of their tenure; and the compliment now paid to the lords of other copyholds, in expressing the tenure to be at their will, was, consequently, in the case of these customary freeholds, long since dropped. That the tenants have not the fee simple in themselves appears evident from the fact, that the right to mines and timber, on the lands held by this tenure, belongs to the lord in the same manner as in other copyholds. Neither can the tenants generally grant leases without the lord's consent. The lands are, moreover, said to be *parcel* of the manors of which they are held, denoting that in law they belong, like other copyholds, to the lord of the manor, and are not merely *held of* him, like the estates of the freeholders. In law, therefore, the estates of these tenants cannot, in respect of their lords, be regarded as any other than estates at will, though this is not now actually expressed. If there should be any customary freeholds in which the above characteristics, or most of them, do not exist, such may with good reason be regarded as the actual freehold estates of the tenants. The tenants would then possess the rights of other freeholders in fee simple, subject only to a customary mode of alienation. That such a state of things may, and in some cases does exist, is the opinion of some very eminent lawyers. But a recurrence to first principles seems to show that the question, whether the freehold is in the lord or in the tenant, is to be answered, not by an appeal to learned *dicta* or conflicting decisions, but by ascertaining in each case whether the well-known rights of freeholders, such as to cut timber and dig mines, are vested in the lord or in the tenant.

It appears then, that with regard to the lord, a copyholder is only a tenant at will. But a copyholder, who has been admitted tenant on the court rolls of a manor, stands, with respect to other copyholders, in a similar position to a freeholder who has the seisin. The legal estate in the copyholds is said to be *in* such a person in the same manner as the legal estate of freeholds belongs to the person who is seised. The necessary changes which are constantly occurring of the persons who from time to time are tenants on the rolls, form occasionally a source of considerable profit to the lords. For by the customs of manors, on every change of tenancy, whether by death or alienation, fines of more or less amount become payable to the lord. By the customs of some manors the fine payable was anciently arbitrary; but in modern times, fines, even when arbitrary by custom, are restrained to two years' improved value of the land after deducting quit rents. Occasionally a fine is due on the change of the lord; but, in this case, the change must be by the act of God and not by any act of the party. The tenants on the rolls, when once admitted, hold customary estates analogous to the estates which may be holden in freeholds. These estates of copyholders are only *quasi* freeholds; but, as nearly as the rights of the lord and the custom of each manor will allow, such estates possess the same incidents as the freehold estates of which we have already spoken. Thus there may be a copyhold estate for life; and some manors admit of no other estates, the lives being continually renewed as they drop. And in those manors in which estates of inheritance, as in fee simple and fee tail, are allowed, a grant to a man simply, without mentioning his heirs, will confer only a customary estate for his life. But as the customs of manors, having frequently originated in mere caprice, are very various, in some manors the words "to him and his," or "to him and his assigns," or "to him and his sequels in right," will create a customary estate in fee simple, although the word *heirs* may not be used.

It will be remembered that, anciently, if a grant had been made of freehold lands to B. simply, without mentioning his heirs, during the life of A., and B. had died first, the first person who entered after the decease of B. might lawfully hold the lands during the residue of the life of A. And this general occupancy was abolished by the Statute of Frauds. But copyhold lands were never subject to any such law. For the seisin or feudal possession of all such lands belongs, as we have seen, to the lord of the manor, subject to the customary rights of occupation belonging to his tenants. In the case of copyholds, therefore, the lord of the manor after the decease of B. would, until lately, have been entitled to hold the lands during the residue of A.'s life; and the Statute of Frauds had no application to such a case. But now, by the act for the amendment of the laws with respect to wills, the testamentary power is extended to copyhold or customary estates *pur autre vie*; and the same provision, as to the application of the estate by the executors or administrators of the grantee, as is contained with reference to freeholds, is extended also to customary and copyhold estates. The grant of an estate *pur autre vie*, in copyholds, may, however, be extended, by express words, to the heirs of the grantee. And in this event the heir will, in case of intestacy, be entitled to hold during the residue of the life of the *cestui que vie*, subject to the debts of his ancestor the grantee.

An estate tail in copyholds stands upon a peculiar in footing, and has a history of its own, which we shall now endeavour to give. This estate, it will be remembered, is an estate given to a man and the heirs of his body. With regard to freeholds, we have seen that an estate given to a man and the heirs of his body was, like all other estates, at first inalienable; so that no act which the tenant could do could bar his issue, or expectant heirs, of their inheritance. But, in an early period of our history, a right of alienation appears gradually to have grown up, empowering every freeholder to whose estate there was an expectant heir to disinherit such heir, by gift or sale of the lands. A man, to whom lands had been granted to hold to him and the heirs of his body, was accordingly enabled to alien the moment a child or expectant heir of his body was born to him; and this right of alienation at last extended to the possibility of reverter belonging to the lord, as well as to the expectancy of the heir; till at length it was so well established as to require an act of parliament for its abolition. The statute *De donis* accordingly restrained all alienation by tenants of lands which had been granted to themselves and the heirs of their bodies; so that the lands might not fail to descend to their issue after their death, or to revert to the donors or their heirs if issue should fail. This statute was passed avowedly to restrain that right of alienation, of the prior existence of which the statute itself is the best proof. And this right, in respect of fee simple estates, was soon afterwards acknowledged and confirmed by the statute of *Quia emptores*. But during all this period copyholders were in a very different state from the freemen, who were the objects of the above statutes. Copyholders were most of them mere slaves, tilling the soil of their lord's demesne, and holding their little tenements at his will. The right of an ancestor to bind his heir, with which right, as we have seen, the power to alienate freeholds commenced, never belonged to a copyholder. And, until the year 1833, copyhold lands in fee simple descended to the customary heir, quite unaffected by any bond debts of his ancestor by which the heir of his freehold estates might have been bound. It would be absurd, therefore, to suppose that the right of alienation of copyhold estates arose in connexion with the right of freeholders. The two classes were then quite distinct. The one were poor and neglected, the other powerful and consequently protected. The one held their tenements at the will of their lords; the other alienated in spite of them. The one were subject to the whims and caprices of their individual masters; the other were governed only by the general laws and customs of the realm.

Now, with regard to an estate given to a copyholder and the heirs of his body, the lords of different manors appear to have acted differently, — some of them permitting alienation on issue being born, and others forbidding it altogether. And from this. difference appears to have arisen the division of manors, in regard to estates tail, into two classes, namely, those in which there is no custom to entail, and those in which such a custom exists. In manors in which there is no custom to entail, a gift of copyholds, to a man and the heirs of his body, will give him an estate analogous to the fee simple conditional which a freeholder would have acquired under such a gift before the passing of the statute *De donis*. Before he has issue, ho will not be able to alien; but after issue are born to him, he may alienate at his pleasure. In this case the right of alienation appears to be of a very ancient origin, having arisen from the liberality of the lord in permitting his tenants to stand on the same footing in this respect as freeholders then stood.

But, as to those manors in which the alienation of the estate in question was not allowed, the history appears somewhat different. The estate, being inalienable, descended, of course, from father to son, according to the customary line of descent. A perpetual entail was thus set up, and a custom to entail established in the manor. But in process of time the original strictness of the lord defeated his own end. For, the evils of such an entail, which had been felt as to freeholds, after the passing of the statute *De donis*, became felt also as to copyholds. And, as the copyholder advanced in importance, different devices were resorted to for the purpose of effecting a bar to the entail; and, in different manors, different means were held sufficient for this purpose. In some, a customary recovery was suffered, in analogy to the common recovery, by which an entail of freeholds had been cut off. In others, the same effect was produced by a preconcerted forfeiture of the lands by the tenant, followed by a re-grant from the lord of an estate in fee simple. And in others, a conveyance by surrender, the ordinary means, became sufficient for the purpose; and the presumption was, that a surrender would bar the estate tail until a contrary custom was shown. Thus it happened that in all manors, in which there existed a custom to entail, a right grew up, empowering the tenant in tail, by some means or other, at once to alienate the lands. He thus ultimately became placed in a better position than the tenant to him and the heirs of his body in a manor where alienation was originally permitted. For, such a tenant can now only alienate after he has had issue. But a tenant in tail, where the custom to entail exists, need not wait for any issue, but may at once destroy the fetters by which his estate has been attempted to be bound.

The beneficial enactment before referred to, by which fines and common recoveries of freeholds were abolished, also contains provisions applicable, to entails of copyholds. Instead of the cumbrous machinery of a customary recovery or a forfeiture and re-grant, it substitutes, in every case, a simple conveyance by surrender, the ordinary means for conveying a customary estate in fee simple. When the estate tail is in remainder, the necessary consent of the protector *may* be given, either by deed, to be entered on the court rolls of the manor, or by the concurrence of the protector in the surrender, in which case the memorandum or entry of the surrender must expressly state that such consent has been given.

The same free and ample power of alienation, which belongs to an estate in fee simple in freehold lands, appertains also to the like estate in copyholds. The liberty of alienation *inter vivos* appears, as to copyholds, to have had little, if any, precedence, in point of time, over the liberty of alienation by will. Both were, no doubt, at first an indulgence, which subsequently ripened into a right. And these rights of voluntary alienation long outstripped the liability to involuntary alienation for the payment of the debts of the tenants; for, till the year 1833, copyhold lands of deceased debtors were under no liability to their creditors, even where the heirs of the debtor were expressly bound. And the crown had no further privilege than any other creditor. But now, all estates in fee simple, whether freehold, customary or copyhold, are rendered liable to the payment of all the just debts of the deceased tenant. Creditors who had obtained judgments against their debtors were also, till the year 1838, unable to take any part of the copyhold lands of their debtors under the writ of *elegit*. But the act, by which the remedies of judgment creditors were extended, enables the sheriff, under the writ of *elegit*, to deliver execution of copyhold or customary, as well as of freehold lands; and purchasers of copyholds thus became bound by all judgments which had been entered up against their vendors. But if any purchaser should have had no notice of any judgment, it would seem that he was protected by the clause in a subsequent act, which provided, that, as to purchasers without notice, no judgment should bind any lands otherwise than it would have bound such purchasers under the old law. By a later act, even if the purchaser had notice of a judgment, he was not bound unless a writ of execution on the judgment should have been issued and registered before the execution of his conveyance and the payment of his purchase-money; nor even then unless the execution should have been put in force within three calendar months from the time when it was registered. And now, as we have seen, the lien of all judgments of a date subsequent to the 29th of July, 1864, has been abolished altogether.

Copyholds are equally liable, with freeholds, to involuntary alienation on the bankruptcy of the tenant. The trustee for the creditors has now power to deal with any property of every description to which the bankrupt is beneficially entitled as tenant in tail, in the same manner as the bankrupt might have dealt with the same. And the Bankruptcy Act, 1869, provides that where any portion of the bankrupt's estate consists of copyhold or customary property, or any like property passing by surrender and admittance or in any similar manner, the trustee shall not be compellable to be admitted to such property, but may deal with the same in the same manner as if such property had been capable of being and had been duly surrendered or otherwise conveyed to such uses as the trustee may appoint; and any appointee of the trustee shall be admitted or otherwise invested with the property accordingly.

The descent of an estate in fee simple in copyholds is governed by the custom of descent which may happen to prevail in the manor; but, subject to any such custom, the provisions contained in the act for the amendment of the law of inheritance apply to copyhold as well as freehold hereditaments, whatever be the customary course of their descent. As, in the case of freeholds, the lands of a person dying intestate descend at once to his heir, so the heir of a copyholder becomes, immediately on the decease of his ancestor, tenant of the lands, and may exercise any act of ownership before the ceremony of his admittance has taken place. But as between himself and the lord, he is not completely a tenant till he has been admitted.

The tenure of an estate in fee simple in copyholds involves, like the tenure of freeholds, an oath of fealty from the tenant, together with suit to the customary court of the manor. Escheat to the lord on failure of heirs is also an incident of copyhold tenure. And before the abolition of forfeiture for treason and felony the lord of a copyholder had the advantage over the lord of a freeholder in this respect, that, whilst freehold lands in fee simple were forfeited to the crown by the treason of the tenant, the copyholds of a traitor escheated to the lord of the manor of which they were held. Rents also of small amount are not unfrequent incidents of the tenure of copyhold estates. And reliefs may, by special custom, be payable by the heir. The other incidents of copyhold tenure depend on the arbitrary customs of each particular manor; for this tenure, as we have seen, escaped the destruction in which the tenures of all freehold lands (except free and common socage, and frankalmoign) were involved by the act of 12 Car. II. c. 24.

A curious incident to be met with in the tenure of some copyhold estates is the right of the lord, on the death of a tenant, to seize the tenant's best beast, or other chattel, under the name of a heriot. Heriots appear to have been introduced into England by the Danes. The heriot of a military tenant was his arms and habiliments of war, which belonged to the lord, for the purpose of equipping his successor. And, in analogy to this feudal custom, the lords of manors usually expected that the best beast or other chattel of each tenant, whether he were a freeman or a villein, should on his decease be left to them. This legacy to the lord was usually the first bequest in the tenant's will; and, when the tenant died intestate, the heriot of the lord was to be taken in the first place out of his effects, unless, indeed, as not unfrequently happened, the lord seized upon the whole of the goods. To the goods of the villein he was indeed entitled, the villein himself being his lord's property. And from the difference between the two classes of freemen and villein has perhaps arisen the circumstance, that, whilst heriots from freeholders seldom occur, heriots from copyholders remain to this day, in many manors, a badge of the ancient servility of the tenure. But the right of the lord is now confined to such a chattel as the custom of the manor, grown into a law, will enable him to take. The kind of chattel which may be taken for a heriot varies in different manors. And in some cases the heriot consists merely of a money-payment.

All kinds of estates in copyholds, as well as in freeholds, may be held in joint tenancy or in common; and an illustration of the unity of a joint tenancy occurs in the fact, that the admission, on the court rolls of a manor, of one joint tenant, is the admission of all his companions; and on the decease of any of them the survivors or survivor, as they take no new estate, require no new admittance. The jurisdiction of the Court of Chancery in enforcing partitions between joint tenants and tenants in common did not formerly extend to copyhold lands. But by an enactment of the present reign this jurisdiction was extended to the partition of copyholds as well as freeholds.

The rights of lords of manors to fines and heriots, rents, reliefs and customary services, together with the lord's interests in the timber growing on copyhold lands, have been found productive of considerable inconvenience to copyhold tenants, without any sufficient corresponding advantage to the lords. An act of parliament was accordingly passed a few years ago, by which the commutation of these rights and interests, together with the lord's rights in mines and minerals, if expressly agreed on, has been greatly facilitated. The machinery of the act is, in many respects, similar to that by which the commutation of tithes was effected. The rights and interests of the lord are changed, by the commutation, into a rent-charge varying or not, as may be agreed on, with the price of corn, together with a small fixed fine on death or alienation, in no case exceeding the sum of five shillings. By the same act facilities were also afforded for the enfranchisement of copyhold lands, or the conveyance of the freehold of such lands from the lord to the tenant, whereby the copyhold tenure, with all its incidents, is for ever destroyed. The enfranchisement of copyholds was authorized to be made, either in consideration of money to be paid to the lord, or of an annual rent charge, varying with the price of corn, issuing out of the lands 'enfranchised, or in consideration of the conveyance of other lands. Provision was also made for charging the money, paid for enfranchisement, on the lands enfranchised, by way of mortgage. The principal object of these enactments, was to provide for the case of the lands being in settlement, or vested in parties not otherwise capable of at once entering into a complete arrangement; but no provision was made for compulsory enfranchisement. More recently, however, acts have been passed to make the enfranchisement of copyholds compulsory at the instance either of the tenant or of the lord. If the enfranchisement be made at the instance of the tenant, the compensation is to be a gross sum of money, to be paid at the time of the completion of the enfranchisement, or to be charged on the land by way of mortgage; and where the enfranchisement is effected at the instance of the lord, the compensation is to be an annual rent charge, to be issuing out of the lands enfranchised; subject to the right of the parties, with the sanction of the commissioners appointed under the act, to agree that the compensation shall be either a gross sum or a yearly rent charge, or a conveyance of land to be settled to the same uses as the manor is settled. It is also provided that in any enfranchisement to be hereafter effected under the before-mentioned act, it shall not be imperative to make the enfranchisement rent charge variable with the prices of grain; but the same may, at the option of the parties or at the discretion of the commissioners, as the case may require, be fixed in money or be made variable as aforesaid. Enfranchisements under these acts are irrespective of the validity of the lord's title. By the Copyhold Act, 1858, an award of enfranchisement, confirmed by the commissioners, has been substituted for the deed of enfranchisement required by the Act of 1852. The acts also provide for the extinguishment of heriots due by custom from tenants of freeholds and customary freeholds. But the curtesy, dower or freebench of persons married before the enfranchisement shall have been completed, is expressly saved: and all the commonable rights of the tenant continue attached to his lands, notwithstanding the same shall have become freehold. And no enfranchisement under these acts is to affect the estate or rights of any lord or tenant in any mines or minerals within or under the lands enfranchised or any other lands, unless with the express consent in writing of such lord or tenant. And nothing therein contained is to interfere with any enfranchisement which may be made irrespective of the acts, where the parties competent to do so shall agree on such enfranchisement. Where all parties are sui juris and agree to an enfranchisement, it may at any time be made by a simple conveyance of the fee simple from the lord to his tenant.

CHAPTER II
OF THE ALIENATION OF COPYHOLDS

The mode in which the alienation of copyholds is at present effected, so far at least as relates to transactions *inter vivos*, still retains much of the simplicity, as well as the inconvenience, of the original method in which the alienation of these lands was first allowed to take place. The copyholder surrenders the lands into the hands of his lord, who thereupon admits the alienee. For the purpose of effecting these admissions, and of informing the lord of the different events happening within his manor, as well as for settling disputes, it was formerly necessary that his Customary Court, to which all the copyholders were suitors, should from time to time be held. At this Court, the copyholders present were called the homage, on account of the ceremony of *homage* which they were all anciently bound to perform to their lord. In order to form a Court, it was formerly necessary that two copyholders at least should be present. But, in modern times, the holding of courts having degenerated into little more than an inconvenient formality, it has been provided by an act of the present reign, that Customary Courts may be holden without the presence of any copyholder; but no proclamation made at any such courts is to affect the title or interest of any person not present, unless notice thereof shall be duly served on him within one month; and it is also provided, that where, by the custom of any manor, the lord is authorized, with the consent of the homage, to grant any common or waste lands of the manor, the Court must be duly summoned and holden as before the act. No Court can lawfully be held out of the manor; but by immemorial custom, Courts for several manors may be held together within one of them. In order that the transactions at the Customary Court may be preserved, a book is provided, in which a correct account of all the proceedings is entered by a person duly authorized. This book, or a series of them, forms the court rolls of the manor. The person who makes the entries is the steward; and the court rolls are kept by him, but subject to the right of the tenants to inspect them. This officer also usually presides at the Court of the manor.

Before adverting to alienation by surrender and admittance, it will be proper to mention, that, whenever any lands which have been demisable time out of mind by copy of court roll, fall into the hands of the lord, he is at liberty to grant them to be held by copy at his will, according to the custom of the manor, under the usual services. These grants may be made by the lord for the time being, whatever be the extent of his interest, so only that it be lawful: for instance, by a tenant for a term of life or years. But if the lord, instead of granting the lands by copy, should once make any conveyance of them at the common law, though it were only a lease for years, his power to grant by copy would for ever be destroyed. The steward, or his deputy, if duly authorized so to do, may also make grants, as well as the lord, whose servant he is. It was formerly doubtful whether the steward or his deputy could make grants of copyholds when out of the manor. But by the act, to which we have before had occasion to refer, it is provided that the lord of any manor, or the steward, or deputy steward, may grant at any time, and at any place, either within or out of the manor, any lands parcel of the manor, to be held by copy of court roll, or according to the custom of the manor, which such lord shall for the time being be authorized and empowered to grant out to be held as aforesaid; so that such lands be granted for such estate, and to such person only, as the lord, steward, or deputy shall be authorized or empowered to grant the same.

When a copyholder is desirous of disposing of his lands, the usual method of alienation is by surrender of the lands into the hands of the lord (usually through the medium of his steward), to the use of the alienee and his heirs, or for any other customary estate which it may be wished to bestow. This surrender generally takes place by the symbolical delivery of a rod, by the tenant to the steward. It may be made either in or out of Court. If made in Court, it is of course entered on the court rolls, together with the other proceedings; and a copy of so much of the roll as relates to such surrender is made by the steward, signed by him and stamped like a purchase deed; it is then given to the purchaser as a muniment of his title. If the surrender should be made out of Court, a memorandum of the transaction, signed by the parties and the steward, is made, in writing, and duly stamped as before. In order to give effect to a surrender made out of Court, it was formerly necessary that due mention, or *presentment*, of the transaction, should be made by the suitors or homage assembled at the next, or, by special custom, at some other subsequent Court. And in this manner an entry of the surrender appeared on the court rolls, the steward entering the presentment as part of the business of the Court. But by the act above mentioned, it is provided that surrenders, copies of which may be delivered to the lord, his steward, or deputy steward, shall be forthwith entered on the court rolls; which entry is to be deemed to be an entry made in pursuance of a presentment by the homage. So that in this case, the ceremony of presentment is now dispensed with. When the surrender has been made, the surrenderor still continues tenant to the lord, until the admittance of the surrenderee. The surrenderee acquires by the surrender merely an inchoate right, to be perfected by admittance. This right was formerly inalienable at law, even by will, until rendered devisable by the new statute for the amendment of the laws with respect to wills; but, like a possibility in the case of freeholds, it may always be released, by deed, to the tenant of the lands.

A surrender of copyholds may be made by a man to the use of his wife, for such a surrender is not a direct conveyance, but operates only through the instrumentality of the lord. And a valid surrender may at any time be made of the lands of a married woman, by her husband and herself: she being on such surrender separately examined, as to her free consent, by the steward or his deputy. The Vendor and Purchaser Act, 1874, now provides that where any copyhold hereditament shall be vested in a married woman, as a bare trustee, she may surrender the same as if she were a feme sole.

When the surrender has been made, the surrenderee has, at any time, a right to procure *admittance* to the lands surrendered to his use; and, on such admittance, he becomes at once tenant to the lord, and is bound to pay him the customary fine. This admittance is usually taken immediately; but, if obtained at any future time, it will relate back to the surrender; so that, if the surrenderor should, subsequently to the surrender, have surrendered to any other person, the admittance of the former surrenderee, even though it should be subsequent to the admittance of the latter, will completely displace his estate. Formerly a steward was unable to admit tenants out of a manor; but, by the act for the improvement of copyhold tenure, the lord, his steward, or deputy, may admit at any time, and at any place, either within or out of the manor, and without holding a Court; and the admission is rendered valid without any presentment of the surrender, in pursuance of which admission may have been granted.

The alienation of copyholds by will was formerly effected in a similar manner to alienation *inter vivos*. It was necessary that the tenant who wished to devise his estate should first make a surrender of it to the use of his will. His will then formed part of the surrender, and no particular form of execution or attestation was necessary. The devisee, on the decease of his testator, was, until admittance, in the same position as a surrenderee. By a statute of Geo. III., a devise of copyholds, without any surrender to the use of the will, was rendered as valid as if a surrender had been made. The act for the amendment of the laws with respect to wills requires that wills of copyhold lands should be executed and attested in the same manner as wills of freeholds. But a surrender to the use of the will is still unnecessary; and a surrenderee, or devisee, who has not been admitted, is now empowered to devise his interest. Formerly, the devisee under a will was accustomed, at the next Customary Court held after the decease of his testator, to bring the will into Court; and a presentment was then made of the decease of the testator, and of so much of his will as related to the devise. After this presentment the devisee was admitted, according to the tenor of the will. But under the act for the improvement of copyhold tenure, the mere delivery to the lord, or his steward, or deputy steward, of a copy of the will is sufficient to authorize its entry on the court rolls, without the necessity of any presentment; and the lord, or his steward, or deputy steward, may admit the devisee at once, without holding any Court for the purpose.

Sometimes, on the decease of a tenant, no person came in to be admitted as his heir or devisee. In this case the lord, after making due proclamation at three consecutive Courts of the manor for any person having right to the premises to claim the same and be admitted thereto, is entitled to seize the lands into his own hands *quousque*, as it is called, that is, *until* some person claims admittance; and by the special custom of some manors, he is entitled to seize the lands absolutely. But as this right of the lord might be very prejudicial to infants, married women, and lunatics or idiots entitled to admittance to any copyhold lands in consequence of their inability to appear, special provision has been made by act of parliament in their behalf. Such persons are accordingly authorized to appear, either in person or by their guardian, attorney or committee, as the case may be; and in default of such appearance, the lord or his steward is empowered to appoint any fit person to be attorney for that purpose only, and by such attorney to admit every such infant, married woman, lunatic or idiot, and to impose the proper fine. If the fine be not paid, the lord may enter and receive the rents till it be satisfied out of them; and if the guardian of any infant, the husband of any married woman, or the committee of any lunatic or idiot, should pay the fine, he will be entitled to a like privilege. But no absolute forfeiture of the lands is to be incurred by the neglect or refusal of any infant, married woman, lunatic or idiot to come in and be admitted, or for their omission, denial or refusal to pay the fine imposed on their admittance.

Although mention has been made of surrenders *to the use* of the surrenderee, it must not, therefore, be supposed that the Statute of Uses has any application to copyhold lands. This statute relates exclusively to freeholds. The seisin or feudal possession of all copyhold land ever remains, as we have seen, vested in the lord of the manor. Notwithstanding that custom has given to the copyholder the enjoyment of the lands, they still remain, in contemplation of law, the lord's freehold. The copyholder cannot, therefore, simply by means of a surrender to his use from a former copyholder, be deemed, in the words of the Statute of Uses, in lawful seisin for such estate as he has in the use; for the estate of the surrenderor is customary only, and the estate of the surrenderee cannot, consequently, be greater. Custom, however, has now rendered the title of the copyholder quite independent of that of his lord. When a surrender of copyholds is made into the hands of the lord *to the use* of any person, the lord is now merely an instrument for carrying the intended alienation into effect; and the title of the lord, so that he be lord *de facto*, is quite immaterial to the validity either of the surrender or of the subsequent admittance of the surrenderee. But if a surrender should be made by one person to the use of another, *upon trust* for a third, the Chancery Division of the High Court would exercise the same jurisdiction over the surrenderee, in compelling him to perform the trust, as it would in the case of freeholds vested in a trustee. And when copyhold lands form the subject of settlement, the usual plan is to surrender them to the use of trustees, as joint tenants of a customary estate in fee simple, upon such trusts as will effect, in equity, the settlement intended. The trustees thus become the legal copyhold tenants of the lord, and account for the rents and profits to the persons beneficially entitled. The equitable estates which are thus created are of a similar nature to the equitable estates in freeholds, of which we have already spoken; and a trust for the separate use of a married woman may be created as well out of copyhold as out of freehold lands. An equitable estate tail in copyholds may be barred by deed, in the same manner in every respect as if the lands had been of freehold tenure. But the deed, instead of being inrolled in the Chancery Division of the High Court, must be entered on the court rolls of the manor. And if there be a protector, and he consent to the disposition by a distinct deed, such deed must be executed by him either on, or any time before, the day on which the deed barring the entail is executed; and the deed of consent must also be entered on the court rolls.

As the owner of an equitable estate has, from the nature of his estate, no legal right to the lands, he is not himself a copyholder. He is not a tenant to the lord: this position is filled by his trustee. The trustee, therefore, is admitted, and may surrender; but the cestui que trust cannot adopt these means of disposing of his equitable interest. To this general rule, however, there have been admitted, for convenience sake, two exceptions. The first is that of a tenant in tail whose estate is merely equitable: by the act for the abolition of fines and recoveries, the tenant of a merely equitable estate tail is empowered to bar the entail, either by deed in the manner above described, or by surrender in the same manner as if his estate were legal. The second exception relates to married women, it being provided by the same act that, whenever a husband and wife shall surrender any copyhold lands in which she alone, or she and her husband in her right, may have any equitable estate or interest, the wife shall be separately examined in the same manner as she would have been, had her estate or interest been at law instead of in equity merely; and every such surrender, when such examination shall be taken, shall be binding on the married woman and all persons claiming under her; and all surrenders previously made of lands similarly circumstanced, where the wife shall have been separately examined by the person taking the surrender, are thereby declared to be good and valid. But these methods of conveyance, though tolerated by the law, are not in accordance with principle; for an equitable estate is, strictly speaking, an estate in the contemplation of equity only, and has no existence anywhere else. As, therefore, an equitable estate tail in copyholds may properly be barred by a deed entered on the court rolls of the manor, so an equitable estate or interest in copyholds belonging to a married woman is more properly conveyed by a deed, executed with her husband's concurrence, and *acknowledged* by her in the same manner as if the lands were freehold. And the act for the abolition of fines and recoveries, by which this mode of conveyance is authorized, does not require that such a deed should be entered on the court rolls.

1. Copyhold estates admit of remainders analogous to those which may be created in estates of freehold. And when a surrender or devise is made to the use of any person for life, with remainders over, the admission of the tenant for life is the admission of all persons having estates in remainder, unless there be in the manor a special custom to the contrary. A vested estate in remainder is capable of alienation by the usual mode of surrender and admittance. Contingent remainders of copyholds have always had this advantage, that they have never been liable to destruction by the sudden determination of the particular estate on which they depend. The freehold, vested in the lord, is said to be the means of preserving such remainders until the time when the particular estate would regularly have expired. In this respect

they resemble contingent remainders of equitable or trust estates of freeholds, as to which we have seen, that the legal seisin, vested in the trustees, preserves the remainders from destruction; but if the contingent remainder be not ready to come into possession the moment the particular estate would naturally and regularly have expired, such contingent remainder will fail altogether. To this rule, however, an exception has now been made by the act to amend the law as to contingent remainders, which extends to hereditaments of any tenure; although it affects only such a contingent remainder as would have been valid as a springing or shifting use, or executory devise or other limitation, had it not had a sufficient estate to support it as a contingent remainder.

Executory devises of copyholds, similar in all respects to executory devises of freeholds, have long been permitted. And directions to executors to sell the copyhold lands of their testator (which directions, we have seen, give rise to executory interests) are still in common use; for, when such a direction is given, the executors, taking only a power and no estate, have no occasion to be admitted; and if they can sell before the lord has had time to hold his three Customary-Courts for making proclamation in order to seize the land *quousque*, the purchaser from them will alone require admittance by virtue of his executory estate which arose on the sale. By this means the expense of only one admittance is incurred; whereas, had the lands been devised to the executors in trust to sell, they must first have been admitted under the will, and then have surrendered to the purchaser, who again must have been admitted under their surrender. And in a recent case, where a testator devised copyholds to such uses as his trustees should appoint, and subject thereto to the use of his trustees, their heirs and assigns for ever, with a direction that they should sell his copyholds, it was decided that the trustees could make a good title without being admitted, even although the lord had in the meantime seized the lands *quousque* for want of a tenant. But it has recently been decided that the lord of a manor is not bound to accept a surrender of copyholds *inter vivos*, to such uses as the surrenderee shall appoint, and, in default of appointment, to the use of the surrenderee, his heirs and assigns. This decision is in accordance with the old rule, which construed surrenders of copyholds in the same manner as a conveyance of freeholds *inter vivos* at common law. If, however, the lord should accept such a surrender, he will be bound by it, and must admit the appointee under the power of appointment, in case such power should be exercised.

With regard to the interest possessed by husband and wife in each other's copyhold lands, the Married Women's Property Act, 1870, provides, as we have seen, that when any copyhold or customary-property shall descend upon any woman married after the passing of that act, as heiress or co-heiress of an intestate, the rents and profits of such property shall, subject and without prejudice to the trusts of any settlement affecting the same, belong to such woman for her separate use. But in cases not affected by this statute, the husband has the whole income of his wife's land during the coverture; although a special custom appears to be necessary to entitle him to be tenant by curtesy. A special custom also is required to entitle the wife to any interest in the lands of her husband after his decease. Where such custom exists, the wife's interest is termed her *freebench*; and it generally consists of a life interest in one divided third part of the lands, or sometimes of a life interest in the entirety; and, like dower under the old law, freebench is paramount to the husband's debts. Freebench, however, usually differs from the ancient right of dower in this important particular, that whereas the widow was entitled to dower of all freehold lands of which her husband was solely seised *at any time* during the coverture, the right to freebench does not usually attach until the actual decease of the husband, and it may be defeated by a devise of the lands by the will of the husband. Freebench, therefore, is in general no impediment to the free alienation by the husband of his copyhold lands, without his wife's concurrence. To this rule the important manor of Cheltenham forms an exception; for, by the custom of this manor, as settled by act of parliament, the freebench of widows attaches, like the ancient right of dower out of freeholds, on all the copyhold lands of inheritance of which their husbands were tenants at any time during the coverture. The act for the amendment of the law relating to dower does not extend to freebench.

PART IV
OF PERSONAL INTERESTS IN REAL ESTATE

The subjects which have hitherto occupied our attention derive a great interest from the antiquity of their origin. We have seen that the difference between freehold and copyhold tenure has arisen from the distinction which prevailed, in ancient times, between the two classes of freemen and villeins; and that estates of freehold in lands and tenements owe their origin to the ancient feudal system. The law of real property, in which term both freehold and copyhold interests are included, is full of rules and principles to be explained only by a reference to antiquity; and many of those rules and principles were, it must be confessed, much more reasonable and useful when they were first instituted than they are at present. The subjects, however, on which we are now about to be engaged, possess little of the interest which arises from antiquity; although their present value and importance are unquestionably great. The principal interests of a personal nature derived from landed property, are a term of years and a mortgage debt. The origin and reason of the personal nature of a term of years in land have been already attempted to be explained; and at the present day, leasehold interests in land, in which amongst other things all building leases are included, form a subject sufficiently important to require a separate consideration. The personal nature of a mortgage debt was not clearly established till long after a term of years was considered as a chattel. But it is now settled that every mortgage, whether with or without a bond or covenant for the repayment of the money, forms part of the personal estate of the lender or mortgagee. And when it is known that the larger proportion of the lands in this kingdom is at present in mortgage, a fact generally allowed, it is evident that a chapter devoted to mortgages cannot be superfluous.

CHAPTER I
OF A TERM OF YEARS

At the present day, one of the most important kinds of chattel or personal interests in landed property is a term of years, by which is understood, not the time merely for which a lease is granted, hut also the interest acquired by the lessee. Terms of years may practically be considered as of two kinds; first, those which are created by ordinary leases, which are subject to a yearly rent, which seldom exceed ninety-nine years, and in respect of which so large a number of the occupiers of lands and houses are entitled to their occupation; and secondly, those which are created by settlements, wills, or mortgage deeds, in respect of which no rent is usually reserved, which are frequently for one thousand years or more, which are often vested in trustees, and the object of which is usually to secure the payment of money by the owner of the land. But although terms of years of different lengths are thus created for different purposes, it must not, therefore, be supposed that a long term of years is an interest of a different nature from a short one. On the contrary, all terms of years of whatever length possess precisely the same attributes in the eye of the law.

The consideration of terms of the former kind, or those created by ordinary leases, may conveniently be preceded by a short notice of a tenancy at will, and a tenancy by sufferance. A tenancy at will may be created by parol, or by deed; it arises when a person lets land to another, to hold at the will of the lessor or person letting. The lessee, or person taking the lands, is called a tenant at will; and, as he may be turned out when his landlord pleases, so he may leave when he likes. A tenant at will is not answerable for mere permissive waste. He is allowed, if turned out by his landlord, to reap what he has sown, or, as it is legally expressed, to take the emblements; and if he should be within the provisions of the Agricultural Holdings (England) Act, 1875, he will be entitled to compensation for improvements, according to the provisions of the act. But as this kind of letting is very inconvenient to both parties, it is scarcely ever adopted; and, in construction of law, a lease at an annual rent, made generally without expressly stating it to be at will, and without limiting any certain period, is not a lease at will, but a lease from year to year, of which we shall presently speak. When property is vested in trustees, the cestui que trust is, as we have seen, absolutely entitled to such property in equity. But as the courts of law did not recognize trusts, they considered the cestui que trust, when in possession, to be merely the tenant at will of his trustees; and as the distinction between law and equity has not been abolished by the Judicature Acts, a cestui que trust, whilst in possession, is still a tenant at will at law, although absolutely entitled in equity. A tenancy by sufferance is when a person, who has originally come into possession by a lawful title, holds such possession after his title has determined.

A lease from year to year is a method of letting very commonly adopted: in most cases it is much more advantageous to both landlord and tenant than a lease at will. The advantage consists in this, that both landlord and tenant are entitled to notice before the tenancy can be determined by the other of them. This notice must be given at least half a year before the expiration of the current year of the tenancy; for the tenancy cannot be determined by one only of the parties, except at the end of any number of whole years from the time it began. So that, if the tenant enter on any quarter day, he can quit only on the same quarter day: when once in possession, he has a right to remain for a year; and if no notice to quit be given for half a year after he has had possession, he will have a right to remain two whole years from the time he came in; and so on from year to year. But where the tenancy is within the Agricultural Holdings (England) Act, 1875, a year's notice, expiring with a year of tenancy, is substituted for the half year's notice formerly required; but this is not to extend to a case where the tenant is adjudged bankrupt, or has filed a petition for a composition or arrangement with his creditors. And the landlord's notice may, with a view to certain improvements to be stated in the notice, relate to part only of the holding; the tenant having the option, by counter notice in writing within twenty-eight days, to accept the same as notice to quit the entire holding. This act does not apply to any holding which is not either wholly agricultural or wholly pastoral, or in part agricultural and as to the residue pastoral, or that is of less extent than two acres. But the act applies to every such contract of tenancy beginning after the 14th of February, 1876, the time of the commencement of the act, unless in any case the landlord and tenant agree in writing, in the contract of tenancy or otherwise, that the act or any part or provision of the act shall not apply to the contract; and in that case the act, or the part or provision thereof to which that agreement refers (as the case may be), shall not apply to the contract. And nothing in the act is to prevent a landlord and tenant, or intending landlord and tenant, from entering into and carrying into effect any such agreement as they think fit, or shall interfere with the operation thereof. The act does not apply to any contract of tenancy current at the commencement of the act, except in the case of a tenancy from year to year or at will; nor does it apply to such a tenancy in case, within two months after the commencement of the act, the landlord or the tenant gave notice in writing to the other to the effect that he (the person giving the notice) desired that the existing contract of tenancy between them should remain unaffected by the act. A lease from year to year can be made by parol or word of mouth, if the rent reserved amount to two-thirds at least of the full improved value of the lands; for if the rent reserved do not amount to so much, the Statute of Frauds declares that such parol lease shall have the force and effect of a lease at will only. A lease from year to year, reserving a less amount of rent, must be made by deed. The best way to create this kind of tenancy is to let the lands to hold "from year to year" simply, for much litigation has arisen from the use of more circuitous methods of saying the same thing.

A lease for a fixed number of years may, by the Statute of Frauds, be made by parol, if the term do not exceed three years from the making thereof, and if the rent reserved amount to two-thirds, at least, of the full improved value of the land. Leases for a longer term of years, or at a lower rent, were required, by the Statute of Frauds, to be put into writing and signed by the parties making the same, or their agents thereunto lawfully authorized by writing. But a lease of a separate incorporeal hereditament was always required to be made by deed. And the act to amend the law of real property now provides that a lease, required by law to be in writing, of any tenements or hereditaments shall be void *at law*, unless made by deed. But such a lease, although void as a lease for want of its being by deed, may be good as an agreement to grant a lease, *ut res magis valeat quam pereat*. It does not require any formal words to make a lease for years. The words commonly employed are, "demise, lease, and to farm let;" but any words indicating an intention to give possession of the lands for a determinate time will be sufficient. Accordingly, it sometimes happened, previously to the act, that what was meant by the parties merely as an agreement to execute a lease, was in law construed as itself an actual lease; and very many law suits arose out of the question, whether the effect of a memorandum was in law an actual lease, or merely an agreement to make one. Thus, a mere memorandum in writing that A. agreed to let, and B. agreed to take, a house or farm for so many years, at such a rent, was, if signed by the parties, as much a lease as if the most formal words had been employed. By such a memorandum a term of years was created in the premises, and was vested in the lessee, immediately on his entry, instead of the lessee acquiring, as at present, merely a right to have a lease granted to him in accordance with the agreement.

There is no limit to the number of years for which a lease may be granted; a lease may be made for 99, 100, 1,000, or any other number of years; the only requisite on this point is, that there be a definite period of time fixed in the lease, at which the term granted must end; and it is this fixed period of ending which distinguishes a *term* from an estate of freehold. Thus, a lease to A. for his life is a conveyance of an estate of freehold, and must be carried into effect by the proper method for conveying the legal seisin; but a lease to A. for ninety-nine years, if he shall so long live, gives him only a term of years, on account of the absolute certainty of the determination of the interest granted, at a given time *fixed in the lease*. Besides the fixed time for the term to end, there must also be a time fixed from which the term is to begin; and this time may, if the parties please, be at a future period. Thus, a lease may be made for 100 years from next Christmas. For, as leases anciently were contracts between the landlords and their husbandmen, and had nothing to do with the freehold or feudal possession, there was no objection to the tenant's right of occupation being deferred to a future time.

When the lease is made, the lessee does not become complete tenant by lease to the lessor until he has entered on the lands let. Before entry, he has no estate, but only a right to have the lands for the term by force of the lease, called in law an *interesse termini*. But if the lease should be made by a bargain and sale, or any other conveyance operating by virtue of the Statute of Uses, the lessee will, as we have seen, have the whole term vested in him at once, in the same manner as if he had actually entered.

The circumstance, that a lease for years was anciently nothing more than a mere contract, explains a curious point of law relating to the creation of leases for years, which does not hold with respect to the creation of any greater interest in land. If a man should by indenture lease lands, in which he has no legal interest, for a term of years, both lessor and lessee will be *estopped* during the term, or forbidden to deny the validity of the lease. This might have been expected. But the law goes further, and holds, that if the lessor should at any time during the lease acquire the lands he has so let, the lease, which before operated only by estoppel, shall now take effect out of the newly-acquired estate of the lessor, and shall become for all purposes a regular estate for a term of years. If, however, the lessor has, at the time of making the lease, any interest in the lands he lets, such interest only will pass, and the lease will have no further effect by way of estoppel, though the interest purported to be granted be really greater than the lessor had at the time power to grant. Thus, if A., a lessee for the life of B., makes a lease for years by indenture, and afterwards purchases the reversion in fee, and then B. dies, A. may at law avoid his own lease, though several of the years expressed in the lease may he still to come; for, as A. had an interest in the lands for the life of B., a term of years determinable on B.'s life passed to the lessee. But if in such a case the lease was made for valuable consideration, Equity would oblige the lessor to make good the term out of the interest he had acquired.

The first kind of leases for years to which we have adverted, namely, those taken for the purpose of occupation, are usually made subject to the payment of a yearly rent, and to the observance and performance of certain covenants, amongst which a covenant to pay the rent is always included. The rent and covenants are thus constantly binding on the lessee, during the whole continuance of the term, notwithstanding any assignment which he may make. On assigning leasehold premises, the assignee is therefore bound to enter into a covenant with the assignor, to indemnify him against the payment of the rent reserved, and the observance and performance of the covenants contained in the lease. The assignee, as such, is liable to the landlord for the rent which may be unpaid, and for the covenants which may be broken during the time that the term remains vested in him, although he may never enter into actual possession, provided that such covenants relate to the premises let; and a covenant to do any act upon the premises, as to build a wall, is binding on the assignee, if the lessee has covenanted for himself *and his assigns* to do the act. But a covenant to do any act upon premises not comprised in the lease cannot be made to bind the assignee. Covenants which are binding on the assignee are said to *run with the land*, the burden of such covenants passing with the land to every one to whom the term is from time to time assigned. But when the assignee assigns to another, his liability ceases as to any future breach. In the same manner the benefit of covenants relating to the land, entered into by the lessor, will pass to the assignee; for, though no contract has been made between the lessor and the assignee individually, yet, as the latter has become the tenant of the former, a *privity of estate* is said to arise between them, by virtue of which the covenants entered into, when the lease was granted, become mutually binding, and may be enforced by the one against the other. This mutual right is also confirmed by an express clause of the statute before referred to, by which assignees of the reversion were enabled to take advantage of conditions of re-entry contained in leases. By the same statute also, the assignee of the reversion is enabled to take advantage of the covenants entered into by the lessee with the lessor, under whom such assignee claims, — an advantage, however, which, in some cases, he is said to have previously possessed.

The payment of the rent, and the observance and performance of the covenants, are usually further secured by a proviso or condition for re-entry, which enables the landlord or his heirs (and the statute above mentioned enables his assigns), on non-payment of the rent, or on non-observance or non-performance of the covenants, to re-enter on the premises let, and repossess them as if no lease had been made. The proviso for re-entry, so far as it relates to the non-payment of rent, has been already adverted to. The proviso for re-entry on breach of covenants was until recently the subject of a curious doctrine; that if an express licence were once given by the landlord for the breach of any covenant, or, if the covenant were, not to do a certain act without licence, and licence were once given by the landlord to perform the act, the right of re-entry was gone for ever. The ground of this doctrine was, that every condition of re-entry is entire and indivisible; and, as the condition had been waived once, it could not be enforced again. So far as this reason extended to the breach of any covenant, it was certainly intelligible; but its application to a licence to perform an act, which was only prohibited when done *without* licence, was not very apparent. This rule, which was well established, was frequently the occasion of great inconvenience to tenants; for no landlord could venture to give a licence to do any act, which might be prohibited by the lease unless done with licence, for fear of losing the benefit of the proviso for re-entry, in case of any future breach of covenant. The only method to be adopted in such a case was, to create a fresh proviso for re-entry on any future breach of the covenants, a proceeding which was of course attended with expense. The term would then, for the future, have been determinable on the new events stated in the proviso; and there was no objection in point of law to such a course; for a term, unlike an estate of freehold, may be made determinable during its continuance, on events which were not contemplated at the time of its creation. By an act of the present reign the inconvenient doctrine above mentioned ceased to extend to licences granted to the tenants of crown lands. And by a subsequent statute it has been provided, that every such licence shall, unless otherwise expressed, extend only to the permission actually given, or to any specific breach of any proviso or covenant made or to be made, or to the actual matter thereby specifically authorized to be done, but not so as to prevent any proceeding for any subsequent breach, unless otherwise specified in such licence. And all rights under covenants and powers of forfeiture and re-entry contained in the lease are to remain in full force, and are to be available as against any subsequent breach or other matter not specifically authorised by the licence, in the same manner as if no such licence had been given; and the condition or right of re-entry is to remain in all respects as if such licence had not been given, except in respect of the particular matter authorized to be done. Provision has also been made that a licence to one of several lessees, or with respect to part only of the property let, shall not destroy the right of re-entry as to the other lessee's, or as to the remainder of the property. It has been further provided that where the reversion upon a lease is severed, and the rent or other reservation is legally apportioned, the assignee of each part of the reversion shall, in respect of the apportioned rent or other reservation allotted or belonging to him, have and be entitled to the benefit of all conditions or powers of re-entry for non-payment of the original rent or other reservation, in like manner as if such conditions or powers had been reserved to him as incident to his part of the reversion in respect of the apportioned rent or other reservation allotted or belonging to him. Before this enactment a grantee of part of the reversion could not take advantage of the condition; as if a lease had been made of three acres, reserving a rent upon condition, and the reversion of two acres were granted, the rent might be apportioned, but the condition was destroyed, "for that it is entire and against common right".

The above enactments, however, failed to provide for the case of an actual waiver of a breach of covenant. On this point the law stood thus. The receipt of rent by the landlord, after notice of a breach of covenant committed by his tenant prior to the rent becoming due, was an implied waiver of the right of re-entry; but if the breach was of a continuing kind, this implied waiver did not extend to the breach which continued after the receipt. An implied waiver of this kind did not destroy the condition of re-entry; but an actual waiver had this effect. Few landlords therefore were disposed to give an actual waiver. The inconvenience which thus arose is now met by a subsequent act, which provides that, where any actual waiver of the benefit of any covenant or condition in any lease on the part of the lessor, or his heirs, executors, administrators, or assigns, shall be proved to have taken place, after the passing of that act, in any one particular instance, such actual waiver shall not be assumed or deemed to extend to any instance, or any breach of covenant or condition, other than that to which such waiver shall specially relate, nor to be a general waiver of the benefit of any such covenant or condition, unless an intention to that effect shall appear.

A condition of re-entry is, evidently, a very serious instrument of oppression in the hands of the landlord, when the property comprised in the lease is valuable, and the tenant by mere inadvertence may have committed some breach of covenant. To forget to pay the annual premium on the insurance of the premises against fire might thus occasion the loss of the whole property; although, on the other hand, the landlord might well consider such forgetfulness inexcusable, since it might end in the loss of the premises by fire whilst uninsured. In this matter some beneficial provisions have been made by recent enactments. The Court has now power to relieve, upon such terms as it may think fit, against a forfeiture for breach of a covenant or condition to insure against fire, where no loss or damage by fire has happened, and the breach has, in the opinion of the Court, been committed through accident or mistake, or otherwise without fraud or gross negligence, and there is an insurance on foot at the time of the application to the Court in conformity with the covenant to insure. But where such relief shall be granted, a record or minute thereof is required to be made by indorsement on the lease or otherwise. And the Court is not to relieve the same person more than once in respect of the same covenant or condition; nor is it to grant any relief where a forfeiture under the covenant, in respect of which relief is sought, shall have been already waived out of Court in favour of the person seeking the relief. It is further provided that the persons entitled to the benefit of a covenant on the part of a lessee or mortgagor to insure against loss or damage by fire shall, on loss or damage by fire happening, have the same advantage from any then subsisting insurance relating to the building covenanted to be insured, effected by the lessee or mortgagor in respect of his interest under the lease or in the property, or by any person claiming under him, but not effected in conformity with the covenant, as he would have from an insurance effected in conformity with the covenant.

It was provided by the Statute of Frauds, that no leases estates or interests, not being copyhold or customary interests, in any lands, tenements or hereditaments, should be assigned, unless by deed or note in writing, signed by the party so assigning, or his agent thereunto lawfully authorized by writing, or by act or operation of law. And now, by the act to amend the law of real property, it is enacted that an assignment of a chattel interest, not being copyhold, in any tenements or hereditaments, shall be void at law unless made by deed.

A very beneficial provision for purchasers of leaseholds is made by the act to which we have already frequently referred.

This act provides that where, on a *bonâ fide* purchase after the passing of the act of a leasehold interest under a lease containing a covenant on the part of the lessee to insure against fire, the purchaser is furnished with a written receipt of the person entitled to receive the rent, or his agent, for the last payment of rent accrued due before the completion of the purchase, and there is subsisting at the time of the completion of the purchase an insurance in conformity with the covenant, the purchaser or any person claiming under him shall not be subject to any liability by way of forfeiture or damages, or otherwise, in respect of any breach of the covenant committed at any time before the completion of the purchase, of which the purchaser had not notice before the completion of the purchase.

Leasehold estates may also be bequeathed by will. As leaseholds are personal property, they devolve in the first place on the executors of the will, in the same manner as other personal property; or, on the decease of their owner intestate, they will pass to his administrator. An explanation of this part of the subject will be found in the author's treatise on the principles of the law of personal property. It was formerly a rule that where a man had lands in fee simple, and also lands held for a term of years, and devised by his will all his lands and tenements, the fee simple lands only passed by the will, and not the leaseholds; but if he had leasehold lands, and none held in fee simple, the leaseholds would then pass, for otherwise the will would be merely void. But the act for the amendment of the laws with respects to wills now provides, that a devise of the land of the testator, or of the land of the testator in any place, or in the occupation of any person mentioned in his will, or otherwise described in a general manner, and any other general devise which would describe a leasehold estate if the testator had no freehold estate which could be described by it, shall be construed to include the leasehold estates of the testator, or his leasehold estates to which such description shall extend, as well as freehold estates, unless a contrary intention shall appear by the will. The act to which we have already referred contains a provision for the exoneration of the executors or administrators of a lessee from liability to the rents and covenants of the lease, similar to that to which we have already referred with respect to their liability to rents-charge in conveyances on rents-charge.

Leasehold estates are also subject to involuntary alienation for the payment of debts. By the act for extending the remedies of creditors against the property of their debtors, they became subject in the same manner as freeholds, to the claims of judgment creditors: with this exception, that, as against purchasers without notice of any judgments, such judgments had no further effect than they would have had under the old law. And, under the old law, leasehold estates, being goods or chattels merely, were not bound by judgments until a writ of execution was actually in the hands of the sheriff or his officer. So that a judgment had no effect as against a purchaser of a leasehold estate without notice, unless a writ of execution on such judgment had actually issued prior to the purchase. And if leaseholds should be considered to be "goods" within the meaning of the Mercantile Law Amendment Act, 1856, then a purchaser without notice was safe at any time before an actual seizure under the writ. And now, as we have seen, no judgment of a date later than the 29th of July, 1864, can affect any land of whatever tenure, until such land shall have been actually delivered in execution by virtue of a writ of elegit or other lawful authority in pursuance of such judgment.

In the event of bankruptcy, leasehold property may now be disclaimed by the trustee for the creditors, with the leave of the Court, notwithstanding he has endeavoured to sell, or has taken possession of such property, or exercised any act of ownership in relation thereto; and the lease shall be deemed to have been surrendered on the same date. But the trustee shall not be entitled to disclaim any property in pursuance of the act in oases where an application in writing has been made to him by any person interested in such property, requiring such trustee to decide whether he will disclaim or not, and the trustee has, for a period of not less than twenty-eight days after the receipt of such application, or such further time as may be allowed by the Court, declined or neglected to give notice whether he disclaims the same or not.

The tenant for a term of years may, unless restrained by express covenant, make an underlease for any part of his term; and any assignment for less than the whole term is in effect an underlease. On the other hand, any assurance purporting to be an underlease, but which comprises the whole term, is, by the better opinion, in effect an assignment. It is true that in some cases, where a tenant for years, having less than three years of his term to run, has verbally agreed with another person to transfer the occupation of the premises to him for the rest of the term, he paying an equivalent rent, this has been regarded as an underlease, and so valid, rather than as an attempted assignment which would be void, formerly for want of a writing, and now for want of a deed. It is, however, held that no distress can be made for the rent thus reserved. But if a tenure be created, the lord, if he have no estate, must at least have a seignory, to which the rent would by law be incident; and being thus rent service, it must by the common law be enforceable by distress. The very fact, therefore, that no distress can be made for the rent by the common law, shows that there can be no tenure between the parties. And, if so, the attempted disposition cannot operate as an underlease. If, however, the disposition be by deed, and be executed by the alienee, it has been decided that the reservation of rent may operate to create a rent-charge, for which the owner may sue, and which he may assign, so as to entitle the assignee to sue in his own name. And if this be so, there seems no good reason why, under these circumstances, the statutory power of distress given to the owner of a rent seck, should not apply to the rent thus created. But on this point also opinions differ.

Every underlessee becomes tenant to the lessee who grants the underlease, and not tenant to the original lessor. Between him and the underlessee, no *privity* is said to exist. Thus the original lessor cannot maintain any action against an underlessee for any breach of the covenants contained in the original lease. His remedy is only against the lessee, or any assignee from him of the whole term. The derivative term, which is vested in the underlessee, is not an estate in the interest originally granted to the lessee: it is a new and distinct term, for a different, because a less, period of time. It certainly arises and takes effect out of the original term, and its existence depends on the continuance of such term, but still, when created, it is a distinct chattel, in the same way as a portion of any moveable piece of goods becomes, when cut out of it, a separate chattel personal.

If a married woman should be possessed of a term of years, her husband may dispose of it at any time during the coverture, either absolutely or by way of mortgage; and in case he should survive her, he will be entitled to it by his marital right. But if he should die in her lifetime it will survive to her, and his will alone will not be sufficient to deprive her of it. And now, by the Married Women's Property Act, 1870, where any woman married after the 9th of August, 1870, the date of the act, shall during her marriage become entitled to any personal property (which would seem to include leaseholds) as next of kin or one of the next of kin of an intestate, such property shall, subject and without prejudice to the trusts of any settlement affecting the same, belong to the woman for her separate use.

In many cases landlords, particularly corporations, are in the habit of granting to their tenants fresh leases, either before or on the expiration of existing ones. In other cases a covenant is inserted to renew the lease on payment of a certain fine for renewal; and this covenant may be so worded as to confer on the lessee a perpetual right of renewal from time to time as each successive lease expires. In all these cases the acceptance by the tenant of the new lease operates as a surrender in law of the unexpired residue of the old term; for the tenant by accepting the new lease affirms that his lessor has power to grant it; and as the lessor could not do this during the continuance of the old term, the acceptance of such new lease is a surrender in law of the former. But if the new lease be void, the surrender of the old one will be void also; and if the new lease be voidable, the surrender will be void if the new lease fail. It appears to be now settled, after much difference of opinion, that the granting of a new lease to another person with the consent of the tenant is an implied surrender of the old term. Whenever a lease, renewable either by favour or of right, is settled in trust for one person for life with remainders over, or in any other manner, the benefit of the expectation or right of renewal belongs to the persons from time to time beneficially interested in the lease; and if any other person should, on the strength of the old lease, obtain a new one, he will be regarded in equity as a trustee for the persons beneficially interested in the old one. So the costs of renewal are apportioned between the tenant for life and remaindermen according to their respective periods of actual enjoyment of the new lease. Special provisions have been made by parliament for facilitating the procuring and granting of renewals of leases when any of the parties are infants, idiots or lunatics. And the provision by which the remedies against under-tenants have been preserved, when leases are surrendered in order to be renewed, has been already mentioned. More recently provisions have been made by parliament enabling trustees of renewable leaseholds to renew their leases, and to raise money by mortgage for that purpose. Provisions have also been made for facilitating the purchase by such trustees of the reversion of the lands, when it belongs to an ecclesiastical corporation, and for raising money for that purpose by sale or mortgage; also for the exchange of part of the lands, comprised in any renewable lease, for the reversion in other part of the same lands, so as thus to acquire the entire fee simple in a part of the lands instead of a renewable lease of the whole.

The Agricultural Holdings (England) Act, 1875, contains provisions for the compensation of tenants, whose tenancies are within the act, for improvements made by them. The improvements are divided into three classes, which are to be considered as exhausted, as to the first class at the end of twenty years, as to the second class at the end of seven years, and as to the third class at the end of two years. A landlord, on paying to the tenant the amount of compensation due to him under the act, may obtain an order from the County Court charging the holding with the repayment of the amount paid, or any part thereof, with such interest and by such instalments, and with such directions for giving effect to the charge, as the Court thinks fit. But where the landlord is not absolute owner, no instalment or interest is to be made payable after the time when the improvement, in respect whercof compensation is made, will for the purposes of the act be taken to be exhausted. There is also a provision for the removal of tenant's fixtures, subject to the landlord's option to purchase the same.

We now come to consider those long terms of years of which frequent use is made in conveyancing, generally for the purpose of securing the payment of money. For this purpose it is obviously desirable that the person who is to receive the money should have as much power as possible of realizing his security, whether by receipt of the rents or by selling or pledging the land; at the same time it is also desirable that the ownership of the land, subject to the payment of the money, should remain as much as possible in the same state as before, and that when the money is paid, the persons to whom it was due should no longer have anything to do with the property. These desirable objects are accomplished by conveyancers by means of the creation of a long term of years, say 1,000, which is vested (when the parties to be paid are numerous, or other circumstances make such a course desirable), in trustees, upon trust out of the rents and profits of the premises, or by sale or mortgage thereof for the whole or any part of the term, to raise and pay the money required, as it may become due, and upon trust to permit the owners of the land to receive the residue of the rents and profits. By this means the parties to be paid have ample security for the payment of their money. Not only have their trustees the right to receive on their behalf (if they think fit) the whole accruing income of the property, but they have also power at once to dispose of it for 1,000 years to come, a power which is evidently almost as effectual as if they were enabled to sell the fee simple. Until the time of payment comes, the owner of the land is entitled, on the other hand, to receive the rents and profits, by virtue of the trust under which the trustees may be compelled to permit him so to do. So, if part of the rents should be required, the residue must be paid over to the owner; but if non-payment by the owner should render a sale necessary, the trustees will be able to assign the property, or any part of it, to any purchaser for 1,000 years without any rent. But until these measures may be enforced, the ownership of the land, subject to the payment of the money, remains in the same state as before. The trustees, to whom the term has been granted, have only a chattel interest; the legal seisin of the freehold remains with the owner, and may be conveyed by him, or devised by his will, or will descend to his heir, in the same manner as if no term existed, the term all the while still hanging over the whole, ready to deprive the owners of all substantial enjoyment, if the money should not be paid.

If, however, the money should be paid, or should not ultimately be required, different methods may be employed of depriving the trustees of all power over the property. The first method, and that most usually adopted in modern times, is by inserting in the deed, by which the term is created, a proviso that the term shall cease, not only at its expiration by lapse of time, but also in the event of the purposes for which it is created being fully performed and satisfied, or becoming unnecessary, or incapable of taking effect. This proviso for *cesser*, as it is called, makes the term endure so long only as the purposes of the trust require; and, when these are satisfied, the term expires without any act to be done by the trustees: their title at once ceases, and they cannot, if they would, any longer intermeddle with the property.

But if a proviso for cesser of the term should not be inserted in the deed by which it is created, there is still a method of getting rid of the term, without disturbing the ownership of the lands which the term overrides. The lands in such cases, it should be observed, may not, and seldom do, belong to one owner for an estate in fee simple. The terms of which we are now speaking are most frequently created by marriage settlements, and are the means almost invariably used for securing the portions of the younger children; whilst the lands are settled on the eldest son in tail. But, on the son's coming of age, or on his marriage, the lands are, for the most part, as we have before seen, resettled on him for life only, with an estate tail in remainder to his unborn eldest son. The owner of the lands is therefore probably only a tenant for life, or perhaps a tenant in tail. But, whether the estate be a fee simple, or an estate tail, or for life only, each of these estates is, as we have seen, an estate of freehold, and, as such, is larger, in contemplation of law, than any term of years, however long. The consequence of this legal doctrine is, that if any of these estates should happen to be vested in any person, who at the same time is possessed of a term of years in the same land, and no other estate should intervene, the estate of freehold will infallibly swallow up the term, and yet be not a bit the larger. The term will, as it is said, be *merged* in the estate of freehold. Thus, let A. and B. be tenants for a term of 1,000 years, and subject to that term let C. be tenant for his life; if now A. and B. should assign their term to C. (which assignment under such circumstances is called a *surrender)*, C. will still be merely tenant for life as before. The term will be gone for ever; yet C. will have no right to make any disposition to endure beyond his own life. He had the legal seisin of the lands before, though A. and B. had the possession by virtue of their term; now, he will have both legal seisin and actual possession during his life, and A. and B. will have completely given up all their interest in the premises. Accordingly, if A. and B. should be trustees for the purposes we have mentioned, a surrender by them of their term to the legal owner of the land, will bring back the ownership to the same state as before. The act to amend the law of real property now provides that a surrender in writing of an interest in any tenements or hereditaments, not being a copyhold interest, and not being an interest which might by law have been created without writing, shall be void at law unless made by deed.

The merger of a term of years is sometimes occasioned by the accidental union of the term and the immediate freehold in one and the same person. Thus, if the trustee of the term should purchase the freehold, or if it should be left to him by the will of the former owner, or descend to him as heir at law, in each of these cases the term will merge. So if one of two joint holders of a term obtain the immediate freehold, his moiety of the term will merge; or conversely if the sole owner of a term obtain the immediate freehold jointly with another, one moiety of the term will merge, and the joint ownership of the freehold will continue, subject only to the remaining moiety of the term. Merger being a *legal* incident of estates, formerly occurred quite irrespectively of the trusts on which they were held; but equity did its utmost to prevent any injury being sustained by a cestui que trust, the estate of whose trustee might accidentally have merged. The Supreme Court of Judicature Act, 1873, however, provides that there shall not, after the commencement of that act, which took place on the 1st of November, 1875, be any merger by operation of law only of any estate, the beneficial interest in which would not be deemed to be merged or extinguished in equity. The law, though it did not recognize the trusts of equity, yet took notice in some few cases of property being held by one person in right of another, or *in autre droit*, as it is called; and in these cases the general rule was, that the union of the term with the immediate freehold would not Cause any merger, if such union were occasioned by the act of law, and not by the act of the party. Thus, if a term were held by a person, to whose wife the immediate freehold afterwards came by descent or devise, such freehold, coming to the husband in right of his wife, would not have caused a merger of the term. So, if the owner of a term made the freeholder his executor, the term would not have merged; for the executor is recognized by the law as usually holding only for the benefit of creditors and legatees; but if the executor himself should be the legatee of the term, it seems that, after all the creditors have been paid, the term will still merge. And if an executor, whether legatee or not, holding a term as executor, should *purchase* the immediate freehold, the better opinion is, that this being his own act, will occasion the merger of the term, except so far as respects the rights of the creditors of the testator.

There was until recently another method of disposing of a term when the purposes for which it was created had been accomplished. If it were not destroyed by a proviso for cesser, or by a merger in the freehold, it might have been kept on foot for the benefit of the owner of the property for the time being. A term, as we have seen, is an instrument of great power, yet easily managed; and in case of a sale of the property, it might have been a great protection to the purchaser. Suppose, therefore, that, after the creation of such a term as we have spoken of, the whole property had been sold. The purchaser, in this case, often preferred having the term still kept on foot, and assigned by the trustees to a new trustee of his own choosing, in trust for himself, his heirs and assigns; or, as it was technically said, *in trust to attend the inheritance*. The reason for this proceeding was that the former owner might, possibly, since the commencement of the term, have created some incumbrance upon the property, of which the purchaser was ignorant, and against which, if existing, he was of course desirous of being protected. Suppose, for instance, that a rent-charge had been granted to be issuing out of the lands, subsequently to the creation of the term: this rent-charge of course could not affect the term itself, but was binding only on the freehold, subject to the term. The purchaser, therefore, if he took no notice of the term, bought an estate, subject not only to the term, but also to the rent-charge. Of the existence of the term, however, we suppose him to have been aware. If now he should have procured the term to be surrendered to himself, the unknown rent-charge, not being any estate in the land, would not have prevented the union and merger of the term in the freehold. The term would consequently have been destroyed, and the purchaser would have been left without any protection against the rent-charge, of the existence of which he had no knowledge, nor any means of obtaining information. The rent-charge, by this means, became a charge, not only on the legal seisin, but also on the possession of the lands, and was said to be accelerated by the merger of the term. The preferable method, therefore, always was to avoid any merger of the term; but, on the contrary, to obtain an assignment of it to a trustee in trust for the purchaser, his heirs and assigns, and to attend the inheritance. The trustee thus became possessed of the lands for the term of 1,000 years; but he was bound, by virtue of the trust, to allow the purchaser to receive the rents, and exercise what acts of ownership he might please. If, however, any unknown incumbrance, such as the rent-charge in the case supposed, should have come to light, then was the time to bring the term into action. If the rent-charge should have been claimed, the trustee of the term would at once have interfered, and informed the claimant that, as his rent-charge was made subsequently to the term, he must wait for it till the term was over, which was in effect a postponement *sine die*. In this manner, a term became a valuable protection to any person on whose behalf it was kept on foot, as well as a source of serious injury to any incumbrancer, such as the grantee of the rent-charge, who might have neglected to procure an assignment of it on his own behalf, or to obtain a declaration of trust in his favour from the legal owner of the term. For it will be observed that, if the grantee of the rent-charge had obtained from the persons in whom the term was vested a declaration of trust in his behalf, they would have been bound to retain the term, and could not lawfully have assigned it to a trustee for the purchaser.

If the purchaser, at the time of his purchase, should have had notice of the rent-charge, and should yet have procured an assignment of the term to a trustee for his own benefit, the Court of Chancery would, on the first principles of equity, have prevented his trustee from making any use of the term to the detriment of the grantee of the rent-charge. Such a proceeding would evidently be a direct fraud, and not the protection of an innocent purchaser against an unknown incumbrance. To this rule, however, one exception was admitted, which reflects no great credit on the gallantry, to say the least, of those who presided in the Court of Chancery. In the common case of a sale of lands in fee simple from A. to B., it was holden that, if there existed a term in the lands, created prior to the time when A.'s seisin commenced, or prior to his marriage, an assignment of this term to a trustee for B. might be made use of for the purpose of defeating the claim of A.'s wife, after his decease, to her dower out of the premises. Here B. evidently had notice that A. was married, and he knew also that, by the law, the widow of A. would, on his decease, be entitled to dower out of the lands. Yet the Court of Chancery permitted him to procure an assignment of the term to a trustee for himself, and to tell the widow that, as her right to dower arose subsequently to the creation of the term, she must wait for her dower till the term was ended. We have already seen, that, as to all women married after the first of January, 1834, the right to dower has been placed at the disposal of their husbands. Such husbands, therefore, had no need to request the concurrence of their wives in a sale of their lands, or to resort to the device of assigning a term, should this concurrence not have been obtained.

When a term had been assigned to attend the inheritance, the owner of such inheritance was not regarded, in consequence of the trust of the term in his favour, as having any interest of a personal nature, even in contemplation of equity; but as, at law, he had a real estate of inheritance in the lands, subject to the term, so, in equity, he had, by virtue of the trust of the term in his favour, a real estate of inheritance in immediate possession and enjoyment. If the term were neither surrendered nor assigned to a trustee to attend the inheritance, it still was considered attendant on the inheritance, by construction of law, for the benefit of all persons interested in the inheritance according to their respective titles and estates.

An act has, however, been passed "to render the assignment of satisfied terms unnecessary". This act provides, that every satisfied term of years which, either by express declaration or by construction of law, shall upon the thirty-first day of December, 1845, be attendant upon the reversion or inheritance of any lands, shall *on that day absolutely cease* and determine as to the land upon the inheritance or reversion whereof such term shall be attendant as aforesaid, except that every such term of years, which shall be so attendant as aforesaid by express declaration, although thereby made to cease and determine, shall afford to every person the same protection against every incumbrance, charge, estate, right, action, suit, claim, and demand, as it would have afforded to him if it had continued to subsist, but had not been assigned or dealt with, after the said thirty-first day of December, 1845, and shall, for the purpose of such protection, *be considered in every Court of law* and of equity *to be a subsisting term*. The act further provides that every term of years then subsisting, or thereafter to be created, becoming satisfied after the thirty-first of December, 1845, and which, either by express declaration or by construction of law, shall after that day become attendant upon the inheritance or reversion of any land, shall, immediately upon the same becoming so attendant, absolutely cease and determine as to the land upon the inheritance or reversion whereof such term shall become attendant as aforesaid. In the two first editions of this work, some remarks on this act were inserted by way of Appendix. These remarks are now omitted, not because the author has changed his opinion on the wording of the act, but because the remarks, being of a controversial nature, seem to him to be scarcely fitted to be continued in every edition of a work intended for the use of students, and also because the act has, upon the whole, conferred a great benefit on the community. Experience has in fact shown that the cases in which purchasers enjoy their property without any molestation are infinitely more numerous than those in which they are compelled to rely on attendant terms for protection; so that the saving of expense to the generality of purchasers seems greatly to counterbalance the inconvenience to which the very small minority may be put, who have occasion to set up attendant terms as a defence against adverse proceedings. And it is very possible that some of the questions to which this act gives rise may never be actually litigated in a Court of justice.

CHAPTER II
OF A MORTGAGE DEBT

Our next subject for consideration is a mortgage debt. The term mortgage debt is here employed for want of one which can more precisely express the kind of interest intended to be spoken of. Every person who borrows money, whether upon mortgage or not, incurs a *debt* of personal obligation to repay out of whatever means he may possess; and this obligation is usually expressed in a mortgage deed in the shape of a covenant by the borrower to repay the lender the money lent, with interest at the rate agreed on. If, however, the borrower should personally be unable to repay the money lent to him, or if, as occasionally happens, it is expressly stipulated that the borrower shall not be personally liable to repay, then the lender must depend solely upon the property mortgaged; and the nature of his interest in such property, here called his mortgage debt, is now attempted to be explained. In this point of view, a mortgage debt may be defined to be an interest in land of a personal nature, which was recognized as such only by the Court of Chancery, in its office of administering equity. We have seen, in the chapter on Uses and Trusts, that the Court of Chancery is now abolished, although the doctrines of equity remain the same. In equity, a mortgage debt is a sum of money, the payment whereof is secured, with interest, on certain lands; and being money, it is personal property, subject to all the incidents which appertain to such property. The Courts of law on the other hand, did not regard a mortgage in the light of a mere security for the repayment of money with interest. A mortgage in law was an absolute conveyance, subject to an agreement for a reconveyance on a certain given event. Thus, let us suppose freehold lands to be conveyed by A., a person seised in fee, to B. and his heirs, subject to a proviso, that on repayment on a given future day, by A. to B., of a sum of money then lent by B. to A., with interest until repayment, B. or his heirs will reconvey the lands to A. and his heirs; and with a further proviso, that until default shall be made in payment of the money, A. and his heirs may hold the land without any interruption from B. or his heirs. Here we have at once a common mortgage of freehold land. A., who conveys the land, is called the mortgagor; B., who lends the money, and to whom the land is conveyed, is called the mortgagee. The conveyance of the land from A. to B. gives to B., as is evident, an estate in fee simple at law. He thenceforth becomes, at law, the absolute owner of the premises, subject to the agreement under which A. has a right of enjoyment, until the day named for the payment of the money; on which day, if the money be duly paid, B. has agreed to reconvey the estate to A. If, when the day comes, A. should repay the money with interest, B. of course must reconvey the lands; but if the money should not be repaid punctually on the day fixed, there is evidently nothing on the face of the arrangement to prevent B. from keeping the lands to himself and his heirs for ever. But upon this arrangement, a very different construction was placed by the Courts of law and by the Courts of equity, a construction which well illustrates the difference between the two.

The Courts of law, adhering, according to their ancient custom, to the strict literal meaning of the terms, held, that if A. did not pay or tender the money punctually on the day named, he should lose the land for ever; and this, according to Littleton, is the origin of the term *mortgage* or *mortuum vadium*, "for that it is doubtful whether the feoffor will pay at the day limited such sum or not; and if he doth not pay, then the land which is put in pledge, upon condition for the payment of the money, is taken from him for ever, and is dead to him upon condition, &c. And if he doth pay the money, then the pledge is dead as to the tenant, &c." Correct, however, as is Littleton's statement of the law, the accuracy of his derivation may be questioned; as the word *mortgage* appears to have been applied, in more early times, to a feoffment to the creditor and his heirs, to be held by him until his debtor paid him a given sum; until which time he received the rents without account, so that the estate was unprofitable or dead to the debtor in the meantime; the rents being taken in lieu of interest, which, under the name of usury, was anciently regarded as an unchristian abomination. This species of mortgage has, however, long been disused, and the form above given is now constantly employed. From the date of the mortgage deed, the legal estate in fee simple belongs, not to the mortgagor, but to the mortgagee. The mortgagor, consequently, is thenceforward unable to create any legal estate or interest in the premises; he cannot even make a valid lease for a term of years, — a point of law too frequently neglected by those whose necessities have obliged them to mortgage their estates. Formerly, when the day named for payment had passed, the mortgagee, if not repaid his money, might at any time have brought an action of ejectment against the mortgagor without any notice, and thus have turned him out of possession; so that, if the debtor had now no greater mercy shown to him than the Courts of law allowed, the smallest want of punctuality in his payment would cause him for ever to lose the estate he had pledged. In modern times, a provision was certainly made by act of parliament for staying the proceedings in any action of ejectment brought by the mortgagee, on payment by the mortgagor, being the defendant in the action, of all principal, interest and costs. But at the time of this enactment, the jurisdiction of equity over mortgages had become fully established; and the act may consequently be regarded as ancillary only to that full relief, which, as we shall see, the Court of Chancery was accustomed to afford to the mortgagor in all such cases. The Supreme Court of Judicature Act, 1873, now provides that a mortgagor entitled for the time being to the possession or receipt of the rents and profits of any land, as to which no notice of his intention to take possession, or to enter into the receipt of the rents and profits thereof shall have been given by the mortgagee, may sue for such possession, or for the recovery of such rents or profits, or to prevent or recover damages in respect of any trespass or other wrong relative thereto, in his own name only, unless the cause of action arises upon a lease or other contract made by him jointly with any other person.

The relative rights of mortgagor and mortgagee appear to have long remained on the footing of the strict construction of their bargain, adopted by the Courts of law. It was not till the reign of James I. that the Court of Chancery took upon itself to interfere between the parties. But at length, having determined to interpose, it went so far as boldly to lay down as one of its rules, that no agreement of the parties, for the exclusion of its interference, should have any effect. This rule, no less benevolent than bold, is a striking instance of that determination to enforce fair dealing between man and man, which raised the Court of Chancery, notwithstanding the many defects in its system of administration, to the power and dignity which it enjoyed. The Court of Chancery accordingly held, that after the day fixed for the payment of the money had passed, the mortgagor had still a right to redeem his estate, on payment to the mortgagee of all principal, interest and costs due upon the mortgage to the time of actual payment. This right still remains, and is called the mortgagor's *equity of redemption*; and no agreement with the creditor, expressed in any terms, however stringent, can deprive the debtor of his equitable right, on payment within a reasonable time. The Judicature Act, 1873, has expressly assigned to the Chancery Division of the High Court of Justice all causes and matters for, amongst other things, the redemption or foreclosure of mortgages. If, therefore, after the day fixed in the deed for payment, the mortgagee should enter into possession of the property mortgaged, the Chancery Division of the High Court will nevertheless compel him to keep a strict account of the rents and profits; and, when he has received so much as will suffice to repay him the principal money lent, together with interest and costs, he will be compelled to re-convey the estate to his former debtor. In equity the mortgagee is properly considered as having no right to the estate, further than is necessary to secure to himself the due repayment of the money he has advanced, together with interest for the loan; the equity of redemption, which belongs to the mortgagor, renders the interest of the mortgagee merely of a personal nature, namely, a security for so much money. At law, the mortgagee is absolutely entitled; and the estate mortgaged may be devised by his will, or, if he should die intestate, will descend to his heir at law; but in equity he has a security only for the payment of money, the right to which will, in common with his other personal estate, devolve on his executors or administrators, for whom his devisee or heir will be a trustee; and, when they are paid, such devisee or heir will be obliged by the Court, without receiving a sixpence for himself, to re-convey the estate to the mortgagor. And, as we shall presently see, the executors or administrators of the mortgagee are now empowered to re-convey on payment of all sums secured by the mortgage.

Indulgent, however, as the Court has shown itself to the debtor, it will not allow him for ever to deprive the mortgagee, his creditor, of the money which is his due; and if the mortgagor will not repay him within a reasonable time, equity will allow the mortgagee for ever to retain the estate to which he is already entitled at law. For this purpose it will be necessary for the mortgagee to bring an action of *foreclosure* against the mortgagor in the Chancery Division of the High Court, claiming that an account may be taken of the principal and interest due to him, and that the mortgagor may be directed to pay the same, with costs, by a day to be appointed by the Court, and that in default thereof he may be foreclosed his equity of redemption. A day is then fixed by the Court for payment; which day, however, may, on the application of the mortgagor, good reason being shown, be postponed for a time. Or, if the mortgagor should be ready to make repayment, before the cause is brought to a hearing, he may do so at any time previously, on making proper application to the Court, admitting the title of the mortgagee to the money and interest. If, however, on the day ultimately fixed by the Court, the money should not be forthcoming, the debtor will then be absolutely deprived of all right to any further assistance from the

Court; in other words, his equity of redemption will be foreclosed, and the mortgagee will be allowed to keep, without further hindrance, the estate which was conveyed to him when the mortgage was first made. By the act to amend the practice and course of proceeding in the Court of Chancery, the Court is empowered, in any suit for foreclosure, to direct a sale of the property at the request of either party instead of a foreclosure. And the equitable jurisdiction of the Court is now extended to the County Courts with respect to all sums not exceeding five hundred pounds.

In addition to the remedy by foreclosure, which, it will be perceived, involves the necessity of an action in the Chancery Division of the High Court, a more simple and less expensive remedy is now usually provided in mortgage transactions; this is nothing more than a power given by the mortgage deed to the mortgagee, without further authority, to sell the premises, in case default should be made in payment. When such a power is exercised, the mortgagee, having the whole estate in fee simple at law, is of course able to convey the same estate to the purchaser; and, as this remedy would be ineffectual, if the concurrence of the mortgagor were necessary, it has been decided that his concurrence cannot be required by the purchaser. The mortgagee, therefore, is at any time able to sell; but, having sold, he has no further right to the money produced by the sale than he had to the lands before they were sold. He is at liberty to retain to himself his principal, interest and costs; and, having done this, the surplus, if any, must be paid over to the mortgagor. And, by a recent act of parliament, a power of sale, a power to insure against fire, and a power to require the appointment of a receiver of the rents, or in default to appoint any person as such receiver, have been rendered incident to every mortgage or charge by deed affecting any hereditaments of any tenure. These powers, however, do not arise until after the expiration of one year from the time when the principal money shall have become payable according to the terms of the deed, or after any interest on such principal money shall have been in arrear for six months, or after any omission to pay any premium on any insurance, which by the terms of the deed ought to be paid by the person entitled to the property subject to the charge. And no sale is to be made until after six months' notice in writing. But none of these powers are to be exercisable, if it be declared in the mortgage deed that they shall not take effect; and where there is no such declaration, then if any variations or limitations of any of the powers are contained in the deed, such powers shall be exercisable only subject to such variations or limitations.

If after the day fixed for the payment of the money is passed, the mortgagor should wish to pay off the mortgage, he must give to the mortgagee six calendar months' previous notice in writing of his intention so to do, and must then punctually pay or tender the money at the expiration of the notice; for if the money should not be then ready to be paid, the mortgagee will be entitled to fresh notice; as it is only reasonable that he should have time afforded him to look out for a fresh security for his money.

Mortgages of freehold lands are sometimes made for long terms, such as 1,000 years. But this is not now often the case, as the fee simple is more valuable, and therefore preferred as a security. Mortgages for long terms, when they occur, are usually made by trustees, in whom the terms have been vested in trust to raise, by mortgage, money for the portions of the younger children of a family, or other similar purposes. The reasons for vesting such terms in trustees for these purposes were explained in the last chapter.

Copyhold, as well as freehold lands, may be the subjects of mortgage. The purchase of copyholds, it will be remembered, is effected by a surrender of the lands from the vendor into the hands of the lord of the manor, to the use of the purchaser, followed by the admittance of the latter as tenant to the lord. The mortgage of copyholds is effected by surrender, in a similar manner, from the mortgagor to the use of the mortgagee and his heirs, subject to a condition, that on payment by the mortgagor to the mortgagee of the money lent, together with interest, on a given day, the surrender shall be void. If the money should be duly paid on the day fixed, the surrender will be void accordingly, and the mortgagor will continue entitled to his old estate; but if the money should not be duly paid on that day, the mortgagee will then acquire at law an absolute right to be admitted to the customary estate which was surrendered to him; subject nevertheless to the equitable right of the mortgagor, confining the actual benefit derived by the former to his principal money, interest and costs. The mortgagee, however, is seldom admitted, unless he should wish to enforce his security, contenting himself with the right to admittance conferred upon him by the surrender; and, if the money should be paid off, all that will then be necessary will be to procure the steward to insert on the court rolls a memorandum of acknowledgment, by the mortgagee, of satisfaction of the principal money and interest secured by the surrender. If the mortgagee should have been admitted tenant, he must of course, on repayment, surrender to the use of the mortgagor, who will then be re-admitted. It is now provided by the Vendor and Purchaser Act, 1874, that the legal personal representative, that is, the executors or administrators, of a mortgagee of a freehold estate, or of a copyhold estate to which the mortgagee shall have been admitted, may, on payment of all sums secured by the mortgage, convey or surrender the mortgaged estate, whether the mortgage be in form an assurance subject to redemption, or an assurance upon trust. Before this enactment, in case of the death of the mortgagee, his heir or the devisee under his will had to reconvey the legal estate, on payment of the mortgage debt and interest, to the legal personal representative of the mortgagee.

Leasehold estates also frequently form the subjects of mortgage. The term of years of which the estate consists is assigned by the mortgagor to the mortgagee, subject to a proviso for redemption or re-assignment on payment, on a given day, by the mortgagor to the mortgagee, of the sum of money advanced with interest; and with a further proviso for the quiet enjoyment of the premises by the mortgagor until default shall be made in payment. The principles of equity as to redemption apply equally to such a mortgage, as to a mortgage of freeholds; but, as the security, being a term, is always wearing out, payment will not be permitted to be so long deferred. A power of sale also is frequently inserted in a mortgage of leaseholds, and the statutory powers given by the act already referred to extend also to leaseholds. From what has been said in the last chapter, it will appear that, as the mortgagee is an assignee of the term, he will be liable to the landlord, during the continuance of the mortgage, for the payment of the rent and the performance of the covenants of the lease; against this liability the covenant of the mortgagor is his only security. In order, therefore, to obviate this liability, when the rent or covenants are onerous, mortgages of leaseholds are frequently made by way of demise or underlease: the mortgagee by this means becomes the tenant only of the mortgagor, and consequently a mere stranger with regard to the landlord. The security of the mortgagee in this case is obviously not the whole term of the mortgagor, but only the new and derivative term created by the mortgage.

In some cases the exigency of the circumstances will not admit of time to prepare a regular mortgage; a deposit of the title deeds is then made with the mortgagee; and, notwithstanding the stringent provision of the Statute of Frauds to the contrary, it was held by the Court of Chancery that such a deposit, even without any writing, operated as an equitable mortgage of the estate of the mortgagor in the lands comprised in the deeds. This doctrine still remains; and the same doctrine applies to copies of court roll relating to copyhold lands, for such copies are the title deeds of copyholders.

When lands are sold, but the whole of the purchase-money is not paid to the vendor, he has a lien in equity on the lands for the amount unpaid, together with interest at four per cent., the usual rate allowed in equity. And the circumstance of the vendor having taken from the purchaser a bond or a note for the payment of the money will not destroy the lien. But if the vendor take a mortgage of part of the estate, or any other independent security, his lien will be gone. If the sale be made in consideration of an annuity, it appears that a lien will subsist for such annuity, unless a contrary intention can be inferred from the nature of the transaction.

A curious illustration of the anxiety of the Court of Chancery to prevent any imposition being practised by the mortgagee upon the mortgagor occurs in the following doctrine: that, if money be lent at a given rate of interest, with a stipulation that, on failure of punctual payment, such rate shall be increased, this stipulation is held to be void as too great a hardship on the mortgagor; whereas, the very same effect may be effectually accomplished by other words. If the stipulation be, that the higher rate shall be paid, but on punctual payment a lower rate of interest shall be accepted, such a stipulation, being for the benefit of the mortgagor, is valid, and will be allowed to be enforced. The highest rate of interest which could be taken upon the mortgage of any lands, tenements or hereditaments, or any estate or interest therein, was formerly 5*l.* per cent. per annum; and all contracts and assurances, whereby a greater rate of interest was reserved or taken on any such security, were deemed to have been made or executed for an illegal consideration. By a modern statute, the previous restriction of the interest of all loans to 5*l.* per cent. was removed, with respect to contracts for the loan or forbearance of money above the sum of 10*l.* sterling; but loans upon the security of any lands, tenements or hereditaments, or any estate or interest therein, were expressly excepted. But, by an act of parliament passed on the 10th of August, 1854, all the laws against usury were repealed; so that, now, any rate of interest may be taken on a mortgage of lands which the mortgagor is willing to pay.

The loan of money on mortgage is an investment frequently resorted to by trustees, when authorized by their trust to make such use of the money committed to their care: in such a case, the fact that they are trustees, and the nature of their trust, are usually omitted in the mortgage deed, in order that the title of the mortgagor or his representatives may not be affected by the trusts. It is, however, a rule of equity, that when money is advanced by more persons than one, it shall be deemed, unless the contrary be expressed, to have been lent in equal shares by each; if this were the case, the executor or administrator of any one of the parties would, on his decease, be entitled to receive his share. In order, therefore, to prevent the application of this rule, it is usual to declare, in all mortgages made to trustees, that the money is advanced by them on a joint account, and that, in case of the decease of any of them in the lifetime of the others, the receipts of the survivors or survivor shall be an effectual discharge for the whole of the money.

We have already defined a mortgage debt as an interest in land of a personal nature; and in accordance with this view, it was held that judgment debts against the mortgagee were a charge upon his interest in the mortgaged lands. But it was afterwards provided, that where any mortgage should have been paid off prior to, or at the time of, the conveyance of the lands to a purchaser or mortgagee for valuable consideration, the lands should be discharged both from the judgment and crown debts of the mortgagee. And by a still more recent statute, to which we have already referred, the lien of all judgments, of a date later than the 29th of July, 1864, has been abolished.

Mortgages are frequently transferred from one person to another. The mortgagee may wish to be paid off, and another person may be willing to advance the same or a further amount on the same security. In such a case the mortgage debt and interest are assigned by the old to the new mortgagee; and the lands which form the security are conveyed, or if leasehold assigned, by the old to the new mortgagee, subject to the equity of redemption which may be subsisting in the premises; that is, subject to the right in equity of the mortgagor or his representatives to redeem the premises on payment of the principal sum secured by the mortgage, with all interest and costs.

During the continuance of a mortgage, the equity of redemption which belongs to the mortgagor is regarded by the Court as an estate, which is alienable by the mortgagor, and descendible to his heir, in the same manner as any other estate in equity; the Court in truth regards the mortgagor as the owner of the same estate as before, subject only to the mortgage. In the event of the decease of the mortgagor, the land mortgaged will consequently devolve on the devisee under his will, or, if he should have died intestate, on his heir. And the mortgage debt, to which the lands are subject, was formerly payable in the first place, like all other debts, out of the personal estate of the mortgagor. As in equity the lands are only a security to the mortgagee, in case the mortgagor should not pay him, so also in equity the lands still devolved as the real estate of the mortgagor, subject only to be resorted to for payment of the debt, in the event of his personal estate being insufficient for the purpose. But by an act of the present reign it was provided, that when any person should, after the 31st of December, 1854, die seised of or entitled to any estate or interest in any land or other hereditaments which should at the time of his death be charged with the payment of any sum of money by way of mortgage, and such person should not, by his will or deed or other document, *have signified any contrary or other intention*, the heir or devisee, to whom such lands or hereditaments should descend or be devised, should not be entitled to have the mortgage debt discharged or satisfied out of the personal estate or any other real estate of such person; but the land or hereditaments so charged should, as between the different persons claiming through or under the deceased person, be primarily liable to the payment of all mortgage debts with which the same should be charged; every part thereof, according to its value, bearing a proportionate part of the mortgage debts charged on the whole thereof; provided that nothing therein contained should affect or diminish any right of the mortgagee to obtain full payment of his mortgage debt either out of the personal estate of the person so dying as aforesaid or otherwise; provided also, that nothing therein contained should affect the rights of any person claiming under any deed, will or document made before the 1st of January, 1855. This act, having given rise to many doubts, was explained by another act, which provided, that in the construction of the will of any person who might die after the 31st of December, 1867, a general direction that the debts, or that all the debts of the testator, should be paid out of his personal estate, should not be deemed to be a declaration of an intention contrary to or other than the rule established by the act, unless such contrary or other intention should be further declared by words expressly or by necessary implication referring to all or some of the testator's debts or debt charged by way of mortgage on any part of his real estate. It was further provided, that the word "mortgage" should be deemed to extend to any lien for unpaid purchase-money upon any lands or hereditaments purchased by a *testator*.

On the construction of these acts it was held that they were inapplicable to leaseholds for years. It was also held that the latter act did not extend the term "mortgage" to a lien for unpaid purchase-money upon lands purchased by a person who died *intestate*. An act has accordingly been passed to amend both of the acts above mentioned. This act provides that these acts shall, as to any testator or intestate dying after the 31st of December, 1877, be held to extend to a testator or intestate dying seised or possessed of or entitled to any land or other hereditaments of whatever tenure, which shall at the time of his death be charged with the payment of any sum or sums of money by way of mortgage or any other equitable charge, including any lien for unpaid purchase-money; and the devisee or legatee or heir shall not be entitled to have such sum or sums discharged or satisfied out of any other estate of the testator or intestate, unless (in the case of a testator) he shall, within the meaning of the said acts, have signified a contrary intention; and such contrary intention shall not be deemed to be signified by a charge of or direction for payment of debts upon or out of residuary real and personal estate, or residuary real estate.

The equity of redemption belonging to the mortgagor may again be mortgaged by him, either to the former mortgagee by way of further charge, or to any other person. In order to prevent frauds by clandestine mortgages, it is provided by an act of William and Mary, that a person twice mortgaging the same lands, without discovering the former mortgage to the second mortgagee, shall lose his equity of redemption. Unfortunately, however, in such cases the equity of redemption, after payment of both mortgages, is generally worth nothing. And if the mortgagor should again mortgage the lands to a third person, the act will not deprive such third mortgagee of his right to redeem the two former mortgages. When lands are mortgaged, as occasionally happens, to several persons, each ignorant of the security granted to the other, the general rule is, that the several mortgages rank as charges on the lands in the order of time in which they were made, according to the maxim *qui prior est tempore, potior est jure*. But as the first mortgagee alone obtains the legal estate, he has this advantage over the others, that if he takes a further charge on a subsequent advance to the mortgagor, without notice of any intermediate second mortgage, he will be preferred to an intervening second mortgagee. And if a third mortgagee, who has made his advance without notice of a second mortgage, can procure a transfer to himself of the first mortgage, he may *tack*, as it is said, his third mortgage to the first, and so postpone the intermediate incumbrancer. For, in a contest between innocent parties, each having equal right to the assistance of the Court, the one who happens to have the legal estate is preferred to the others; the maxim being, that when the equities are equal, the law shall prevail. The doctrine thus established was, however, very seriously broken in upon by the 7th section of the Vendor and Purchaser Act, 1874, which provided that, after the commencement of that act, no priority or protection should be abolished, given or allowed to any estate, right or interest in land, by reason of such estate, right or interest being protected by or tacked to any legal or other estate or interest in such land: provided always, that this section should not take away from any estate, right, title or interest any priority or protection which, but for this section, would have been given or allowed thereto, as against any estate or interest existing before the commencement of the act. This was a very objectionable enactment, in the absence of any general registry of title deeds; and it has been repealed by the Land Transfer Act, 1875, as from the date at which it came into operation, except as to any thing duly done thereunder before the commencement of that act.

A mortgage may be made for securing the payment of money which may thereafter become due from the mortgagor to the mortgagee. Where a mortgage extends to future advances, it has been decided, that the mortgagee cannot safely make such advances, if he have notice of an intervening second mortgage.

It was formerly a rule of equity that a solicitor could not take from his client a mortgage to secure future costs, lest he should be tempted on the strength of it to run up a long bill. This illiberal rule has now been abolished by the Attorneys and Solicitors' Act, 1870, which provides, that an attorney or solicitor may take security from his client for his future fees, charges and disbursements, to be ascertained by taxation or otherwise.

There is one case in which the rules of equity singularly and, as the writer thinks, unduly favour the mortgagee. If one person should mortgage lands to another for a sum of money, and subsequently mortgage other lands to the same person for another sum of money, the mortgagee is placed by the rules of equity in the same favourable position as if the whole of the lands had been mortgaged to him for the sum total of the money advanced. The mortgagor cannot redeem either mortgage without also redeeming the other; and the mortgagee may enforce the payment of the whole of the principal and interest due to him on both mortgages out of the lands comprised in either. This rule, known as the doctrine of consolidation of securities, has been extended to the case of mortgages of different, lands made to different persons by the same mortgagor becoming vested by assignment in the same mortgagee, even when the equities of redemption of the different lands have become vested in different persons. It follows, therefore, that no person can safely lend money on a second mortgage. For, in addition to the risk of some third mortgagee getting in and *tacking* the first mortgage, there is this further danger, that if the mortgagor should have mortgaged some other estate to some other person for more than its value, the holder of the deficient security may take a transfer of the first mortgage, and, consolidating his own security with it, exclude the second mortgagee. The purchaser of an equity of redemption is exposed to similar risks. Hence, it follows, that, in the words of an eminent judge, "it is a very dangerous thing at any time to buy equities of redemption or to deal with them at all".

PART V
OF TITLE

It is evident that the acquisition of property is of little benefit, unless accompanied with a prospect of retaining it without interruption. In ancient times conveyances were principally made from a superior to an inferior, as from the great baron to his retainer, or from a father to his daughter on her marriage. The grantee became the tenant of the grantor; and if any consideration were given for the grant, it more frequently assumed the form of an annual rent, than the immediate payment of a large sum of money. Under these circumstances, it may readily be supposed, that, if the grantor were ready to warrant the grantee quiet possession, the title of the former to make the grant would not be very strictly investigated; and this appears to have been the practice in ancient times; every charter or deed of feoffment usually ending with a clause of warranty, by which the feoffor agreed that he and his heirs would warrant, acquit, and for ever defend the feoffee and his heirs against all persons. Even if this warranty were not expressly inserted, still it would seem that the word *give*, used in a feoffment, had the effect of an implied warranty; but the force of such implied warranty was confined to the feoffor only, exclusive of his heirs, whenever a feoffment was made of lands to be holden of the chief lord of the fee. Under an express warranty, the feoffor, and also his heirs, were bound, not only to give up all claim to the lands themselves, but also to give to the feoffee or his heirs other lands of the same value, in case of the eviction of the feoffee or his heirs by any person having a prior title; and this warranty was binding on the heir of the feoffor, whether he derived any lands by descent from the feoffor or not, except only in the case of the warranty commencing, as it was said, by disseisin; that is, in the case of the feoffor making a feoffment with warranty of lands of which he, by that very act, disseised some person, in which case it was too palpable a hardship to make the heir answerable for the misdeed of his ancestor. But, even with this exception, the right to bind the heir by warranty was found to confer on the ancestor too great a power; thus, a husband, whilst tenant by the curtesy of his deceased wife's lands, could, by making a feoffment of such lands with warranty, deprive his son of the inheritance; for the eldest son of the marriage would usually be heir both to his mother and to his father; as heir to his mother he would be entitled to her lands, but as heir of his father he was bound by his warranty. This particular case was the first in which a restraint was applied by parliament to the effect of a warranty, it having been enacted, that the son should not, in such a case, be barred by the warranty of his father, unless any heritage descended to him of his father's side, and then he was to be barred only to the extent of the value of the heritage so descended. The force of a warranty was afterwards greatly restrained by other statutes, enacted to meet other cases; and the clause of warranty having long been disused in modern conveyancing, its chief force and effect have now been removed by clauses of two modern statutes, passed at the recommendation of the real property commissioners.

In addition to an express warranty, there were formerly some words used in conveyancing, which in themselves implied a covenant for quiet enjoyment; and one of these words, namely, the word *demise*, still retains this power. Thus, if one man demises and lets land to another for so many years, this word *demise* operates as an absolute covenant for the quiet enjoyment of the land by the lessee during the term. But if the lease should contain an express covenant by the lessor for quiet enjoyment, limited to his own acts only, such express covenant, showing clearly what is intended, will nullify the implied covenant, which the word *demise* would otherwise contain. So, as we have seen, the word *give* formerly implied a personal warranty; and the word *grant* was supposed to have implied a warranty, unless followed by an express covenant, imposing on the grantor a less liability. An exchange and a partition between coparceners have also until recently implied a mutual right of re-entry, on the eviction of either of the parties from the lands exchanged or partitioned. And, by the Registry Acts for Yorkshire, the words *grant, bargain and sell*, in a deed of *bargain and sale* of an estate in fee simple, inrolled in the Register Office, imply covenants for the quiet enjoyment of the lands against the bargainor, his heirs and assigns, and all claiming under him, and also for further assurance thereof by the bargainor, his heirs and assigns, and all claiming under him, unless restrained by express words.

The word *grant*, by virtue of some other acts of parliament, also implies covenants for the title. But the act to amend the law of real property now provides that an exchange or a partition of any tenements or hereditaments made by deed shall not imply any condition in law; and that the word *give* or the word *grant* in a deed shall not imply any covenant in law in respect of any tenements or hereditaments, except so far as the word *give* or the word *grant* may by force of any act of parliament imply a covenant. The author is not aware of any act of parliament by force of which the word *give* implies a covenant.

The absence of a warranty is principally supplied in modern times by a strict investigation of the title of the person who is to convey; although, in most cases, covenants for title, as they are termed, are also given to the purchaser. On the sale or mortgage of copyhold lands these covenants are usually contained in a deed of covenant to surrender, by which the surrender itself is immediately preceded, the whole being regarded as one transaction. By these covenants, the heirs of the vendor are always expressly bound; but, like all other similar contracts, they are binding on the heir or devisee of the covenantor to the extent only of the property which may descend to the one, or be devised to the other. Unlike the simple clause of warranty in ancient days, modern covenants for title are five in number, and few conveyancing forms can exceed them in the luxuriant growth to which their verbiage has attained. The first covenant is, that the vendor is scised in fee simple; the next, that he has good right to convey the lands; the third, that they shall be quietly enjoyed; the fourth, that they are free from incumbrances; and the last, that the vendor and his heirs will make any further assurance for the conveyance of the premises which may reasonably be required. At the present day, however, the first covenant is usually omitted, the second being evidently quite sufficient without it; and the length of the remaining covenants has of late years much diminished. These covenants for title vary in comprehensiveness, according to the circumstances of the case. A vendor never gives absolute covenants for the title to the lands he sells, but always limits his responsibility to the acts of those who have been in possession since the last sale of the estate; so that if the land should have been purchased by his father, and so have descended to the vendor, or have been left to him by his father's will, the covenants will extend only to the acts of his father and himself: but if the vendor should himself have purchased the lands, he will covenant only as to his own acts, and the purchaser must ascertain by an examination of the previous title, that the vendor purchased what he may properly re-sell. A mortgagor, on the other hand, always gives absolute covenants for title; for those who lend money are accustomed to require every possible security for its repayment; and, notwithstanding these absolute covenants, the title is investigated on every mortgage, with equal, and indeed with greater strictness, than on a purchase. When a sale is made by trustees, who have no beneficial interest in the property themselves, they merely covenant that they have respectively done no act to encumber the premises. If the money is to be paid over to A. or B., or any persons in fixed amounts, the persons who take the money are expected to covenant for the title; but, if the money belongs to infants, or other persons who cannot covenant, or is to be applied in payment of debts or for any similar purpose, the purchaser must rely for the security of the title solely on the accuracy of his own investigation.

The period for which the title was formerly investigated was the last sixty years; and every vendor of freehold property was bound, at his own expense, to furnish the intended purchaser with an abstract of all the deeds, wills and other instruments which had been executed, with respect to the lands in question, during that period; and also to give him an opportunity of examining such abstract with the original deeds, and with the probates or office copies of the wills; for, in every agreement to sell was implied by law an agreement to make a good title to the property to be sold. The proper length of title to an advowson was, however, 100 years, as the presentations, which are the only fruits of the advowson, and, consequently, the only occasions when the title is likely to be contested, occur only at long intervals. On a purchase of copyhold lands, an abstract of the copies of court roll, relating to the property for the last sixty years, was delivered to the purchaser. And even on a purchase of leasehold property, the purchaser was strictly entitled to a sixty years' title; that is, supposing the lease to have been granted within the last sixty years, so much of the title of the lessor was required to be produced as, with the title to the term since its commencement, would make up the full period of sixty years. If the lease were more than sixty years old, the lease was required to be produced or its absence accounted for, and evidence given of the whole of its contents. But intermediate assignments upwards of sixty years old were not required to be produced. The Vendor and Purchaser Act, 1874, however, now provides, that in the completion of any contract of sale of land made after the 31st day of December, 1874, and subject to any stipulation to the contrary in the contract, forty years shall be substituted as the period of commencement of title which a purchaser may require, in place of sixty years, the present period of such commencement; nevertheless earlier title than forty years may be required in cases similar to those in which earlier title than sixty years may now be required. The act uses the word "land," which has a statutory meaning when used in an act of parliament, including tenements and hereditaments of any tenure, unless there are words to restrict the meaning to tenements of some particular tenure. Now an advowson is certainly an hereditament; but as the act substitutes the period of forty years "in place of sixty years the present period," and as one hundred years and not sixty years was, when the act passed, the proper period for the deduction of the title to an advowson, it is presumed that the act was not intended to apply to advowsons, and that the title to an advowson must, therefore, still be deduced for one hundred years. The act further provides, that in the completion of any such contract as aforesaid, and subject to any stipulation to the contrary in the contract, under a contract to grant or assign a term of years, whether derived or to be derived out of a freehold or leasehold estate, the intended lessee or assign shall not be entitled to call for the title to the freehold. The act further provides, that in the completion of any such contract, and subject to any stipulation to the contrary, recitals, statements and descriptions of facts, matters and parties contained in deeds, instruments, acts of parliament, or statutory declarations twenty years old at the date of the contract, shall, unless and except so far as they shall be proved to be inaccurate, be taken to be sufficient evidence of the truth of such facts, matters and descriptions. The last provision adopts, as a general rule, a stipulation which had been usually inserted in conditions of sale, and in the absence of which the purchaser had a right to require evidence of the truth of the matters recited.

It is not easy to say how the precise term of sixty years came to be fixed on as the time for which an abstract of the title should be required. It is true, that by a statute of the reign of Henry VIII., the time within which a writ of right (a proceeding now abolished) might be brought for the recovery of lands was limited to sixty years; but still in the case of remainders after estates for life or in tail, this statute did not prevent the recovery of lands long after the period of sixty years had elapsed from the time of a conveyance by the tenant for life or in tail; for it is evident, that the right of a remainderman, after an estate for life or in tail, to the possession of the lands does not accrue until the determination of the particular estate. A remainder after an estate tail may, however, be barred by the proper means; but a remainder after a mere life estate cannot. The ordinary duration of human life was therefore, if not the origin of the rule requiring a sixty years' title, at least a good reason for its continuance. For, so long as the law permits of vested remainders after estates for life, and forbids the tenant for life, by any act, to destroy such remainders, so long must it be necessary to carry the title back to such a point as will afford a reasonable presumption that the first person mentioned as having conveyed the property was not a tenant for life merely, but a tenant in fee simple. The recent shortening of the period from sixty to forty years appears justifiable only from the fact that in practice purchasers are generally found willing to accept a forty years' title; in like manner as, in the purchase of leasehold estates, a condition to dispense with the title to the freehold was usually submitted to.

The abstract of the title will of course disclose the names of all parties, who, besides the vendor, may be interested in the lands; and the concurrence of these parties must be obtained by him, in order that an unincumbered estate in fee simple may be conveyed to the purchaser. Thus, if the lands be in mortgage, the mortgagee must be paid off out of the purchase-money, and must join to relinquish his security and convey the legal estate. If the wife of the vendor would, on his decease, be entitled to dower out of the lands, she must release her right and separately acknowledge the purchase deed. And when lands were sold by trustees, and the money was directed to be paid over by them to certain given persons, it was formerly obligatory on the purchaser to see that such persons were actually paid the money to which they were entitled, unless it were expressly provided by the instrument creating the trust, that the receipt of the trustees alone should be an effectual discharge. The duty thus imposed being often exceedingly inconvenient, and tending greatly to prejudice a sale, a declaration, that the receipt of the trustees should be an effectual discharge, was usually inserted, as a common form, in all settlements and trust deeds. The act to simplify the transfer of property provided that the *bonâ fide* payment to, and the receipt of, any person, to whom any money should be payable upon any express or implied trust, or for any limited purpose, should effectually discharge the person paying the same from seeing to the application or being answerable for the misapplication thereof, unless the contrary should be. expressly declared by the instrument creating the trust. But this act was shortly afterwards repealed, without, however, any provision being made for such instruments as had been drawn without any receipt clause upon the faith of this enactment. Subsequently it was enacted that the *bonâ fide* payment to and the receipt of any person to whom any purchase or mortgage money should be payable upon any express or implied trust, should effectually discharge the person paying the same from seeing to the application or being answerable for the misapplication thereof, unless the contrary should be expressly declared by the instrument creating the trust or security. And at length it has again been generally provided that the receipts in writing of any trustees or trustee for any money payable to them or charges. him, by reason or in the exercise of any trusts or powers reposed or vested in them or him, shall be sufficient discharges for the money therein expressed to be received, and shall effectually exonerate the persons paying such money from seeing to the application thereof, or from being answerable for any loss or misapplication thereof.

Supposing, however, that through carelessness in investigating the title, or from any other cause, a man should happen to become possessed of lands, to which some other person is rightfully entitled; in this case it is evidently desirable that the person so rightfully entitled to the lands should be limited in the time during which he may bring an action to recover them. To deprive a man of that which he has long enjoyed, and still expects to enjoy, will be generally doing more harm than can arise from forbidding the person rightfully entitled, but who has long been ignorant or negligent as to his rights, to agitate claims which have long lain dormant. Various acts for the limitation of actions and suits relating to real property have accordingly been passed at different times. By a statute of the reign of George III. The rights of the crown in all lands and hereditaments are barred after the lapse of sixty years. With respect to other persons, the act now m force was passed in the reign of King William IV., at the suggestion of the real property commissioners. By this act, no person can bring an action for the recovery of lands but within twenty years next after the time at which the right to bring such action shall have first accrued to him, or to some person through whom he claims; and, as to estates in reversion or remainder, or other future estates, the right shall be deemed to have first accrued at the time at which any such estate became an estate in possession. But a written acknowledgment of the title of the person entitled, given to him or his agent, signed by the person in possession, will extend the time of claim to twenty years from such acknowledgment. If, however, when the right to bring an action first accrues, the person entitled should be under disability to sue by reason of infancy, coverture (if a woman), idiocy, lunacy, unsoundness of mind, or absence beyond seas, ten years are allowed from the time when the person entitled shall have ceased to be under any disability, or shall have died, notwithstanding the period of twenty years above mentioned may have expired, yet so that the whole period do not, including the time of disability, exceed forty years; and no further time is allowed on account of the disability of any other person than the one to whom the right of action first accrues. When any land or rent is vested in a trustee upon any express trust, the right of the *cestui que trust*, or any party claiming through him to bring a suit against the trustee, or any person claiming through him, to recover such land or rent, is deemed to have first accrued at and not before the time at which such land or rent shall have been conveyed to a purchaser for a valuable consideration, and shall then be deemed to have accrued only as against such purchaser and any person claiming through him. And it is enacted by the Supreme Court of Judicature Act, 1873, that no claim of a *cestui que trust* against his trustee for any property held on an express trust, or in respect of any breach of such trust, shall be held to be barred by any Statute of Limitations. The act of King William

IV. further provides, that in every case of a concealed fraud, the right of any person to bring a suit in Equity for the recovery of any land or rent, of which he, or any person through whom he claims, may have been deprived by such fraud, shall be deemed to have first accrued at and not before the time at which such fraud shall be, or with reasonable diligence might have been, first known or discovered; provided that nothing in that clause contained shall enable any owner of lands or rents to have a suit in Equity for the recovery thereof, or for setting aside any conveyance thereof on account of fraud, against any *bonâ fide* purchaser for valuable consideration, who has not assisted in the commission of such fraud, and who at the time he made the purchase did not know and had no reason to believe that any such fraud had been committed. And nothing in the act contained shall be deemed to interfere with any rule or jurisdiction of Courts of Equity in refusing relief, on the ground of acquiescence or otherwise, to any person whose right to bring a suit may not be barred by virtue of that act. The act further provides, that whenever a mortgagee has obtained possession of the land comprised in his mortgage, the mortgagor shall not bring a suit to redeem the mortgage but within twenty years next after the time when the mortgagee obtained possession, or next after any written acknowledgment of the title of the mortgagor, or of his right to redemption, shall have been given to him, or his agent, signed by the mortgagee. By the same act the time for bringing an action or suit to enforce the right of presentation to a benefice is limited to three successive incumbencies, all adverse to the right of presentation claimed, or to the period of sixty years, if the three incumbencies do not together amount to that time; but whatever the length of the incumbencies, no such action or suit can be brought after the expiration of 100 years from the time at which adverse possession of the benefice shall have been obtained. Money secured by mortgage or judgment, or otherwise charged upon land, and also legacies, are to be deemed satisfied at the end of twenty years, if no interest should be paid, or written acknowledgment given in the meantime. The right to rents, whether rents service or rents charge, and also the right to tithes when in the hands of laymen, is subject to the same period of limitation as the right to land. And in every case where the period limited by the act is determined, the right of the person who might have brought any action or suit for the recovery of the land, rent or advowson in question within the period, is extinguished.

A new Statute of Limitations has now been passed, which, however, does not come into operation until the 1st of January, 1879. It is called the Real Property Limitation Act, 1874. This act shortens the period of twenty years given by the act of Will. IV. to twelve years. It also shortens further the time allowed to estates in reversion or remainder or other future estates, in cases where time has begun to run against the owner of the particular estate; giving twelve years only from that time, or six years from the vesting in possession, whichever period shall be the longer; and if the particular tenant is barred, every reversioner claiming under any deed, will or settlement, executed or taking effect after the time when the right first accrued to the particular tenant, is barred also. The period of ten years allowed by the former statute in cases of disability is shortened to six years. And absence beyond seas is removed from the list of disabilities. The total period of forty years allowed by the former act is reduced to thirty. And the law as to express trusts is again altered by an enactment, that, after the commencement of that act, no action, suit or other proceeding shall he brought to recover any sum of money or legacy charged upon or payable out of any land or rent at law or in equity, and secured by an express trust, or to recover any arrears of rent or of interest in respect of any sum of money or legacy so charged or payable and so secured, or any damages in respect of such arrears, except within the time within which the same would be recoverable if there were not any such trust.

The title to incorporeal rights, whether appendant, appurtenant or in gross, depends upon grant or upon prescription from immemorial user, by which a grant is implied. The time of legal memory was long since fixed at the beginning of the reign of King Richard I. by analogy to the time which, by a statute of Edward I., was fixed for the limitation of the old writ of right. And in the absence of an express grant, a man might either prescribe that he and his ancestors had from time immemorial exercised a certain right in gross, or that he, being seised in fee of certain lands, and all those whose estate he had, had from time immemorial exercised as appendant or appurtenant to their own lands certain rights, such as rights of common or way, over certain other lands. In both of these cases proof of a user as of right, for twenty years or upwards, was formerly considered to afford a presumption of immemorial enjoyment. But this presumption might be effectually rebutted by proof that the enjoyment had in fact commenced within the time of legal memory; in which case the enjoyment for centuries would go for nothing. This is still the law with regard to prescriptions of the former kind, namely, prescriptions of immemorial user by a man and his ancestors. But with regard to prescriptions of the latter kind, where the owner of one tenement, some-tunes called the dominant tenement, claims to exercise some right over another tenement, called the servient tenement, he may either still prove his rights as before, or he may have recourse to an act of King William IV., which has materially shortened the proof required, in all cases where a recent uninterrupted user as of right can be shown. By this act no right of common or other profit or benefit, called in law French *profit à prendre*, to be taken and enjoyed from or upon land (except tithes, rent and services), shall, if actually taken and enjoyed by any person claiming right thereto without interruption for thirty years, be defeated by showing only that it was first enjoyed prior thereto; and if enjoyed for sixty years the right is made absolute and indefeasible, unless it shall appear that the same was taken and enjoyed by some consent or agreement expressly made or given for that purpose by deed or writing. For rights of way and other easements, watercourses and the use of water, the terms arc twenty and forty years respectively instead of thirty and sixty years. And when the access and use of light for any dwelling-house, workshop, or other building, shall have been actually enjoyed therewith for the full period of twenty years without interruption, the right thereto shall he deemed absolute and indefeasible, any local usage or custom to the contrary notwithstanding, unless it shall appear that the same was enjoyed by some consent or agreement expressly made or given for that purpose by deed or writing. The periods mentioned are periods next before some action or suit in which the claim is brought in question; and no act is deemed an interruption unless submitted to or acquiesced in for one year after the party interrupted shall have had notice thereof and of the person making or authorizing the same to be made. The time during which any person, otherwise capable of resisting any claim, shall be an infant, idiot, non com-pos mentis, feme covert or tenant for life, or during which any action or suit shall have been pending, and which shall have been diligently prosecuted until abated by the death of any party thereto, is excluded from the above periods, except when the claim is declared absolute and indefeasible; provided that in the case of ways and watercourses where the servient tenement shall be held for term of life or years exceeding three years, the time of enjoyment of the way or watercourse during such term is excluded from the computation of the period of forty years, in case the claim shall, within three years next after the end or sooner determination of such term, be resisted by any person entitled to any reversion expectant on the determination thereof. The rights above mentioned may be lost by abandonment, of which non-user for twenty years or upwards is generally sufficient evidence, although a shorter period will suffice if an intent to abandon appear.

On any sale or mortgage of lands, all the title-deeds in the hands of the vendor or mortgagor, which relate exclusively to the property sold or mortgaged, are handed over to the purchaser or mortgagee. The possession of the deeds is of the greatest importance; for if the deeds were not required to be delivered, it is evident that property might be sold or mortgaged over and over again to different persons, without much risk of discovery. The only guarantee, for instance, which a purchaser has that the lands he contracts to purchase have not been mortgaged, is that the deeds are in the possession of the vendor. It is true that, in the counties of Middlesex and York, registries have been established, a search in which will lead to the detection of all dealings with the property; but these registries, though existing in Scotland and Ireland, do not extend to the remaining counties of England or to Wales. Generally speaking, therefore, the possession of the deeds is all that a purchaser has to depend on: in most cases this protection, coupled with an examination of the title they disclose, is found to be sufficient: but there are certain circumstances in which the possession of the deeds can afford no security. Thus, the possession of the deeds is no safeguard against an annuity or rent-charge payable out of the lands; for the grantee of a rent-charge has no right to the deeds. So the possession of the deeds, showing the conveyance to the vendor of an estate in fee simple, is no guarantee that the vendor is not now actually seised only of a life estate; for, since he acquired the property, he may, very possibly, have married; and on his marriage he may have settled the lands on himself for his life, with remainder to his children. Being then tenant for life, he will, like every other tenant for life, be entitled to the custody of the deeds; and if he should be fraudulent enough to suppress the settlement, he might make a conveyance from himself, as though seised in fee, deducing a good title, and handing over the deeds; but the purchaser, having actually acquired by his purchase nothing more than the life interest of the vendor, would be liable, on his decease, to be turned out of possession by his children; for, as marriage is a valuable consideration, a settlement then made cannot be set aside by a subsequent sale made by the settlor. Against such a fraud as this the registration of deeds seems the only protection. In some cases, also, persona are entitled to an interest, which they would like to sell, but are prevented, from not having any deeds to hand over. Thus if lands be settled on A. for his life, with remainder to B. in fee, A. during his life will be entitled to the deeds; and B. will find great difficulty in disposing of his reversion at an adequate price; because, having no deeds to give up, he has no means of satisfying a purchaser that the reversion has not previously been sold or mortgaged to some other person. If, therefore, B.'s necessities should oblige him to sell, he will find the want of a registry for deeds the cause of a considerable deduction in the price he can. obtain. It may here be remarked, that as few people would sell a reversion unless they were in difficulties, equity, whenever a reversion was sold, threw upon the purchaser the onus of showing that he gave the fair market price for it. But it is now provided that no purchase, made *bonâ fide*, and without fraud or unfair dealing, of any reversionary interest in real or personal estate shall hereafter be opened or set aside merely on the ground of undervalue.

Where the title-deeds relate to other property, and cannot consequently be delivered over to the purchaser, he is entitled, at the expense of the vendor, to attested copies of such of them as are not enrolled in any court of record; but as the expense thus incurred is usually great, it is in general thrown on the purchaser, by express stipulation in the contract. The purchaser was also formerly entitled to a covenant for the production of the title-deeds, whenever required in support of his title; and the expense of this covenant formerly fell on the vendor, unless thrown on the purchaser by express stipulation. But the Vendor and Purchaser Act, 1874, now provides that in the completion of any contract of sale of land made after the 31st of December, 1874, and subject to any stipulation to the contrary in the contract, the inability of the vendor to furnish the purchaser with a legal covenant to produce and furnish copies of documents of title shall not be an objection to title, in case the purchaser will, on the completion of the contract, have an equitable right to the production of such documents; and further that such covenants for production as the purchaser can and shall require shall be furnished at his expense, but the vendor shall bear the expense of perusal and execution on behalf of and by himself and necessary parties, other than the purchaser; and further that when the vendor retains any part of an estate to which any documents of title relate, he shall be entitled to retain such documents. The covenant for the production of the deeds will run, as it is said, with the land; that is, the benefit of such a covenant will belong to every legal owner of the land sold for the time being; and the better opinion is, that the obligation to perform the covenant will also be binding on every legal owner of the land, in respect of which the deeds have been retained. Accordingly, when a purchase is made without delivery of the title-deeds, the only deeds that can accompany the lands sold are the actual conveyance of the land to the purchaser, and the deed of covenant to produce the former title-deeds. On a future sale, therefore, these deeds will be delivered to the new purchaser; and the covenant, running with the land, will enable him at any time to obtain production of the former deeds to which the covenant relates.

When the lands sold are situated in either of the counties of Middlesex or York, search is made in the registries established for those counties: this search is usually confined to the period which has elapsed from the last purchase-deed, — the search presumed to have been made on behalf of the former purchaser being generally relied on as a sufficient guarantee against latent incumbrances prior to that time; and a memorial of the purchase-deed is of course duly registered as soon as possible after its execution. As to lands in all other counties, also, there are certain matters affecting the title, of which every purchaser can readily obtain information. Thus, if any estate tail has existed in the lands, the purchaser can always learn whether or not it has been barred; for the records of all fines and recoveries, by which the bar was formerly effected, are preserved in the offices of the Court of Common Pleas; and, now, the deeds which have been substituted for those assurances are enrolled in the Chancery Division of the High Court. Conveyances by married women can also be discovered by a search in the index, which is kept in the Common Pleas Division of the High Court, of the certificates of the acknowledgment of all deeds executed and acknowledged by married women. So, we have seen, that debts due from the vendor, or any former owner, to the crown, prior to the 1st of November, 1865, or secured by judgment prior to the 23rd of July, 1860, together with suits which may be pending concerning the land, all which are incumbrances on the land, are always sought for in the indexes provided for the purpose in the office of the Common Pleas Division. Life annuities, also, which may have been charged on the land for money or money's worth prior to August, 1854, may generally be discovered by a search in the office of the Chancery Division, amongst the memorials of such annuities. And those which have been granted since the 26th of April, 1855, otherwise than by marriage-settlement or will, may be found in the registry established in the Common Pleas Division. And, lastly, the bankruptcy or insolvency of any vendor or mortgagor may be discovered by a search in the records of the Bankrupt or Insolvent Courts; and it is the duty of the purchaser's or mortgagee's solicitor to make such search, if he has any reason to believe that the vendor or mortgagor is or has been in embarrassed circumstances. The acts for relief of insolvent debtors are now repealed and the court abolished.

Some mention should here be made of the acts which have been passed with a view to the simplification of titles, and to facilitate the transfer of land. An act has been passed "for obtaining a declaration of title". This act empowers persons claiming to be entitled to land in possession for an estate in fee simple, or claiming power to dispose of such an estate, to apply to the Court of Chancery, now represented by the Chancery Division of the High Court, by petition in a summary way for a declaration of title. The title is then investigated by the Court; and if the Court shall be satisfied that such a title is shown as it would have compelled an unwilling purchaser to accept, an order is made establishing the title, subject, however, to appeal as mentioned in the act. This act, though seldom resorted to, does not appear to have been repealed. Another act of the same session is intituled "An Act to facilitate the Proof of Title to and the Conveyance of Real Estates". This act established an office of land registry, and contained provisions for the official investigation of titles, and for the registration of such as appeared to be good and marketable. It has, however, now been superseded by the Land Transfer Act, 1875, which provides that after the commencement of that act, which took place on the 1st of January, 1876, application for the registration of an estate under the former act shall not be entertained. For the provisions of this act reference should be made to the act itself. Registration under this act is optional, and its success is too doubtful to justify any lengthened account of it in an elementary work like the present. The system of official investigation of title once for all is a good one, provided it be made by competent persons and under sufficient safeguards. Compensation, however, ought to be made to those whose estates may by any error be taken from them in their absence. When land is once registered under this act, it ceases, if situate in Middlesex or Yorkshire, to be subject to the county registry of deeds. If the act should lead to an efficient system of registration of assurances throughout the kingdom, it would, in the author's opinion, be the means of conferring a great benefit on the community. This, however, cannot be advantageously done without resort to the printing of registered deeds and of probates of wills, and the abolition of payment by length. The author's views on this subject will be found in a paper read by him before the Juridical Society, on the 24th of March, 1862, intituled "On the true Remedies for the Evils which affect the Transfer of Land", and to which he begs to refer the reader.

Such is a very brief and exceedingly imperfect outline of the methods adopted in this country for rendering secure the enjoyment of real property when sold or mortgaged. It may perhaps serve to prepare the student for the course of study which still lies before him in this direction. The valuable treatise of Lord St. Leonards on the law of vendors and purchasers of estates will be found to afford nearly all the practical information necessary on this branch of the law. The title to purely personal property depends on other principles, for an explanation of which the reader is referred to the author's treatise on the principles of the law of personal property. From what has already been said, the reader will perceive that the law of England has two different systems of rules for regulating the enjoyment and transfer of property; that the laws of real estate, though venerable for their antiquity, are in the same degree ill adapted to the requirements of modern society: whilst the laws of personal property, being of more recent origin, are proportionably suited to modern times. Over them both has arisen the jurisdiction of the Court of Chancery, by means of which the ancient strictness and simplicity of our real property laws have been in a measure rendered subservient to the arrangements and modifications of ownership, which the various necessities of society have required. Added to this have been continual enactments, especially of late years, by which many of the most glaring evils have been remedied, but by which, at the same time, the symmetry of the laws of real property has been greatly impaired. Those laws cannot indeed be now said to form a system: their present state is certainly not that in which they can remain. For the future, perhaps, the wisest course to be followed would be to aim as far as possible at a uniformity of system in the laws of both kinds of property; and, for this purpose, rather to take the laws of personal estate as the model to which the laws of real estate should be made to conform, than on the one hand to preserve untouched all the ancient rules, because they once were useful, or, on the other, to be annually plucking off, by parliamentary enactments, the fruit which such rules must, until eradicated, necessarily produce.

Made in United States
Troutdale, OR
11/03/2026

56844487R00166